General Equilibrium Theory of Value

General Equilibrium
Theory of Value

Yves Balasko

PRINCETON UNIVERSITY PRESS
PRINCETON AND OXFORD

Published by Princeton University Press, 41 William Street, Princeton, New Jersey 08540
In the United Kingdom: Princeton University Press, 6 Oxford Street, Woodstock,
Oxfordshire OX20 1TW

press.princeton.edu

Library of Congress Cataloging-in-Publication Data

Balasko, Yves.
General equilibrium theory of value / Yves Balasko.
   p. cm.
Includes bibliographical references and index.
ISBN 978-0-691-14679-9 (hardback)
1. Value. 2. Equilibrium (Economics) I. Title.
HB201.B18 2011
338.5'21—dc22   2011015440

British Library Cataloging-in-Publication Data is available

This book has been composed in Sabon

Printed on acid-free paper. ∞

Printed in the United States of America

10 9 8 7 6 5 4 3 2 1

Contents

Preface

The publication of Debreu's *Theory of Value* dates back to more than 50 years ago. In that book, Debreu elegantly combined axiomatic rigor and advanced mathematics to prove two major properties of economies with private ownership of production: the existence of equilibrium and the two theorems of welfare economics. Existence is a necessary step. The two theorems of welfare economics are more interesting from an economic perspective. The first theorem states that every equilibrium allocation is Pareto efficient, a theorem understood as evidence of the efficiency of competition in market economies. The second theorem states that every Pareto efficient allocation can be realized as the equilibrium allocation of some competitive economy after suitable redistribution of individual resources, a property expressing the neutrality of competitive markets.

The proofs worked out by Arrow, Debreu, and McKenzie in the 1950s were considered to be such breakthroughs that many textbooks still limit themselves to the existence and welfare theorems and ignore all the developments that have been going on in the theory of general equilibrium since the publication of Debreu's book.

My goal is to give a much needed update on the properties of economies with private ownership of production. The initial impetus for the study of the general equilibrium model from the differentiable point of view came from Debreu's 1970 landmark paper. The results of that paper, which were limited to the exchange model, were rapidly extended to more general versions of the equilibrium model. Production was dealt with by Fuchs, T. Kehoe, Mas-Colell, and Smale in particular. Further results were also proved for the exchange model by Delbaen, Dierker, and myself. My own work started with the study of the equilibrium manifold. It rapidly evolved into a program focused on the study of the projection map from the equilibrium manifold onto the parameter space. That approach proved to be highly fruitful. That line of research was also pursued by Bonnisseau, Crès, Ghiglino, Jofre, Jouini, Keiding, Rivera, and Tvede among others for the standard version of the general equilibrium model. I have extended it with K. Shell and D. Cass in research on the overlapping-generations model and the general equilibrium model with incomplete asset markets.

This book is limited to the general equilibrium model with private ownership of production, the very model considered in Debreu's *Theory of Value*. Independently of its intrinsic interest, this model is crucial for the study of the more specialized versions of the general equilibrium model that address overlapping-generation or incomplete asset markets for example.

The existence and welfare theorems can be proved with point-set topology and elementary convex analysis as they are in Debreu's book. Most other properties of the equilibrium equation, however, exploit the differentiability of that equation. The appropriate mathematical tools are then the implicit function theorem, Sard's theorem about the set of singular values of smooth maps, and the stratified structure of semi-algebraic sets. Except for the implicit function theorem, none of these theorems are taught at the undergraduate level. In addition, these theorems have the reputation of being difficult. The consequence is that very few economists feel comfortable with the differentiable approach. Properties like the multiplicity and discontinuities of market prices in competitive economies are all too often ignored at both theoretical and applied levels.

One goal of this book is therefore to facilitate the access to the differentiable point of view in the study of the general equilibrium model. Mathematics are simplified as much as possible. A real effort has been made to explain the key concepts so that prior knowledge is not necessary. The mathematical prerequisites for this book are on a par with those required by most other advanced economic books: linear algebra, multivariate calculus, and point-set topology.

This book should convince its readers that our understanding of the general equilibrium model with private ownership of production has significantly progressed during the last 50 years.

This book can serve as a modern introduction to general equilibrium theory. It is based on the experience of teaching general equilibrium theory at various levels. Its content is appropriate for a set of approximately 20 one-hour lectures for first-year graduate students.

CHAPTER 1

Goods and Prices

1.1 INTRODUCTION

The aim of this chapter is to develop the main aspects of the economic environment in which economic agents operate. There are two categories of economic agents, consumers and firms. Consumers buy and sell goods with the ultimate goal of consuming those goods. Firms buy goods that they transform into other goods that they later sell. An economy is made up of these consumers and firms. After having developed models of the consumers and firms, we will combine them into a model of an economy with private ownership of production. Before developing these models, it is necessary to be somewhat more explicit about the economic goods and their prices that define the economic environment.

1.2 GOODS

THE CHARACTERISTICS OF AN ECONOMIC GOOD

Economic goods are defined by their "physical" characteristics or properties. These physical characteristics, which have to be taken in a very broad sense, may include all forms of services. But economic goods often feature other aspects than their physical properties. For example, the location and the date of delivery of an economic good are sufficiently important to be specified for each economic good. The conditions under which delivery takes place is also specified in many general equilibrium models, especially those that involve uncertainty. In these models, the delivery may depend on the realization of some state of nature. Such goods are known as contingent goods. To sum up, economic goods are defined by their characteristics, which may include many more things than just the physical properties of the goods.

THE MEASURABILITY REQUIREMENT

Goods that have a price like all the goods traded in markets have to be measurable. Measurability is a concept that comes from physics. For an economic good to be measurable, it is necessary to have a meaningful definition of the equality and the sum of two quantities of that good. In that regard, not all economic goods are measurable. For example, some public goods like national defense are typically not measurable because it is almost impossible to define the equality of two levels of national defense. Needless to say, the sum of two levels of national defense is even harder to conceive.

The goods considered in general equilibrium models are measurable. They are also divisible. Units are defined once and for all for each good in the economy.

THE COMMODITY SPACE

The number of goods is finite and denoted by ℓ, a number greater than or equal to 2. The commodity bundle $x = (x^1, \ldots, x^\ell)$ consists of x^1 units of the first good, x^2 units of the second good, up to x^ℓ units of the ℓ-th good. The *commodity space* is the Euclidean space $\mathbb{R}^\ell$. Quantities of goods in a commodity bundle like x can be positive, negative, or equal to zero.

1.3 PRICES

We associate with every commodity j a price p_j. Prices are strictly positive. The price p_j of commodity j is actually the price of one *unit* of commodity j.

THE PRICE VECTOR

The price vector $p = (p_1, \ldots, p_j, \ldots, p_\ell) \in \mathbb{R}^\ell$ has for coordinates the prices $p_j > 0$ of the various goods.

VALUE OF A COMMODITY BUNDLE FOR A GIVEN PRICE SYSTEM

Let $x = (x^1, \ldots, x^\ell) \in \mathbb{R}^\ell$ be a commodity bundle and $p = (p_1, \ldots, p_\ell) \in \mathbb{R}^\ell_{++}$ some arbitrary price vector. The *value* of the commodity bundle $x \in \mathbb{R}^\ell$ given the price vector $p \in \mathbb{R}^\ell_{++}$ is equal to the inner product

$$w = p \cdot x = p_1 x^1 + \cdots + p_\ell x^\ell.$$

1.4 RELATIVE PRICES

Given the price vector $p = (p_1, \ldots, p_\ell) \in \mathbb{R}^\ell_{++}$, the price of good h relative to the price of good k is defined by the ratio p_h/p_k.

Relative prices depend only on the direction defined by the price vector $p = (p_1, \ldots, p_h, \ldots, p_k, \ldots, p_\ell) \in \mathbb{R}^\ell_{++}$, not on its length. An important assumption that will be made in future chapters will be that consumption and production decisions depend only on relative prices or, in other words, on the direction defined by the price vector. It has therefore become customary to use some kind of normalization for the price vectors $p \in \mathbb{R}^\ell_{++}$.

1.5 PRICE NORMALIZATION

There are quite a few ways to normalize the price vector $p \in \mathbb{R}^\ell_{++}$. Mathematicians tend to choose some norm on the vector space $\mathbb{R}^\ell$ and to set that norm equal to one.

THE EUCLIDEAN NORMALIZATION

One example of such a normalization is to set the Euclidean norm $\|p\| = \left((p_1)^2 + \cdots + (p_\ell)^2\right)^{1/2}$ to one. Perfectly satisfactory from a mathematical perspective, this normalization has little economic appeal. We will not use this normalization in the book.

THE SIMPLEX NORMALIZATION

Another normalization that is particularly handy when dealing with the behavior of consumers and firms when some prices tend to zero is the *simplex normalization*.

Definition 1.1. *The price vector* $p = (p_1, \ldots, p_\ell) \in \mathbb{R}^\ell_{++}$ *is simplex normalized if* $\sum_k p_k = 1$. *We denote by* S_Σ *the set* $\{p \in X \mid \sum_k p_k = 1\}$ *of simplex normalized prices.*

Note that all prices are strictly positive for $p \in S_\Sigma$. The closed price simplex $\overline{S_\Sigma}$ consists of the price vector $p = (p_1, \ldots, p_\ell)$ where some coordinates can be equal to zero. The boundary $\partial S_\Sigma = \overline{S_\Sigma} \setminus S_\Sigma$ consists of the price vectors $p \in \overline{S_\Sigma}$ that have at least one coordinate equal to zero.

THE NUMERAIRE NORMALIZATION

Another price normalization has the favor of many economists. It consists in giving to some good the role played by money for expressing the prices of the other goods in quantities of that good. Such a good is known as the *numeraire*.

Numeraire is not money because money, paper money (also known as fiat money) is not an economic good in our sense. Paper money cannot be consumed physically like an orange or a banana. Paper money is not an argument of the utility functions considered by the classical theory of the consumer, a theory that we address in chapter 2. Similarly, paper money is not a direct input of the production process in the classical theory of the firm considered in chapter 5. If the numeraire cannot be confused with paper money, gold has many attributes of a numeraire. In the times of the Gold Exchange Standard, prices were expressed in quantities of gold, an argument of consumers' utility functions and producers' production processes.

In practice, having a numeraire amounts to setting the price of the numeraire commodity to one. In this book, we choose the ℓ-th commodity to be the numeraire: $p_\ell = 1$.

Definition 1.2. *The price vector $p = (p_1, \ldots, p_\ell) \in \mathbb{R}_{++}^\ell$ is numeraire normalized if $p_\ell = 1$. We denote by S the set $\{p \in \mathbb{R}_{++}^\ell \mid p_\ell = 1\}$ of numeraire normalized prices.*

Unless the contrary is specified, all price vectors from now on are numeraire normalized. The main problem with the numeraire price normalization is that it treats goods asymmetrically, which may not be very satisfactory from a mathematical perspective. This defect is more than compensated by the relative simplicity it gives to the computation of derivatives of demand and supply functions with respect to prices, operations that we will do extensively in later chapters.

1.6 NOTES AND COMMENTS

This introductory chapter is very similar to the first chapter of Debreu's *Theory of Value* [23].

The necessity of measurability for the goods that claim to have market prices is often neglected. Most public goods and environmental goods are not measurable. This has not prevented Samuelson and his followers to treat public goods as if they were measurable [7, 57].

Some mathematicians use the Euclidean normalization of the price vector because the price vector then belongs to the sphere of unit radius. Then, the aggregate excess demand of an exchange economy can be viewed as defining a vector field on the sphere, which enables the application of several powerful theorems of algebraic topology to the study of this vector field [26].

CHAPTER 2

Preferences and Utility

CLASSICAL CONSUMER THEORY is essentially the theory of utility maximization under a budget constraint. This theory starts with the definition of consumers' preferences. In classical consumer theory, preferences are assumed to be transitive, complete, monotone and convex. These preferences can then be represented by utility functions. The latter are mathematically easier to handle than preferences. Another reason for being interested in utility functions goes back to the early phases of economic theory. Then, it was thought that utility functions could be used as a measure of consumer's satisfaction or utility. Pareto suggested the term of "ophelimité" instead of utility to avoid any misleading interpretation. This chapter is devoted to a presentation of the basic issues regarding preferences and their representability by utility functions.

2.1 CONSUMPTION SETS

The first item to be defined is the consumption set. It is usually defined as the set of commodity bundles that can be physically consumed. In such a case, the consumption set should be the non-negative orthant or some subset of the non-negative orthant. However, negative consumption can also be interpreted as the delivery to the market of some positive quantities of goods, in which case the consumption set can contain commodity bundles with negative coordinates. Negative consumption is explicitely mentioned by Debreu [23]. It is observed in financial markets and, more generally, in markets where short sales are permitted and when goods are not necessarily bought for immediate physical consumption.

This leads us to take all consumption sets equal to the full commodity space $\mathbb{R}^\ell$. Furthermore, this choice is the only one that is really consistent with the existence of preferences since the commodity bundles that are "feasible" will always be preferred to those that are not feasible.

Assumption 2.1. *The consumption set of every consumer is the full commodity space $\mathbb{R}^\ell$.*

2.2 BINARY RELATIONS

Preferences are represented by binary relations defined on consumption sets. Being complete preorders, these relations are representable by utility functions. Other main properties of preferences are monotonicity and convexity. The goal of classical consumer theory is to derive properties of demand functions that come to play a crucial role in the general equilibrium model from the properties of consumer's preference relations.

2.2.1 Properties of Binary Relations

We first define a binary relation on some set $\mathcal{P}$. In applications to consumer theory, this set will be the consumption set $\mathbb{R}^\ell$.

The binary relation $\preccurlyeq_i$ on the set $\mathcal{P}$ consists in the definition of a subset $\mathcal{B}_i$ of the Cartesian product $\mathcal{P} \times \mathcal{P}$. An element of $\mathcal{B}_i$ is an ordered pair (x, y) where the elements x and y of $\mathcal{P}$ are by definition "related" to each other if the pair (x, y) belongs to the set $\mathcal{B}_i$. One then writes $x \preccurlyeq_i y$.

Definition 2.2. *The binary relation* $\preccurlyeq_i$ *is* transitive, reflexive, symmetric, antisymmetric, *and* complete *if it satisfies the following properties:*

Transitivity: $x \preccurlyeq_i y$ *and* $y \preccurlyeq_i z$ *imply* $x \preccurlyeq_i z$;
Reflexivity: $x \preccurlyeq_i x$ *is true for every* $x \in \mathcal{P}$;
Symmetry: $x \preccurlyeq_i y$ *implies* $y \preccurlyeq_i x$;
Antisymmetry: $x \preccurlyeq_i y$ *and* $y \preccurlyeq_i x$ *imply the equality* $x = y$;
Completeness: *for any* x *and* y *in* $\mathcal{P}$, *either* $x \preccurlyeq_i y$ *or* $y \preccurlyeq_i x$ *is satisfied.*

2.2.2 Examples of Binary Relations

Note that not all properties defined above are to be simultaneously satisfied. For example, the combination of symmetry and antisymmetry implies that the binary relation $\preccurlyeq_i$ is in fact the equality $x = y$. Therefore, all binary relations on $\mathcal{P}$ that are different from the equality cannot be simultaneously symmetric and antisymmetric.

PREORDERS

Definition 2.3. *A* complete preorder $\preccurlyeq_i$ *on* $\mathcal{P}$ *is a binary relation that is transitive, reflexive, and complete.*

ORDERS

Definition 2.4. *A* complete order $\preccurlyeq_i$ *on* $\mathcal{P}$ *is a binary relation that is transitive, reflexive, antisymmetric, and complete.*

EQUIVALENCE RELATIONS

Definition 2.5. *An equivalence relation $\sim_i$ on $\mathcal{P}$ is a binary relation that is transitive, reflexive, and symmetric.*

A useful concept is the one of equivalence class. Let x be an element of $\mathcal{P}$. The equivalence class $C_i(x)$ is the subset of $\mathcal{P}$ consisting of the elements $y \in \mathcal{P}$ that are equivalent to x:

$$C_i(x) = \{z \in \mathcal{P} \mid z \sim_i x\}.$$

Equivalence classes have the remarkable property of partitioning the set $\mathcal{P}$ by which it is meant: 1) two equivalence classes $C_i(x)$ and $C_i(y)$ are either disjoint (i.e., their intersection is empty) or identical depending on whether x and y are equivalent or not; 2) the union of all equivalence classes $C_i(x)$ for $x \in \mathcal{P}$ is equal to the set $\mathcal{P}$.

The set of equivalence classes is denoted by $\mathcal{P}/\sim_i$ and is known as the *quotient set* of $\mathcal{P}$ by the equivalence relation $\sim_i$.

Equality is a typical equivalence relation but its equivalence classes consist of only one element each.

A preorder differs from an equivalence relation by not being symmetric.

2.2.3 Equivalence Relation Associated with a Preorder

Let $\preccurlyeq_i$ be a complete preorder on the set $\mathcal{P}$. The binary relation $x \sim_i y$ is then defined by $x \preccurlyeq_i y$ and $y \preccurlyeq_i x$.

Proposition 2.6. *The binary relation $\sim_i$ associated with the preorder $\preccurlyeq_i$ is an equivalence relation on $\mathcal{P}$.*

Proof. Let us prove that the binary relation $\sim_i$ is reflexive, symmetric, and transitive. Reflexivity $x \sim_i x$ follows from $x \preccurlyeq_i x$ that can be read from left to right and from right to left. Symmetry means that $x \sim_i y$ implies $y \sim_i x$. Relations $x \preccurlyeq_i y$ and $y \preccurlyeq_i x$ are both implied by $x \sim_i y$. These relations can also be read in the order $y \preccurlyeq_i x$ and $x \preccurlyeq_i y$, which then implies $y \sim_i x$. Transitivity means that $x \sim_i y$ and $y \sim_i z$ implies $x \sim_i z$. We reformulate these relations in terms of the preorder $\preccurlyeq_i$. We therefore have $x \preccurlyeq_i y$, $y \preccurlyeq_i x$, $y \preccurlyeq_i z$ and $z \preccurlyeq_i y$. Transitivity of the preorder $\preccurlyeq_i$ then implies $x \preccurlyeq_i z$ and $z \preccurlyeq_i x$, which is the same thing as $x \sim_i z$. $\square$

Proposition 2.7. *The preorder $\preccurlyeq_i$ defines an order on the set of equivalence classes $\mathcal{P}/\sim_i$.*

Proof. This is obvious. $\square$

EXERCISES

2.1. Show that the transitivity of $\preccurlyeq_i$ is equivalent to: $(x, y) \in \mathcal{B}_i$ and $(y, z) \in \mathcal{B}_i$ imply $(x, z) \in \mathcal{B}_i$.

2.2. Show that the antisymmetry of $\preccurlyeq_i$ is equivalent to: $(x, y) \in \mathcal{B}_i$ and $(y, x) \in \mathcal{B}_i$ imply $x = y$.

2.3. Show that reflexivity of $\preccurlyeq_i$ is equivalent to: the diagonal $\Delta = \{(x, x) \mid x \in \mathcal{P}\}$ is contained in $\mathcal{B}_i$.

2.4. Show that completeness of $\preccurlyeq_i$ is equivalent to: for all $(x, y) \in \mathcal{P} \times \mathcal{P}$, either $(x, y) \in \mathcal{B}_i$ or $(y, x) \in \mathcal{B}_i$.

2.5. The relation $x \equiv y$ modulo p is defined on the set of relative integers $\mathbb{Z}$ by the condition that $x - y$ is divisible by the integer $p \neq 0$. Prove that this is an equivalence relation.

2.6. Let $\mathbb{Q}$ denote the set of rational numbers (i.e., real numbers equal to the ratio p/q of two integers p and $q \neq 0$). Let $x = (x^q)$ and $y = (y^q)$ be two sequences with values in $\mathbb{Q}$. Define the relation $x \sim y$ by $\lim_{q \to \infty}(x^q - y^q) = 0$. A sequence $x = (x^q)$ is said to be a Cauchy sequence if, for every $\varepsilon > 0$, there exists an integer N such that, for $p, q \geq N$, the inequality $|x^p - x^q| < \varepsilon$ is satisfied. Let $\mathcal{Q}$ denote the set of Cauchy sequences with values in $\mathbb{Q}$. Show that the quotient set $\mathcal{Q}/\sim$ can be identified to the set of real numbers $\mathbb{R}$.

2.3 CONSUMERS' PREFERENCES

The preference relation of consumer i is a binary relation $\preccurlyeq_i$ defined on the consumption set $\mathbb{R}^\ell$ where $x \preccurlyeq_i y$ means that consumer i prefers the commodity bundle y to the commodity bundle x. Let $\sim_i$ be the equivalence relation on $\mathbb{R}^\ell$ associated with the preorder $\preccurlyeq_i$. Consumer i is said to be indifferent between the two commodity bundles x and y when they are equivalent, i.e., $x \sim_i y$.

By definition, the commodity bundle y is strictly preferred to x if consumer i prefers y to x and is not indifferent between x and y: $x \preccurlyeq_i y$ and $x \not\sim_i y$. The relation of strict preference between y and x is denoted by $x \prec_i y$.

SETS OF PREFERRED AND STRICTLY PREFERRED ALLOCATIONS

The following sets associated with $x_i \in \mathbb{R}^\ell$ represent the commodity bundles that are preferred and strictly preferred to x_i respectively:

- $P_i(x_i) = \{x \in \mathbb{R}^\ell \mid x_i \preccurlyeq_i x\}$;
- $S_i(x_i) = \{x \in \mathbb{R}^\ell \mid x_i \prec_i x\}$.

INDIFFERENCE SETS

The indifference set associated with x_i is the set

- $I_i(x_i) = \{x \in \mathbb{R}^\ell \mid x_i \sim_i x\}$.

It consists of the commodity bundles $x \in \mathbb{R}^\ell$ such that consumer i is indifferent between x and x_i. In the case of two goods, this set is the usual indifference curve of elementary textbooks.

Obviously, we have $P_i(x_i) = S_i(x_i) \cup I_i(x_i)$. We now define properties that are going to add substance to the concept of a preference relation.

2.3.1 Properties of Preference Relations

The economic message carried by the concept of a preference relation that would just be a binary relation is rather weak. Asking for the preference relation to be a preorder is not terribly demanding. We will see later on that transitivity can even be dropped without impairing the most important properties of general equilibrium models. This makes it all the more important that we give more flesh to the concept of preference relation.

CONTINUITY

Definition 2.8. *The preference relation $\preccurlyeq_i$ is continuous if the sets $\{y \in \mathbb{R}^\ell \mid x \preccurlyeq_i y\}$ and $\{y \in \mathbb{R}^\ell \mid y \preccurlyeq_i x\}$ are closed in $\mathbb{R}^\ell$ for every $x \in \mathbb{R}^\ell$.*

The continuity property says that if the sequence (y^q) converges to y^0 and is such that y^q is preferred or indifferent to x, then its limit y^0 is also preferred or indifferent to x. Similarly, if y is preferred or indifferent to y^q, then y is also preferred or indifferent to y^0.

Proposition 2.9. *Let $\preccurlyeq_i$ be a continuous relation. The sets $\{y \in \mathbb{R}^\ell \mid x \prec_i y\}$ and $\{y \in \mathbb{R}^\ell \mid y \prec_i x\}$ are open in $\mathbb{R}^\ell$.*

Proof. The set $\{y \in \mathbb{R}^\ell \mid x \prec_i y\}$ is open because its complement in $\mathbb{R}^\ell$ is the set $\{y \in \mathbb{R}^\ell \mid y \preccurlyeq_i x\}$, a set closed by the continuity of $\preccurlyeq_i$. A similar proof applies to the set $\{y \in \mathbb{R}^\ell \mid y \prec_i x\}$. □

The openness property of the first set can be reformulated as follows: If y is strictly preferred to x and if z is close enough to y, then z is also strictly preferred to x. A similar statement holds true for the second set.

MONOTONICITY

Definition 2.10. *The binary relation $\preccurlyeq_i$ is monotone if the inclusion*

$$x + \mathbb{R}^\ell_+ \setminus \{0\} \subset \{y \in \mathbb{R}^\ell \mid x \prec_i y\}$$

is satisfied for every $x \in \mathbb{R}^\ell$.

Monotonicity is easy to interpret. It says that consumer i strictly prefers the commodity bundle y to the commodity bundle x if y contains at least as much of each commodity as x, with a strict inequality in the quantities of at least one commodity. Though widely true in the real world, there exists a class of "goods" that contradict monotonicity. This class includes for example the "goods" associated with pollution effects. In such cases, it is sufficient to change the formal definition of a commodity by taking its opposite to recover the monotonicity of preferences. For example, one substitutes silence to noise, leisure to labor, etc. This transformation is mathematically equivalent to changing the sign in the mathematical representation of the commodity.

Monotonicity excludes any satiation effect. Satiation exists in the real world for immediate physical consumption but disappears at once if the technology of consumption is improved by, for example, the possibility of stockpiling goods. Monotonicity is therefore a reasonable property for a general theory of markets and production.

CONVEXITY

Definition 2.11. *The preference relation $\preccurlyeq_i$ is convex (resp. strictly convex) if the set $P_i(x)$ of bundles preferred or indifferent to x is convex (resp. strictly convex) for every $x \in \mathbb{R}^\ell$.*

For a definition of the convexity and strict convexity of a set, see appendix E. Strict convexity of preferences means that, if x and y are distinct commodity bundles between which consumer i is indifferent, then he strictly prefers the combination $(x + y)/2$, the average of the two bundles, to x and y. This property is necessary and sufficient.

Convexity is not always satisfied in the real world. However, lack of convexity is more often the result of indivisibilities than the consequence of genuine non-convexities. For example, ordering a fourth or a half of a course in a restaurant is rather exceptional. It suffices to make minor changes to the conventions that rule consumption to bring convexity back.

Remark 2.1. *Though this remark may seem premature, monotonicity and convexity are the properties of preferences that have the most far-reaching implications for the resulting general equilibrium model. Dropping either convexity or monotonicity from the picture leads to relatively impoverished theories.*

BOUNDEDNESS FROM BELOW

Definition 2.12. *The preference relation $\preccurlyeq_i$ is bounded from below if the set $P_i(x)$ of bundles preferred or indifferent to x is bounded from below for every $x \in \mathbb{R}^\ell$.*

Boundedness from below just says that there exists a bundle $B_i \in \mathbb{R}^\ell$ such that the inequality $B_i \leq y$ is satisfied for every y in $P_i(x)$.

Boundedness from below means that it is not possible to compensate the consumption of arbitrarily large negative quantities of some good by sufficiently large positive quantities of other goods. This property is mathematically convenient. Nevertheless, it could be weakened quite significantly without impairing the main construction and properties of the theory of general equilibrium. In other words, this property is more convenient than essential.

2.3.2 Representation of Preference Preorders by Utility Functions

Utility functions are a mathematically convenient way of representing preference relations that are preorders. As far as economic substance is concerned, the two concepts are equivalent.

Definition 2.13. *The utility function of consumer i is a map $u_i : \mathbb{R}^\ell \to \mathbb{R}$ that satisfies the following property:*

$$x_i \preccurlyeq_i y_i \quad \text{is equivalent to} \quad u_i(x_i) \leq u_i(y_i).$$

The following condition is sufficient for a preference preorder to be representable by a continuous utility function.

Proposition 2.14. *The continuous and monotone preorder $\preccurlyeq_i$ on $\mathbb{R}^\ell$ is representable by a continuous surjective utility function $u_i : \mathbb{R}^\ell \to \mathbb{R}$.*

Proof. Let $\mathbf{1} = (1, 1, \ldots, 1) \in \mathbb{R}^\ell$ the vector with all coordinates equal to 1. Let $x \in \mathbb{R}^\ell$ be some commodity bundle. We define the real number $u_i(x)$ (which does not necessarily mean that such number exists at the moment) by the condition that the bundle $u_i(x)\mathbf{1}$ is indifferent to the bundle x. In a first step, let us show that $u_i(x)$ exists and is unique for any $x \in \mathbb{R}^\ell$.

Let $A_+ = \{t \in \mathbb{R} \mid x \preccurlyeq_i t\mathbf{1}\}$ and $A_- = \{t \in \mathbb{R} \mid t\mathbf{1} \preccurlyeq_i x\}$. It follows from the continuity of preferences that the two sets A_+ and A_- are closed. Let us show that they are not empty. Let $x = (x^1, \ldots, x^\ell)$. It follows from monotonicity that if t is larger than $\sup\{x^1, \ldots, x^\ell\}$, the upper bound of the coordinates of x, then $t\mathbf{1}$ is preferred to x and t belongs to the set A_+. Similarly, the real number $t < \inf\{x^1, \ldots, x^\ell\}$ belongs to A_-. The union $A_+ \cup A_-$ is equal to $\mathbb{R}$. It then follows from the connectedness of $\mathbb{R}$ combined with the non-emptiness of A_+ and A_- that their intersection, the set $\{t \in \mathbb{R} \mid t\mathbf{1} \sim_i x\}$, is not empty. By monotonicity, this set can contain only one element. We have therefore proved existence and uniqueness of $u_i(x)$ for every $x \in \mathbb{R}^\ell$.

The function $u_i : \mathbb{R}^\ell \to \mathbb{R}$ is surjective (or onto) because the equality $u_i(t1) = t$ is satisfied for every $t \in \mathbb{R}$.

Let us now show that function $u_i : \mathbb{R}^\ell \to \mathbb{R}$ represents the preferences defined by the preorder $\preccurlyeq_i$. Take x and y that satisfy $x \preccurlyeq_i y$. Since x and y are indifferent to $u_i(x)1$ and $u_i(y)1$ respectively, this yields the relation $u_i(x)1 \preccurlyeq_i u_i(y)1$. The inequality $u_i(x) \le u_i(y)$ then follows from monotonicity. Conversely, monotonicity and the inequality $u_i(y) \le u_i(x)$ imply the relation $u_i(x)1 \preccurlyeq_i u_i(y)1$, hence the relation $x \preccurlyeq_i y$. This proves the equivalence between $x \preccurlyeq_i y$ and $u_i(x) \le u_i(y)$.

Continuity of the utility function u_i still has to be established. It suffices to show that the inverse image by u_i of any open subset of $\mathbb{R}$ is open. Since an open subset of $\mathbb{R}$ can always be described as the union of open intervals, and since the inverse image of a union of sets is the union of the inverse images of these sets, one only has to show that the inverse image of any open interval (α, β) is open.

Let x_α and x_β be two bundles in $\mathbb{R}^\ell$ that satisfy $u_i(x_\alpha) = \alpha$ and $u_i(x_\beta) = \beta$ respectively. These bundles exist, the utility function u_i being onto. Furthermore, we have

$$u_i^{-1}\big((\alpha, \beta)\big) = \{x \in \mathbb{R} \mid x_\alpha \prec_i x \prec_i x_\beta\}.$$

This set is open as being the intersection of the two sets $\{x \in \mathbb{R}^\ell \mid x_\alpha \prec_i x\}$ and $\{x \in \mathbb{R}^\ell \mid x \prec_i x_\beta\}$, sets that are open by the continuity of $\preccurlyeq_i$. $\qquad \square$

The existence of a continuous utility function representing a preorder relation can be proved for continuous preorders defined on $\mathbb{R}^\ell$ that are not necessarily monotone. Nevertheless, Proposition 2.14 is sufficient to our purpose.

2.3.3 Sets of Preferred Allocations and Utility Functions

Proposition 2.15. *Let u_i be a continuous utility function representing the continuous and monotone preorder $\preccurlyeq_i$. We then have*

- $P_i(x_i) = \{x \in \mathbb{R}^\ell \mid x_i \preccurlyeq_i x\} = \{x \in \mathbb{R}^\ell \mid u_i(x_i) \le u_i(x)\};$
- $S_i(x_i) = \{x \in \mathbb{R}^\ell \mid x_i \prec_i x\} = \{x \in \mathbb{R}^\ell \mid u_i(x_i) < u_i(x)\};$
- $I_i(x_i) = \{x \in \mathbb{R}^\ell \mid x_i \sim_i x\} = \{x \in \mathbb{R}^\ell \mid u_i(x_i) = u_i(x)\};$
- *The interior $\overset{o}{\widehat{P_i(x_i)}}$ is the set $S_i(x_i)$.*

Proof. Only the equality $\overset{o}{\widehat{P_i(x_i)}} = S_i(x_i)$ requires a proof.

Inclusion $\overset{o}{\overparen{P_i(x_i)}} \subset S_i(x_i)$. Let $x \in \overset{o}{\overparen{P_i(x_i)}}$. Since x belongs to the interior of $P_i(x_i)$, there exists an open ball $B(x; r)$ of radius $r > 0$ that is contained in the set $P_i(x_i)$. Let $\mathbf{1} = (1, 1, \ldots, 1)$ be the vector with coordinates all equal to 1. Then, the point $y = x - \varepsilon\mathbf{1}$ belongs to the open ball $B(x; r)$ for $\varepsilon > 0$ small enough and, therefore, to $P_i(x_i)$. (It suffices to take $\varepsilon < r$ with the sup norm.) The inequality $u_i(x_i) \le u_i(y)$ is then satisfied. The strict inequality $u_i(y) < u_i(x)$ is satisfied by the monotonicity assumption 2.16. The combination of these two inequalities yields the strict inequality $u_i(x_i) < u_i(x)$, which proves that x belongs to the set $S_i(x_i)$.

Inclusion $S_i(x_i) \subset \overset{o}{\overparen{P_i(x_i)}}$. The set $S_i(x_i) = \{x \in \mathbb{R}^\ell \mid u_i(x_i) < u_i(x)\}$ is the preimage of the open interval $\big(u_i(x_i), +\infty\big)$ by the continuous map $u_i : \mathbb{R}^\ell \to \mathbb{R}$. The set $S_i(x_i)$ is therefore open by the continuity of u_i. The inclusion $S_i(x_i) \subset \overset{o}{\overparen{P_i(x_i)}}$ then follows from the property that the interior $\overset{o}{\overparen{P_i(x_i)}}$ of the set $P_i(x_i)$ contains all open subsets of $P_i(x_i)$. $\qquad\square$

2.3.4 Ordinal Utility Functions

Let the map $\phi : \mathbb{R} \to \mathbb{R}$ be a smooth function with a strictly positive derivative. The composition $\phi \circ u_i : \mathbb{R}^\ell \to \mathbb{R}$ represents the same preference relation $\preccurlyeq_i$ as the smooth utility function $u_i : \mathbb{R}^\ell \to \mathbb{R}$. The properties of u_i that are invariant by composition with any function like $\phi : \mathbb{R} \to \mathbb{R}$ are in fact properties of the underlying preference preorder $\preccurlyeq_i$. The utility function $u_i : \mathbb{R}^\ell \to \mathbb{R}$ does not make the utility $u_i(x_i)$ of the commodity bundle $x_i \in \mathbb{R}^\ell$ a measurable quantity. Let y_i be a commodity bundle that gives a utility level that is twice the utility of x_i for u_i: $u_i(y_i) = 2\,u_i(x_i)$. After composition with some smoothly increasing map $\phi : \mathbb{R} \to \mathbb{R}$, the equality $\phi\big(u_i(y_i)\big) = 2\,\phi\big(u_i(x_i)\big)$ is not satisfied in general. Economists express this lack of measurability by saying that the function u_i that represents the preference preorder $\preccurlyeq_i$ is an *ordinal utility function* and not a *cardinal utility function*, the latter utility functions carrying some aspects of measurability.

EXERCISES

2.7. Prove the equivalence of the following properties: i) $x \sim_i x_i$; ii) $P_i(x) = P_i(x_i)$; iii) $I_i(x) = I_i(x_i)$; iv) $S_i(x) = S_i(x_i)$.

2.8. Prove the equivalence between $x_i \preccurlyeq_i x$ and $P_i(x) \subset P_i(x_i)$ when $\preccurlyeq_i$ is a complete preorder. Is this property true for a non-transitive binary relation $\preccurlyeq_i$?

2.4 SMOOTH UTILITY FUNCTIONS

2.4.1 Smoothness

We now assume that consumer i's preferences are represented by a smooth utility function $u_i : \mathbb{R}^\ell \to \mathbb{R}$. This means that the utility function u_i has partial derivatives of any order, partial derivatives that are also differentiable. Smoothness implies continuity.

The economic interpretation of continuity is easy. Two commodity bundles that are close yield utility levels that are also close. Differentiability (smoothness) implies continuity.

Continuity, however, is not sufficient if one wants to study properties of the economic model that go beyond existence and the two welfare theorems. Smoothness is necessary. In that regard, economics is not different from physics. The justification for the use of smooth utility functions lies in the property that *continuous* functions can be approximated by *smooth* functions. There exist many approximation theorems of this kind. The best-known one is the Stone-Weierstrass theorem [28]. These theorems state that for suitable topologies, smooth functions are dense in sets of continuous functions.

Because of this density property, there is no loss of economic substance in restricting the class of utility functions to smooth functions.

2.4.2 Smooth Monotonicity

Smooth monotonicity is expressed as a property of the first order derivatives of the utility function. For a definition of the gradient vector, see section A.2 of the Appendix A.

Definition 2.16. *The utility function u_i is smoothly monotone if its gradient vector $Du_i(x_i)$ is strictly positive for any $x_i \in \mathbb{R}^\ell$.*

In other words, all first order partial derivatives of u_i at $x_i \in \mathbb{R}^\ell$ are strictly positive.

Smooth monotonicity of the utility function u_i obviously implies the monotonicity of the associated preference relation $\preccurlyeq_i$.

INDIFFERENCE SETS AS SMOOTH HYPERSURFACES

An important and immediate consequence of the smoothness and monotonicity assumptions deals with the shape and, more generally, with the geometrical properties of indifference sets $I_i(x_i) = \{x \in \mathbb{R}^\ell \mid u_i(x_i) = u_i(x)\}$ for any $x_i \in \mathbb{R}^\ell$.

Proposition 2.17. *The indifference sets $I_i(x_i)$ are smooth hyper-surfaces in $\mathbb{R}^\ell$.*

Hypersurfaces are a special class of submanifolds of $\mathbb{R}^\ell$. We can take it as a definition that a smooth hypersurface is defined by an equation of the form $h(x_i) = 0$ where h is a smooth map from $\mathbb{R}^\ell$, or from some open subset of $\mathbb{R}^\ell$, into $\mathbb{R}$ such that the gradient vector $Dh(x_i)$ is different from 0 at every point x_i of the hypersurface. Often, we use the terms surface and plane instead of hypersurface and hyperplane though, rigorously speaking, surfaces should be two-dimensional smooth sub-manifolds in three-dimensional spaces, planes two-dimensional affine spaces, and hyperplanes codimension one affine spaces in Euclidean spaces.

The hypersurface defined by equation $h(x_i) = 0$ has a tangent hyperplane at every point x_i. That tangent hyperplane is the set $\{x \in \mathbb{R}^\ell \mid Dh(x_i)^T(x - x_i) = 0\}$. Note that the inner product $Dh(x_i)^T(x - x_i)$ is the first order term of the Taylor expansion at the point x_i of the function $h : x \to h(x)$. This explains that the tangent hyperplane represents the best possible linear approximation of the hypersurface at the point x_i.

Proof of Proposition 2.17. The indifference set $I_i(x_i)$ is the set of zeros of the smooth function $h(x) = u_i(x) - u_i(x_i)$ (where x_i is fixed). That function is smooth since u_i is smooth. Its gradient vector $Dh(x) = Du_i(x)$ is different from 0 for any $x \in \mathbb{R}^\ell$ (and therefore for $x \in I_i(x_i)$) by Assumption 2.16. $\qquad\Box$

TANGENT HYPERPLANES TO INDIFFERENCE HYPERSURFACES

The pictures of indifference curves found in introductory textbooks for the case of two goods help develop the intuition about preferences. The goal of this section is to extend that intuition to higher dimensions where it is not so easy to draw pictures. This is our first inroad into smooth manifold territory. Here, the manifolds are very simple objects, namely curves in the two-dimensional plane, surfaces in the three-dimensional space, and more generally smooth hypersurfaces defined by a smooth equation in the ℓ-dimensional Euclidean space $\mathbb{R}^\ell$.

Proposition 2.18. *The tangent hyperplane $T_i(x_i)$ to the indifference hypersurface $I_i(x_i)$ at x_i is the set $\{x \in \mathbb{R}^\ell \mid Du_i(x_i)^T(x - x_i) = 0\}$. This tangent hyperplane is perpendicular to the gradient vector $Du_i(x_i)$.*

Proof. The equation of the indifference surface $I_i(x_i)$ is $u_i(x) - u_i(x_i) = 0$. The gradient vector at x_i of the map $x \to u_i(x) - u_i(x_i)$ is equal to

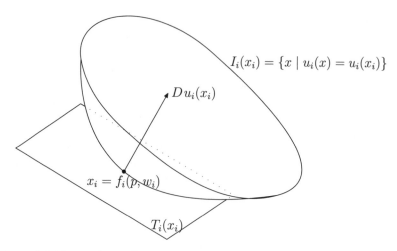

Figure 2.1 Tangent hyperplane $T_i(x_i)$ to the indifference hypersurface $I_i(x_i)$

$Du_i(x_i)$. It follows from the properties of the tangent hyperplane to a hypersurface that the hyperplane $T_i(x_i)$ that is tangent to the indifference hypersurface $I_i(x_i)$ at x_i is defined by equation $Du_i(x_i)^T(x - x_i) = 0$.

The perpendicularity of the gradient vector $Du_i(x)$ with the vector $x - x_i$ for all x belonging to the hyperplane $T_i(x_i)$ follows from the inner product $Du_i(x_i)^T(x - x_i)$ being equal to 0. □

2.4.3 Smooth Quasi-concavity

Definition 2.19. *The utility function $u_i : \mathbb{R}^\ell \to \mathbb{R}$ is smoothly quasi-concave if the function u_i is smoothly (strictly) concave in the sense of Definition E.6 of the Appendix E.*

Proposition 2.20. *The smoothly quasi-concave utility function $u_i : \mathbb{R}^\ell \to \mathbb{R}$ is strictly concave.*

Proof. This is just Proposition E.7 of the Appendix E. □

Smooth quasi-concavity is to strict quasi-concavity what smooth monotonicity is to strict monotonicity.

STRICT CONVEXITY OF SETS OF PREFERRED ALLOCATIONS

Proposition 2.21. *The set $P_i(x_i) = \{x \in \mathbb{R}^\ell \mid u_i(x_i) \leq u_i(x)\}$ is strictly convex for every $x_i \in \mathbb{R}^\ell$.*

Proof. Smooth quasi-concavity implies strict quasi-concavity. The proposition then follows from the definition of strict quasi-concavity: Section E.2 of the Appendix E. □

Proposition 2.22. *Let $u_i : \mathbb{R}^\ell \to \mathbb{R}$, a smooth function. The function u_i is smoothly quasi-concave if and only if, for any $x_i \in \mathbb{R}^\ell$, the only solution to*

$$\begin{cases} Z^T D^2 u_i(x_i) \, Z & \geq 0 \\ Du_i(x_i)^T Z & = 0 \end{cases}$$

is $Z = 0 \in \mathbb{R}^\ell$.

Proof. This is essentially Proposition E.8 of the Appendix E. □

THE BORDERED HESSIAN MATRIX OF A SMOOTH QUASI-CONCAVE UTILITY FUNCTION

Definition 2.23. *The bordered Hessian matrix associated with the utility function u_i at $x_i \in \mathbb{R}^\ell$ is the $(\ell + 1) \times (\ell + 1)$ matrix*

$$H_i(x_i) = \begin{bmatrix} D^2 u_i(x_i) & Du_i(x_i) \\ Du_i(x_i)^T & 0 \end{bmatrix}$$

The bordered Hessian matrix is symmetric like the Hessian matrix $D^2 u_i(x_i)$. It is neither negative definite nor negative semi-definite. The determinant of that matrix, however, has an interesting and useful property:

Proposition 2.24. *Let u_i be a smooth quasi-concave utility function. Its bordered Hessian matrix $H_i(x_i)$ is invertible for every $x_i \in \mathbb{R}^\ell$.*

Proof. This is essentially Proposition E.10 of the Appendix E. □

2.4.4 Boundedness from Below

Definition 2.25. *The utility function $u_i : \mathbb{R}^\ell \to \mathbb{R}$ is bounded from below if the set $P_i(x_i) = \{x \in \mathbb{R}^\ell \mid u_i(x_i) \leq u_i(x)\}$ is bounded from below in $\mathbb{R}^\ell$ for any $x_i \in \mathbb{R}^\ell$.*

This definition is equivalent to the associated preference relation $\precsim_i$ being bounded from below in the sense of Definition 2.12.

2.4.5 Standard Utility Functions

We now define the class of utility functions at the heart of classical consumer theory.

Definition 2.26. *A standard utility function $u_i : \mathbb{R}^\ell \to \mathbb{R}$ satisfies the following properties: smoothness, smooth monotonicity, smooth (strict) quasi-concavity, and boundedness from below.*

We denote by $\mathcal{U}$ the set of these standard utility functions.

2.5 CONCLUSION

The use of (ordinal) utility functions is widespread in economic theory. But we will see in the next chapters that the main properties that we now know to be satisfied by the general equilibrium model do not require such a restrictive setup. This is why the next chapter is devoted to a theory of the consumer based on demand functions that do not necessarily result from the budget constrained maximization of some utility function.

2.6 NOTES AND COMMENTS

The introduction of utility as the determinant of the consumer's economic behavior is known as the marginalist revolution. For details, see [60], pp. 1053–1073. The resulting economic theory is known as neoclassical economics to avoid any confusion with classical economic theory that is essentially based on Ricardo's labor theory of value. The marginalist revolution is traditionally associated with the names of Jevons, Menger, and Walras who came independently to the model of the consumer as a utility maximizer subject to a budget constraint at approximately the same time. The mathematical model of the consumer enables Walras to close the model of an economy already considered by Cournot in his pathbreaking book [22], but a model that was then limited to firms. The equation system of the general equilibrium model formulated by Walras in [67] has the same level of generality as the most recent versions of the model.

At first, utility is cardinal, which is more or less equivalent to the measurability of utility. Edgeworth was the first to promote the use of indifference curves instead of cardinal utility functions. But it was Pareto who observed more than 30 years after the publication of Walras' book that the main properties of the Walrasian general equilibrium model remain true when the assumption of measurability of utility conveyed by the cardinal utility functions is dropped. With ordinal utility, utility levels are only compared, not measured. The better relevance of ordinal utility over cardinal utility is obvious. The important point made by Pareto is that ordinal utilities are enough to develop the theory of general equilibrium.

If the cardinality assumption can be dropped at almost no cost as far as the properties of the general equilibrium model are concerned, this is not true for all the models that address issues of public economics like optimal taxation or the pricing of public goods. There, interpersonal comparisons of individual utility levels are particularly handy. Nevertheless, methods that continue to rely on interpersonal comparisons of utility are considered by current theoretical standards to be deeply flawed.

CHAPTER 3

Demand Functions

3.1 INTRODUCTION

Rational consumers are assumed to maximize their preferences subject to the constraints they perceive. With preferences that are representable by utility functions, the consumer's problem is modeled as one of maximizing a standard utility function subject to a budget constraint. This maximization problem determines the consumer's demand, a demand that is a function of the consumer's wealth and market prices.

These demand functions feature several remarkable properties that make up the bulk of classical consumer theory. The most important ones are Walras law, the weak axiom of revealed preferences (WARP), and the negative definiteness of the Slutsky matrices (ND). An important part of consumer theory is devoted to establishing these properties of demand functions when the latter come from the budget constrained maximization of standard utility functions. The main part of this chapter is devoted to this classical part of the theory. In a final section, however, we drop the straitjacket of utility maximization to characterize consumer's demand functions simply by their properties, namely Walras law (W), boundedness from below (B), desirability (A), the weak axiom of revealed preferences (WARP), and the negative definiteness of not necessarily symmetric Slutsky matrices (ND).

3.2 CONSTRAINED UTILITY MAXIMIZATION

Let consumer i's preferences be defined by a smooth, smoothly monotone, smoothly quasi-concave, and bounded from below utility function $u_i : \mathbb{R}^\ell \to \mathbb{R}$. In other words, we have $u_i \in \mathcal{U}$.

3.2.1 An Optimization Problem

THE CONSUMER'S BUDGET SET

Given the price vector $p \in S$ and income $w_i \in \mathbb{R}$, the budget set of consumer i consists of the commodity bundles $x_i \in \mathbb{R}^\ell$ that the consumer can afford or, in other words, that have a value less than or equal to the income w_i. This is the set

$$\{x_i \in \mathbb{R}^\ell \mid p \cdot x_i \leq w_i\}.$$

THE CONSUMER'S OBJECTIVE FUNCTION: UTILITY

The main assumption of consumer theory is that consumer's demand $x_i \in \mathbb{R}^\ell$ maximizes the utility $u_i(x_i)$ subject to the budget constraint $p \cdot x_i \leq w_i$.

THE CONSUMER'S CONSTRAINED OPTIMIZATION PROBLEM

The mathematical formulation of consumer i's problem is therefore:

$$\begin{cases} \text{Maximize} & u_i(x_i) \\ \text{subject to} & p \cdot x_i \leq w_i. \end{cases}$$

Given the price vector $p \in S$ and wealth $w_i \in \mathbb{R}$, consumer i's demand is a solution of this constrained maximization problem.

3.2.2 Existence and Uniqueness of the Solution

Proposition 3.1. *Consumer i's constrained optimization problem has a unique solution for any price vector $p \in S$ and $w_i \in \mathbb{R}$.*

Proof. Let y_i be an element of $\mathbb{R}^\ell$ such that the inner product $p \cdot y_i$ is less than or equal to w_i. Every x_i solution of consumer i's optimization problem satisfies the inequality $u_i(x_i) \geq u_i(y_i)$. The solution set of consumer i's constrained optimization problem is therefore not modified by the addition of the constraint $u_i(x_i) \geq u_i(y_i)$.

We now show that the subset K of $\mathbb{R}^\ell$ defined by the two constraints $p \cdot x_i \leq w_i$ and $u_i(x_i) \geq u_i(y_i)$ is compact. This is equivalent to showing that the set K is closed and bounded in $\mathbb{R}^\ell$.

The set K is closed in $\mathbb{R}^\ell$ as the intersection of two closed sets, namely $\{x_i \in \mathbb{R}^\ell \mid u_i(x_i) \geq u_i(y_i)\}$ and the halfspace $\{x_i \in \mathbb{R}^\ell \mid p \cdot x_i \leq w_i\}$. To prove compactness, it suffices to show that K is bounded.

The set K is a subset of $\{x_i \in \mathbb{R}^\ell \mid u_i(y_i) \leq u_i(x_i)\}$, which itself is bounded from below. This proves that K is bounded from below.

There exists some $B \in \mathbb{R}^\ell$ such that $B \leq x_i$ for any $x_i \in K$. Since the coordinates of the price vector $p \in S$ are all strictly positive, we get for coordinate k the inequality $p_k B^k \leq p_k x_i^k$. This implies the inequality

$$p_1 x_i^1 + p_2 B^2 + \cdots + B^\ell \leq p_1 x_i^1 + p_2 x_i^2 + \cdots + x_i^\ell.$$

The combination of this inequality with the inequality $p \cdot x_i \leq w_i$ yields

$$p_1 x_i^1 \leq w_i - (p_2 B^2 + \cdots + B^\ell),$$

which proves that x_i^1 is bounded from above. Similar reasoning shows that x_i^k is also bounded from above for every k between 1 and ℓ.

The utility function u_i being continuous, it reaches its maximum on the compact set K.

We now prove the uniqueness of the utility maximizing solution. We argue by contradiction. Let x_i and x_i' with $x_i \neq x_i'$ be two solutions. The equality $u_i(x_i) = u_i(x_i')$ is satisfied by the definition of x_i and x_i'. Let $x_i'' = (x_i + x_i')/2$. The budget constraint is obviously satisfied by x_i''. The inequality $u_i(x_i'') > u_i(x_i) = u_i(x_i')$ is satisfied by the strict quasi-concavity of u_i by Proposition E.1 of the Appendix. Therefore, x_i'' belongs to K. The strict inequality $u_i(x_i'') > u_i(x_i)$ then contradicts the definition of x_i as a solution of the utility maximization problem. □

3.2.3 Binding Budget Constraints

Proposition 3.2. *The budget constraint $p \cdot x_i \leq w_i$ is binding in consumer i's maximization problem.*

This proposition tells us that, if x_i is the solution to consumer i's utility maximization problem, then the equality $p \cdot x_i = w_i$ is satisfied.

Proof. Let us assume the contrary, i.e., that we have $p \cdot x_i < w_i$. The difference $\varepsilon = w_i - p \cdot x_i$ is > 0. Define the commodity bundle $x = (x^1, x^2, \ldots, x^\ell)$ by the conditions

$$x^1 = x_i^1, \ x^2 = x_i^2, \ldots, \ x^{\ell-1} = x_i^{\ell-1}, \ x^\ell = x_i^\ell + \varepsilon.$$

It follows from the definition of ε (combined with the numeraire assumption, i.e., the equality $p_\ell = 1$) that we have $p \cdot x \leq w_i$ (actually, there is equality), while the inequality $u_i(x) > u_i(x_i)$ follows from the monotonicity of u_i, a contradiction with the definition of x_i as the solution to the constrained utility maximization problem. □

3.2.4 First-order Conditions for Consumer i's Budget Constrained Utility Maximization Problem

Optimization of a smooth function yields first order conditions that have to be satisfied by its first order derivatives at solutions of the optimization problem. These conditions can be necessary or sufficient depending on the nature of the objective function and constraint. Here, we focus on the first order conditions associated with consumer i's constrained optimization problem when consumer i' utility function is standard, i.e., belongs to the set $\mathcal{U}$.

Proposition 3.3. *The element $x_i \in \mathbb{R}^\ell$ is the solution to consumer i's budget constrained utility maximization problem if and only if there exists a real number $\lambda_i > 0$ such that*

$$\begin{cases} Du_i(x_i) - \lambda_i p = 0, \\ p \cdot x_i - w_i = 0. \end{cases}$$

The proof of this proposition is standard in constrained optimization theory and is included here only for the sake of completeness. Most readers will skip it.

Proof.
The condition is necessary.
Let us show that the vectors p and $Du_i(x_i)$ are collinear. Let $H(p)$ be the hyperplane of $\mathbb{R}^\ell$ that is perpendicular to the price vector $p \in S$. It then suffices that we show that the vector $Du_i(x_i)$ is perpendicular to the hyperplane $H(p)$.

Let $\mathbf{u}$ be an arbitrary vector in $H(p)$. That vector satisfies $p \cdot \mathbf{u} = 0$. Let $x = x_i + t\mathbf{u}$ with $t > 0$. From $p \cdot x = p \cdot x_i + tp \cdot \mathbf{u} = p \cdot x_i = w_i$, the inequality $u_i(x) \leq u_i(x_i)$ is satisfied.

Let

$$u_i(x) = u_i(x_i) + Du_i(x_i)(x - x_i) + \epsilon(x)$$

be a first order Taylor expansion of u_i at x_i. The rest term $\epsilon(x)$ satisfies

$$\lim_{\|x - x_i\| \to 0} \frac{|\epsilon(x)|}{\|x - x_i\|} = 0. \tag{1}$$

Combined with inequality $u_i(x) \leq u_i(x_i)$, we get

$$u_i(x_i) + Du_i(x_i)(x - x_i) + \epsilon(x) \leq u_i(x_i),$$

and therefore

$$tDu_i(x_i) \cdot \mathbf{u} + \epsilon(x) \leq 0.$$

After division by $t > 0$, let us have t tend to 0. The above inequality becomes, given (1), $Du_i(x_i) \cdot \mathbf{u} \leq 0$.

We now repeat the same line of reasoning with the vector $-\mathbf{u}$. This yields the inequality $Du_i(x_i) \cdot (-\mathbf{u}) \leq 0$, which, after multiplication by -1, yields the inequality $Du_i(x_i) \cdot \mathbf{u} \geq 0$. The combination of the two opposite inequalities yields the equality $Du_i(x_i) \cdot \mathbf{u} = 0$ for every vector $\mathbf{u} \in H(p)$, which proves that the vector $Du_i(x_i)$ is perpendicular to the hyperplane $H(p)$.

The condition is sufficient.

Let $(x_i, \lambda_i) \in \mathbb{R}^\ell \times \mathbb{R}_{++}$ that satisfies the first order conditions. Let us show that x_i solves the consumer i's budget constrained utility optimization problem.

We use a contradiction argument. Assume that x_i does not solve the optimization problem. There exists some $x \in \mathbb{R}^\ell$ that satisfies the strict inequality $u_i(x_i) < u_i(x)$ and the inequality $p \cdot x \leq w_i = p \cdot x_i$. By the strict quasi-concavity of u_i, the strict inequality $Du_i(x_i)^T(x - x_i) > 0$ follows from Proposition E.2 in the Appendix. The second inequality can be written as $p \cdot (x - x_i) \leq 0$ which, after multiplication by $\lambda_i > 0$, becomes $Du_i(x_i)^T(x - x_i) \leq 0$, hence a contradiction. □

These first order conditions take a simple form with the help of the (numeraire) normalized gradient of the utility u_i defined in Section A.2 of the Appendix:

Corollary 3.4. *Let x_i be the solution of the problem of maximizing $u_i(x_i')$ subject to the constraint $p \cdot x_i' \leq p \cdot x_i$. Then, we have $D_n u_i(x_i) = p$.*

EXERCISE

3.1. Let $x_i \in \mathbb{R}^\ell$. Define $p = D_n u_i(x_i)$ and $w_i = p \cdot x_i$. Show that x_i maximizes $u_i(x_i')$ subject to the constraint $p \cdot x_i' \leq w_i$.

3.3 THE INDIVIDUAL DEMAND FUNCTION

Consumer i's *demand* is uniquely determined by the price vector $p \in S$ and the wealth $w_i \in \mathbb{R}$. We denote by $f_i(p, w_i)$ this commodity bundle. Consumer i's *demand function* is the map $f_i : S \times \mathbb{R} \to \mathbb{R}^\ell$.

Definition 3.5. *Let $\mathcal{D}$ denote the set of demand functions $f_i : S \times \mathbb{R} \to \mathbb{R}^\ell$ that result from the maximization subject to a budget constraint of some standard utility function $u_i \in \mathcal{U}$.*

Our goal is to uncover several properties of the functions that belong to $\mathcal{D}$ and in particular those properties that play a crucial role in the analysis of general equilibrium models. Some of these properties will involve the Slutsky matrices of these demand functions, matrices that we now define.

3.3.1 *The Slutsky Matrix of a Smooth Demand Function*

In the following definition, the price vector $p \in \mathbb{R}^{\ell}_{++}$ is not normalized. The demand function $f_i(p, w_i)$ is then homogenous of degree zero. The Slutsky matrix is usually defined for non-normalized price vectors:

Definition 3.6. *The (non-normalized) Slutsky matrix* $Sf_i(p, w_i) = \left(s_{jk}(p, w_i)\right)$ *associated with the map* $f_i : S \times \mathbb{R} \to \mathbb{R}^{\ell}$ *is defined for the non-normalized price vector* $p = (p_1, \ldots, p_{\ell})$ *by*

$$s_{jk}(p, w_i) = \frac{\partial f_i^j}{\partial p_k}(p, w_i) + \frac{\partial f_i^j}{\partial w_i}(p, w_i) \, f_i^k(p, w_i)$$

for $1 \le j, k \le \ell$.

3.3.2 *Slutsky Matrix (Numeraire Normalized)*

With numeraire normalized prices $p \in S$, the numeraire normalized Slutsky matrix is defined as follows:

Definition 3.7. *The* $(\ell - 1) \times (\ell - 1)$ *(numeraire normalized) Slutsky matrix* $S_{\ell\ell}f_i(p, w_i)$ *of the function* $f_i \in D$ *is the matrix defined by the first* $\ell - 1$ *rows and columns of the (non-normalized) Slutsky matrix* $Sf_i(p, w_i)$.

EXERCISE

3.2. Let $Sf_i(p, w_i)$ be the non-normalized Slutsky matrix of the function $f_i \in D$. Prove the equality $p^T Sf_i(p, w_i) = Sf_i(p, w_i) \, p = 0$.

3.4 Properties of Demand Functions in D

3.4.1 *Smoothness (S)*

Proposition 3.8. *Every function* $f_i \in D$ *is smooth (S)*.

Proof. The proof of this proposition will be our first application of the implicit function theorem. That theorem is a very convenient tool for proving that the solution of an equation system depends smoothly on the parameters defining that equation system.

We use the equation system of Proposition 3.3 defined by the first order conditions of the budget constrained utility maximization problem:

$$Du_i(x_i) - \lambda_i p = 0 \quad \text{and} \quad p \cdot x_i - w_i = 0.$$

The implicit function theorem tells us that the solution (x_i, λ_i) is a smooth function of p and w_i if the matrix obtained by taking the derivatives of the above equation system with respect to the coordinates of x_i and λ_i at the point (x_i, λ_i, p, w_i) is invertible.

This matrix is equal to

$$\begin{bmatrix} D^2 u_i(x_i) & -p \\ p & 0 \end{bmatrix}.$$

We do not change invertibility by multiplying the last column by -1, which yields

$$\begin{bmatrix} D^2 u_i(x_i) & p \\ p & 0 \end{bmatrix};$$

and, again, by multiplying the last row and column by $\lambda_i \neq 0$, we get

$$\begin{bmatrix} D^2 u_i(x_i) & Du_i(x_i) \\ Du_i(x_i)^T & 0 \end{bmatrix}.$$

This matrix is invertible by Proposition 2.24.

The solution (x_i, λ_i) is therefore a smooth function of $(p, w_i) \in S \times \mathbb{R}_{++}$. This implies that the component x_i of (x_i, λ_i) is also a smooth function of (p, w_i). $\qquad\square$

The smoothness property of individual demand functions can be strengthened as follows:

Proposition 3.9. *Every function $f_i \in \mathcal{D}$ is a diffeomorphism.*

This statement means that, in addition to being smooth, the demand function $f_i \in \mathcal{D}$ is a bijection and its inverse $g_i = f_i^{-1}$ (whose existence is ensured by the property that the function f_i is a bijection) is also smooth.

Proof. Recall that $D_n u_i(x_i)$ denotes the normalized gradient of u_i. Let us define the map $g_i : \mathbb{R}^\ell \to S \times \mathbb{R}$ by the formula

$$g_i(x_i) = \left(D_n u_i(x_i), D_n u_i(x_i)^T x_i\right).$$

The map $x_i \to D_n u_i(x_i)$ is smooth. The inner product $(x, y) \to x \cdot y = x^T y = y^T x$ is bilinear, hence smooth. Therefore, the map $x_i \to D_n u_i(x_i)^T x_i$ is also smooth. This proves that the map g_i is smooth.

Let us establish that the maps f_i and g_i are inverse, i.e., that the relations $f_i \circ g_i = \mathrm{id}_{\mathbb{R}^\ell}$, and $g_i \circ f_i = \mathrm{id}_{S \times \mathbb{R}}$ are satisfied.

Computation of $f_i \circ g_i$. Let us compute $f_i \circ g_i(x_i)$, where x_i is in $\mathbb{R}^\ell$. Let $p = D_n u_i(x_i)$ and $w_i = D_n u_i(x_i)^T x_i$. We have $g_i(x_i) = (p, w_i)$ and, therefore, $f_i \circ g_i(x_i) = f_i(p, w_i)$. We observe that x_i then satisfies the normalized first order conditions, which implies the equality $x_i = f_i(p, w_i)$.

Computation of $g_i \circ f_i$. Let $x_i = f_i(p, w_i)$. We then have $g_i \circ f_i(p, w_i) = g_i(x_i)$. By Corollary 3.4, we have $D_n u_i\big(f_i(p, w_i)\big) = p$ and, by Walras law (W), $p \cdot x_i = p \cdot f_i(p, w_i) = w_i$, which proves the equality $g_i(x_i) = (p, w_i)$.

We have therefore established that the maps f_i and g_i are bijections, which are inverse to each other, and that the map g_i is smooth. Finally, it also follows from Proposition 3.8 that the map f_i is smooth. □

Corollary 3.10. *The Jacobian matrix of the map $f_i : S \times \mathbb{R} \to \mathbb{R}^\ell$ is invertible.*

Proof. Taking the derivatives of the maps $f_i \circ g_i = \mathrm{id}_{\mathbb{R}^\ell}$ and $g_i \circ f_i = \mathrm{id}_{S \times \mathbb{R}}$ yields the equalities

$$D(f_i \circ g_i) = D(\mathrm{id}_{\mathbb{R}^\ell}) = \mathrm{id}_{\mathbb{R}^\ell} \quad \text{and} \quad D(g_i \circ f_i) = D(\mathrm{id}_{S \times \mathbb{R}}) = \mathrm{id}_{S \times \mathbb{R}}.$$

The chain rule gives $D(f_i \circ g_i) = D(f_i) \circ D(g_i)$ and $D(g_i \circ f_i) = D(g_i) \circ D(f_i)$. The linear maps Df_i and Dg_i are therefore inverse to each other. In other words, the map f_i has an invertible Jacobian matrix, the matrix of the map Df_i. □

The following matrix is computed at $(p, w_i) \in S \times \mathbb{R}$.

Corollary 3.11.

$$\det \begin{bmatrix} \dfrac{\partial f_i^1}{\partial p_1} & \dfrac{\partial f_i^1}{\partial p_2} & \cdots & \dfrac{\partial f_i^1}{\partial p_{\ell-1}} & \dfrac{\partial f_i^1}{\partial w_i} \\[2ex] \dfrac{\partial f_i^2}{\partial p_1} & \dfrac{\partial f_i^2}{\partial p_2} & \cdots & \dfrac{\partial f_i^2}{\partial p_{\ell-1}} & \dfrac{\partial f_i^2}{\partial w_i} \\[2ex] \vdots & \vdots & \ddots & \vdots & \vdots \\[2ex] \dfrac{\partial f_i^{\ell-1}}{\partial p_1} & \dfrac{\partial f_i^{\ell-1}}{\partial p_2} & \cdots & \dfrac{\partial f_i^{\ell-1}}{\partial p_{\ell-1}} & \dfrac{\partial f_i^{\ell-1}}{\partial w_i} \\[2ex] \dfrac{\partial f_i^\ell}{\partial p_1} & \dfrac{\partial f_i^\ell}{\partial p_2} & \cdots & \dfrac{\partial f_i^\ell}{\partial p_{\ell-1}} & \dfrac{\partial f_i^\ell}{\partial w_i} \end{bmatrix} \neq 0.$$

Proof. This matrix is the Jacobian matrix $Df_i(p, w_i)$ of the individual demand function f_i at (p, w_i). It is invertible by Corollary 3.10; its determinant is therefore different from 0. □

3.4.2 Walras Law (W)

Proposition 3.12. *Every function $f_i \in \mathcal{D}$ satisfies the identity*

$$p \cdot f_i(p, w_i) = w_i \quad for all (p, w_i) \in S \times \mathbb{R}.$$

This identity is known as Walras law (W).

Proof. The identity $p \cdot f_i(p, w_i) = w_i$ is equivalent to the budget constraint $p \cdot x_i \leq w_i$ being binding in consumer i's budget constrained maximization problem, a property established in Proposition 3.2. □

IDENTITIES INVOLVING THE FIRST-ORDER DERIVATIVES OF THE
DEMAND FUNCTION $f_i \in \mathcal{D}$

Proposition 3.13. *The following identities are satisfied by the first-order derivatives of the individual demand function $f_i \in \mathcal{D}$.*

$$p \cdot \frac{\partial f_i}{\partial w_i}(p, w_i) = 1; \tag{2}$$

$$p \cdot \frac{\partial f_i}{\partial p_j}(p, w_i) = -f_i^j(p, w_i) \tag{3}$$

with $j = 1, 2, \ldots, \ell - 1$.

Proof. Equality (2) is obtained by taking the derivative of Walras law $p \cdot f_i(p, w_i) = w_i$ with respect to w_i. By taking the derivative with respect to p_j, one gets $f_i^j(p, w_i) + p \cdot \frac{\partial f_i}{\partial p_j}(p, w_i) = 0$, hence Equality (3). □

3.4.3 Boundedness from Below (B)

Definition 3.14. *The function $f_i \in \mathcal{D}$ satisfies boundedness from below (B) if, for any compact subset $K_i \subset \mathbb{R}^\ell$, the set $\{f_i(p, p \cdot \omega_i) \mid \omega_i \in K_i$ and $p \in S\}$ is bounded from below.*

Boundedness from below (B) means the demand for all goods is bounded from below when endowments are bounded from below.

Proposition 3.15. *Every function $f_i \in \mathcal{D}$ satisfies boundedness from below (B).*

Proof. Let K_i be a compact subset of $\mathbb{R}^\ell$. There exists $B_i \in \mathbb{R}^\ell$ such that $B_i \leq \omega_i$ for any $\omega_i \in K_i$. For any $p \in S$, the utility $u_i(f_i(p, p \cdot \omega_i))$ is larger than or equal to $u_i(\omega_i)$ by the definition of the demand $f_i(p, p \cdot \omega_i)$, and the utility $u_i(\omega_i)$ is larger than or equal to $u_i(B_i)$ by the monotonicity of the utility function u_i. Therefore, the inequality $u_i(B_i) \leq u_i(f_i(p, p \cdot \omega_i))$ is satisfied for any $p \in S$ and $\omega_i \in K_i$. We conclude by observing that the set $\{x \in \mathbb{R}^\ell \mid u_i(B_i) \leq u_i(x)\}$ is bounded from below. □

3.4.4 Desirability (A)

The following property is stated for price vectors that are simplex normalized, i.e., $p \in S_\Sigma$ or $\sum_k p_k = 1$. The reason is that this property deals with the behavior of demand when the relative prices of some goods tend to zero, and the numeraire may be one of these goods. Recall that we use the same notation for the function f_i whether it is homogenous of degree zero and defined on $\mathbb{R}^\ell_{++} \times \mathbb{R}$, or defined on $S \times \mathbb{R}$, or on $S_\Sigma \times \mathbb{R}$.

Definition 3.16. *The function $f_i \in \mathcal{D}$ satisfies desirability (A) if, for any sequence $(p^q, w_i^q) \in S_\Sigma \times \mathbb{R}$ of simplex normalized price vectors and income converging to $(p^0, w_i^0) \in \partial S_\Sigma \times \mathbb{R}$ (where $\partial S_\Sigma = \overline{S_\Sigma} \setminus S_\Sigma$; in other words, some coordinates of p^0 are equal to zero), then $\limsup \|f_i(p^q, w_i^q)\| = +\infty$.*

We then have:

Proposition 3.17. *Every function $f_i \in \mathcal{D}$ satisfies desirability (A).*

Proof. The function $f_i : S \times \mathbb{R} \to \mathbb{R}^\ell$ is a diffeomorphism by Proposition 3.9, with an inverse map denoted by $g_i : \mathbb{R}^\ell \to S_\Sigma \times \mathbb{R}$. Let us argue by contradiction. Define $x_i^q = f_i(p^q, w_i^q)$ where (p^q, w_i^q) satisfies the assumptions of the proposition. Assume that the sequence (x_i^q) is bounded. Then, there exists a subsequence that converges to some $x_i^0 \in \mathbb{R}^\ell$ and there is no loss of generality in considering only this subsequence. It follows from the continuity of g_i that the sequence $g_i(x_i^q) = (p^q, w_i^q)$ converges to $g_i(x_i^0) = (p^0, w_i^0) \in S_\Sigma \times \mathbb{R}$. Therefore, we have $p^0 \in S_\Sigma$, a contradiction. □

3.4.5 The Property of Revealed Preferences (WARP)

Proposition 3.18. *Let (p, w_i) and (p', w_i') be two (distinct) price-income pairs with $f_i(p, w_i) \neq f_i(p', w_i')$. When satisfied, the inequality*

$p \cdot f_i(p', w_i') \leq w_i$ *implies the strict inequality* $p' \cdot f_i(p, w_i) > w_i'$. *This property is known as (WARP).*

Proof. The inequality $p \cdot f_i(p', w_i') \leq w_i$ means that $f_i(p', w_i')$ satisfies the budget constraint $p \cdot x_i \leq w_i$. Since $f_i(p, w_i)$ maximizes the utility $u_i(x_i)$ subject to the budget constraint $p \cdot x_i \leq w_i$, the inequality

$$u_i(f_i(p', w_i')) \leq u_i(f_i(p, w_i)), \tag{4}$$

is therefore satisfied.

This inequality is strict because the solution $f_i(p, w_i)$ that maximizes the utility $u_i(x_i)$ subject to the constraint budget constrained $p \cdot x_i \leq w_i$ is unique, while $f_i(p, w_i)$ and $f_i(p', w_i')$ are distinct.

We have therefore proved that the inequality $p \cdot f_i(p', w_i') \leq w_i$ implies the strict inequality $u_i\left(f_i(p', w_i')\right) < u_i\left(f_i(p, w_i)\right)$. In order to show that the inequality $p' \cdot f_i(p, w_i) > w_i'$ is satisfied, we argue by contradiction. Let us assume that the opposite inequality is satisfied, i.e., that we have $p' \cdot f_i(p, w_i) \leq w_i'$. By following the same line of reasoning as above, this inequality implies the strict inequality $u_i\left(f_i(p, w_i)\right) < u_i\left(f_i(p', w_i')\right)$, a contradiction with inequality (4). $\qquad\square$

The acronym (WARP) stands for the Weak Axiom of Revealed Preferences and has become the traditional name of the above property.

3.4.6 *Negative Definiteness of the Slutsky Matrix (ND)*

Proposition 3.19. *The* $(\ell - 1) \times (\ell - 1)$ *(numeraire normalized) Slutsky matrix* $S_{\ell\ell}f_i(p, w_i)$ *of the demand function* $f_i \in \mathcal{D}$ *is negative definite for all* $(p, w_i) \in S \times \mathbb{R}$. *This property is known as (ND).*

Note that (ND) says nothing about the symmetry of the Slutsky matrix $S_{\ell\ell}f_i(p, w_i)$. We shall see in a moment that the Slutsky matrix $S_{\ell\ell}f_i(p, w_i)$ is also symmetric for $f_i \in \mathcal{D}$. However, the symmetry property will play no major role in the study of the general equilibrium model.

The proof requires three lemmata:

Lemma 3.20. *Let* $\omega_i = f_i(p, w_i)$ *for* $(p, w_i) \in S \times \mathbb{R}$. *The function* $p' \in S \to h_i(p') = u_i\left(f_i(p', p' \cdot \omega_i)\right)$ *reaches an absolute minimum at* $p' = p$.

Proof. By definition, $x_i' = f_i(p', p' \cdot \omega_i)$ maximizes $u_i(x)$ subject to the budget constrained $p' \cdot x \leq p' \cdot \omega_i$. Obviously, ω_i satisfies the budget constraint, which implies the inequality $u_i(\omega_i) \leq u_i\left(x_i'\right)$ for $p' \in S$. $\qquad\square$

Lemma 3.21. *The Hessian matrix of $p' \to h_i(p')$ at $p' = p$ is equal to* $-\lambda S_{\ell\ell} f_i(p, w_i)$, *where* $\lambda > 0$.

Proof. Define $\lambda_i(x_i') = \dfrac{\partial u_i}{\partial x^\ell}(x_i')$ for $x_i' \in \mathbb{R}^\ell$. Recall that we have $Du_i(x_i') = \lambda_i(x_i')D_n u_i(x_i')$. The function $x_i' \to \lambda_i(x_i')$ is smooth.

The computation of the first-order derivative at $p' \in S$ exploits the chain rule, which yields:

$$\frac{\partial h_i}{\partial p_j} = Du_i(x_i')^T \frac{df_i}{dp_j} = \lambda_i(x_i')\, p' \cdot \left(\frac{\partial f_i^j}{\partial p_j} + \frac{\partial f_i^j}{\partial w_i} \omega_i^j \right)$$

which, by Proposition 3.13, yields

$$\frac{\partial h_i}{\partial p_j} = -\lambda_i(x_i') \left(f_i^j(p', p' \cdot \omega_i) - \omega_i^j \right).$$

The second-order derivative at $p' \in S$ is equal to

$$\frac{\partial^2 h_i}{\partial p_j \partial p_k} = -\frac{d\lambda_i}{dp_k}(x_i') \left(f_i^j(p', p' \cdot \omega_i) - \omega_i^j \right) - \lambda_i(x_i') \frac{df_i^j}{dp_k}(p', p' \cdot \omega_i).$$

For $p' = p$, we have $f_i^j(p, p \cdot \omega_i) = \omega_i^j$, from which follows the equality

$$\left. \frac{\partial^2 h_i}{\partial p_j \partial p_k} \right|_{p'=p} = -\lambda_i(\omega_i)\left(\frac{\partial f_i^j}{\partial p_k}(p, p \cdot \omega_i) + \frac{\partial f_i^j}{\partial w_i}(p, p \cdot \omega_i)\omega_i^k \right) = -\lambda_i(\omega_i)s_{jk}.$$

It then suffices to observe that $\lambda = \lambda_i(\omega_i)$ is > 0. $\square$

Lemma 3.22. *The Slutsky matrix has a non-zero determinant:*

$$\det S_{\ell\ell} f_i(p, w_i) \neq 0.$$

Proof. The Jacobian matrix of the individual demand function f_i: $(p, w_i) \to f_i(p, w_i)$ is invertible by Corollary 3.11. This Jacobian matrix is equal to

$$\begin{bmatrix} \dfrac{\partial f_i^1}{\partial p_1} & \dfrac{\partial f_i^1}{\partial p_2} & \cdots & \dfrac{\partial f_i^1}{\partial p_{\ell-1}} & \dfrac{\partial f_i^1}{\partial w_i} \\[2ex] \dfrac{\partial f_i^2}{\partial p_1} & \dfrac{\partial f_i^2}{\partial p_2} & \cdots & \dfrac{\partial f_i^2}{\partial p_{\ell-1}} & \dfrac{\partial f_i^2}{\partial w_i} \\[2ex] \vdots & \vdots & \vdots & \vdots & \vdots \\[2ex] \dfrac{\partial f_i^\ell}{\partial p_1} & \dfrac{\partial f_i^\ell}{\partial p_2} & \cdots & \dfrac{\partial f_i^\ell}{\partial p_{\ell-1}} & \dfrac{\partial f_i^\ell}{\partial w_i} \end{bmatrix}.$$

The determinant of this (Jacobian) matrix does not change if we add to the last row some linear combination of the other rows of the matrix. Therefore, let us add to the last row the first row multiplied by p_1, the second row multiplied by p_2, ..., the $\ell - 1$th row multiplied by $p_{\ell-1}$. It follows from Proposition 3.13 that this yields a last row equal to

$$\begin{bmatrix} -f_i^1 & -f_i^2 & \cdots & -f_i^{\ell-1} & 1 \end{bmatrix}.$$

Again, the value of the determinant does not change by adding to the first column the last column multiplied by f_i^1, to the second column the last column multiplied by f_i^2, etc., up to the $\ell - 1$th column to which is added the last column multiplied by $f_i^{\ell-1}$. This operation yields the matrix

$$\begin{bmatrix} S_{\ell\ell}f_i(p, w_i) & \vdots \\ 0\ldots0 & 1 \end{bmatrix},$$

whose determinant is therefore equal to the determinant of the (numeraire normalized) Slutsky matrix $S_{\ell\ell}f_i(p, w_i)$. □

Proof of Proposition 3.19. By Lemma 3.20, the function $p' \to h_i(p')$ reaches an absolute minimum at $p' = p$. Therefore, the Hessian matrix of h_i at $p' = p$ is positive semidefinite. This Hessian matrix is equal to the Slutsky matrix multiplied by a negative real number by Lemma 3.21. This implies that the Slutsky matrix $S_{\ell\ell}f_i(p, w_i)$ is negative semidefinite. In order to be negative definite, it suffices that its determinant is different from zero, which follows from Lemma 3.22. □

Proposition 3.23. *The Slutsky matrix $S_{\ell\ell}f_i(p, w_i)$ of the demand function $f_i \in \mathcal{D}$ is symmetric.*

Proof. This follows readily from the proof of Proposition 3.19, the Hessian matrix of the map $p' \to h(p')$ being symmetric. □

3.5 DEMAND-BASED CONSUMER THEORY

Demand functions do not have to result from budget constrained utility maximization to satisfy some of the properties (S), (W), (B), (A), (WARP), and (ND) properties to which we add (NSD), the negative semidefiniteness of $S_{\ell\ell}f_i(p, w_i)$, a slightly weaker form of (ND). At variance with preferences and utility functions, demand functions are observable. This has led to a theory of the consumer that is based directly on demand functions satisfying some or all of the above properties.

The class of these demand functions is much larger than the set $\mathcal{D}$ of demand functions derived from the budget constrained maximization of utility functions.

3.5.1 Sets of Demand Functions

We denote by $\mathcal{F}$ the set of functions $f_i : S \times \mathbb{R} \to \mathbb{R}^\ell$ that satisfy smoothness (S) and Walras law (W). Let (P) denote one of the properties (A), (B), (WARP), etc., or their conjunctions as, for example, $(A \wedge B)$ meaning (A) and (B).

Definition 3.24. *Let (P) be a property of the maps $f_i \in \mathcal{F}$, we denote by $\mathcal{F}_P$ the subset of $\mathcal{F}$ that consists of the maps $f_i \in \mathcal{F}$ that satisfy (P).*

For example, $\mathcal{F}_{A \wedge B}$ denotes the set of maps $f_i \in \mathcal{F}$ that satisfy properties (A) and (B). Similarly, $\mathcal{F}_{A \wedge B \wedge ND}$ denotes the set of maps $f_i \in \mathcal{F}$ that satisfy properties (A), (B), and (ND).

3.5.2 The Set $\mathcal{F}_B$

Boundedness from below (B) excludes the possibility for the demand of some goods to tend to $-\infty$ when endowments are bounded from below. We need this property because consumption is not restricted to be positive nor even bounded from below in our setup. The following lemma is often useful:

Lemma 3.25. *Let $f_i \in \mathcal{F}_B$. For K_i compact subset of $\mathbb{R}^\ell$ and L, a compact interval of $[0, +\infty)$, there exists $B'_i \in \mathbb{R}^\ell$ such that $B'_i \le f_i(p, p \cdot \omega_i + w_i)$ for $\omega_i \in K_i$, $w_i \in L$, and $p \in S$.*

Proof. There exist x_i and $x'_i \in \mathbb{R}^\ell$ such that $x_i \le \omega_i \le x'_i$ for all $\omega_i \in K_i$. Let $\alpha_i > 0$ such that $0 \le \lambda \le \alpha_i$ for $\lambda \in L$. Let $e_\ell = (0, 0, \ldots, 0, 1)$ be the unit vector parallel to the ℓ-th coordinate axis. Let $x''_i = x'_i + \alpha_i e_\ell$. The union of the two line segments $K'_i = [x_i, x'_i] \cup [x'_i, x''_i]$ is compact. For any $p \in S$, the intersection $K'_i \cap \{z_i \in \mathbb{R}^\ell \mid p \cdot z_i = p \cdot \omega_i + w_i\}$ is reduced to a point, a point that we denote by ω_i'. Then, $f_i(p, p \cdot \omega_i + w_i) = f_i(p, p \cdot \omega_i')$. It then suffices to apply (B) to the compact set K_i'. $\qquad\square$

3.5.3 The Set $\mathcal{F}_A$

By definition, a map is proper if the preimage of every compact set is compact: see Definition B.1 of the Appendix. Properness is a very powerful and useful property.

Proposition 3.26. *Every function $f_i \in \mathcal{F}_A$ is proper.*

Proof. Let K_i be some compact subset of $\mathbb{R}^\ell$. The preimage $f_i^{-1}(K_i)$ is closed in $S \times \mathbb{R}$ by the continuity of f_i. Let us show that any sequence (p^q, w_i^q) in $f_i^{-1}(K_i)$ has a subsequence that converges to some $(p^0, w_i^0) \in f_i^{-1}(K_i)$.

Let $(\tilde{p}^q, \tilde{w}_i^q)$ be the simplex price normalized sequence corresponding to the numeraire normalized sequence (p^q, w_i^q). It follows from the compactness of $\overline{S_\Sigma}$ that we can find a subsequence such that $(\tilde{p}^q)$ converges to some $\tilde{p}^0 \in \overline{S_\Sigma}$. The map $(\tilde{p}, \omega_i) \to \tilde{w}_i = \tilde{p} \cdot \omega_i$ is continuous. Therefore, the image of the compact set $\overline{S_\Sigma} \times K_i$ by this map is a compact subset of $\mathbb{R}$. The sequence $(\tilde{w}_i^q)$ belongs to that compact subset. Therefore, by considering a suitable subsequence again, we can assume without loss of generality that the wealth sequence $(\tilde{w}_i^q)$ converges to some real number $\tilde{w}_i^0$.

It follows from desirability (A) that, if the limit $\tilde{p}^0$ of the sequence $(\tilde{p}^q)$ has some coordinates equal to zero, then $\lim \sup_{q \to \infty} \|f_i(\tilde{p}^q, \tilde{w}_i^q)\| = +\infty$, which would contradict the boundedness of K_i. This implies that $\tilde{p}^0$ belongs to S_Σ and, therefore, p^0 to S and (p^0, w_i^0) to $f^{-1}(K)$ by the closedness of $f^{-1}(K)$. $\qquad\square$

3.5.4 The Sets $\mathcal{F}_{NSD}$, $\mathcal{F}_{ND}$ and $\mathcal{F}_{WARP}$

Proposition 3.27. *The following inclusions are satisfied:*

$$\mathcal{F}_{ND} \subset \mathcal{F}_{WARP} \subset \mathcal{F}_{NSD}.$$

Proof. Let us show that (WARP) implies (NSD), which is equivalent to the inclusion $\mathcal{F}_{WARP} \subset \mathcal{F}_{NSD}$. Let $(p, w_i) \in S \times \mathbb{R}$ and $\omega_i = f_i(p, w_i)$. For $p' \in S$, it comes

$$p' \cdot f_i(p, p \cdot \omega_i) = p' \cdot f_i(p, w_i) \leq p' \cdot \omega_i = w_i'.$$

The inequality $p \cdot (f_i(p', p' \cdot \omega_i) - \omega_i) \geq 0$ follows from (WARP) and is strict if $f_i(p, w_i) \neq f_i(p', w_i')$ and becomes $0 = 0$ if $f_i(p', w_i') = f_i(p, w_i)$. The function $p' \to p \cdot (f_i(p', p' \cdot \omega_i) - \omega_i)$ then reaches an absolute minimum at $p' = p$. The Hessian matrix of second derivatives of that function at $p' = p$ is then negative semi-definite. Straightforward computations show that this Hessian matrix is the sum $S_{\ell\ell} f_i(p, w_i) + (S_{\ell\ell} f_i(p, w_i))^T$ and defines, up to a factor 2, the same quadratic form as $S_{\ell\ell}(p, w_i)$. This proves (NSD).

The proof that (ND) implies (WARP), which is equivalent to the inclusion $\mathcal{F}_{ND} \subset \mathcal{F}_{WARP}$, is slightly beyond the scope of this book and can be found in [35] or [42]. $\qquad\square$

3.5.5 The Set $\mathcal{F}_{ND}$

SUBMERSIONS

By definition, the smooth map $f_i \in \mathcal{F}$ is a submersion if the Jacobian matrix $Df_i(p, w_i)$ is invertible for any $(p, w_i) \in S \times \mathbb{R}$. We have:

Proposition 3.28. *Every function $f_i \in \mathcal{F}_{ND}$ is a submersion.*

Proof. Let $Df_i(p, w_i)$ denote the Jacobian matrix of $f_i : S \times \mathbb{R} \to \mathbb{R}^\ell$ at (p, w_i). (Prices are numeraire normalized.) This $\ell \times \ell$ matrix is equal to

$$
\begin{bmatrix}
\dfrac{\partial f_i^1}{\partial p_1} & \dfrac{\partial f_i^1}{\partial p_2} & \cdots & \dfrac{\partial f_i^1}{\partial p_{\ell-1}} & \dfrac{\partial f_i^1}{\partial w_i} \\[2ex]
\dfrac{\partial f_i^2}{\partial p_1} & \dfrac{\partial f_i^2}{\partial p_2} & \cdots & \dfrac{\partial f_i^2}{\partial p_{\ell-1}} & \dfrac{\partial f_i^2}{\partial w_i} \\[2ex]
\vdots & \vdots & \ddots & \vdots & \vdots \\[2ex]
\dfrac{\partial f_i^{\ell-1}}{\partial p_1} & \dfrac{\partial f_i^{\ell-1}}{\partial p_2} & \cdots & \dfrac{\partial f_i^{\ell-1}}{\partial p_{\ell-1}} & \dfrac{\partial f_i^{\ell-1}}{\partial w_i} \\[2ex]
\dfrac{\partial f_i^\ell}{\partial p_1} & \dfrac{\partial f_i^\ell}{\partial p_2} & \cdots & \dfrac{\partial f_i^\ell}{\partial p_{\ell-1}} & \dfrac{\partial f_i^\ell}{\partial w_i}
\end{bmatrix}.
$$

The value of the determinant of this matrix does not change by substituting to the last row the sum of the first row multiplied by p_1, the second row by p_2, up to the ℓ-th row by p_ℓ. It follows from $p \cdot \dfrac{\partial f_i}{\partial p_k} = -f_i^k(p, w_i)$

for $1 \leq k \leq \ell - 1$ that this new matrix is equal to

$$
\begin{bmatrix}
\dfrac{\partial f_i^1}{\partial p_1} & \dfrac{\partial f_i^1}{\partial p_2} & \cdots & \dfrac{\partial f_i^1}{\partial p_{\ell-1}} & \dfrac{\partial f_i^1}{\partial w_i} \\[2ex]
\dfrac{\partial f_i^2}{\partial p_1} & \dfrac{\partial f_i^2}{\partial p_2} & \cdots & \dfrac{\partial f_i^2}{\partial p_{\ell-1}} & \dfrac{\partial f_i^2}{\partial w_i} \\[2ex]
\vdots & \vdots & \ddots & \vdots & \vdots \\[2ex]
\dfrac{\partial f_i^{\ell-1}}{\partial p_1} & \dfrac{\partial f_i^{\ell-1}}{\partial p_2} & \cdots & \dfrac{\partial f_i^{\ell-1}}{\partial p_{\ell-1}} & \dfrac{\partial f_i^{\ell-1}}{\partial w_i} \\[2ex]
-f_i^1(p, w_i) & -f_i^2(p, w_i) & \cdots & f_i^{\ell-1}(p, w_i) & 1
\end{bmatrix}
$$

The value of the determinant of this matrix does not change by adding to the first column the last column multiplied by $f_i^1(p, w_i)$, by adding to the second column the last column multiplied by $f_i^2(p, w_i)$, and so on up to the $\ell - 1$th column to which is added the last column multiplied by $f_i^{\ell-1}(p, w_i)$. This gives us the matrix

$$
\begin{bmatrix}
 & & & & * \\
 & S_{\ell\ell} f_i(p, w_i) & & & * \\
 & & & & \vdots \\
0 & 0 & \cdots & 0 & 1
\end{bmatrix}
$$

with determinant equal to $\det S_{\ell\ell} f_i(p, w_i)$, which is different from zero. □

3.5.6 The Set $\mathcal{F}_{A \wedge ND}$

Proposition 3.29. *Every function $f_i \in \mathcal{F}_{A \wedge ND}$ is a diffeomorphism.*

Proof. The map f_i is a proper submersion. It therefore defines a covering of $\mathbb{R}^\ell$. It follows from the connectedness of $S \times \mathbb{R}$ and the simple connectedness of $\mathbb{R}^\ell$ that this covering is actually a diffeomorphism. (See Proposition D.11 of the Appendix.) □

EXERCISE

3.3. Let $\ell = 2$. Let $\omega_i \in \mathbb{R}^\ell$ be given. 1) Show that consumer i's demand curve $p_1 \in \mathbb{R}_{++} \to f_i\left((p_1, 1), p_1 \omega_i^1 + \omega_i^2\right) \in \mathbb{R}^2$ has two infinite branches corresponding to $p_1 \to 0$ and $p_1 \to \infty$. 2) Use the intermediate value theorem to show that there exists at least one price vector $p \in S$ such that $f_i(p, p \cdot \omega_i) = \omega_i$.

3.6 CONCLUSION

The list of properties of the demand functions considered in this chapter is far from exhaustive. For example, we have made no mention of the strong axiom of revealed preferences (SARP). In the same vein, there are no definitions and interpretations of the income and substitution effects, a pillar of classical consumer theory. The main reason is that the only properties that have been developed in this chapter are those that play a role in the study of general equilibrium models, properties that do not require utility maximization.

3.7 NOTES AND COMMENTS

The classical theory of the consumer is essentially a theory of the maximization of the consumer's utility function subject to a budget constraint. The observation that demand functions are observable while preferences or utility functions are not is made by Samuelson in a paper that marks the beginning of the theory of revealed preferences [54]. One objective of the classical theory of the consumer is the characterization of the demand functions that belong to the set $\mathcal{D}$ of functions from $S \times \mathbb{R}$ into $\mathbb{R}^{\ell}$ that result from the budget constrained maximization of standard utility functions.

Samuelson thinks at first that the weak axiom of revealed preferences (WARP) characterizes the elements of $\mathcal{D}$, an equivalence that he proves in the case of two goods [54, 56]. But Houthakker and Uzawa show that this equivalence does not hold in the case of more than two goods. The weak axiom of revealed preferences (WARP) has to be strengthened into the strong axiom (SARP) [36, 65]. The implication (ND) $\implies$ (WARP) $\implies$ (NSD) is proved by Kihlstrom, Mas-Colell, and Sonnenschein, and Hildenbrand and Jerison [35, 42]. The relations between (WARP) and preference maximization are explored by Al-Najjar and Quah who show that demand functions satisfying (WARP) can be derived from the budget constrained maximization of non-transitive convex preferences, but that the latter are not uniquely determined by the demand functions [1, 52].

The property of desirability (A) was introduced under that name by Debreu for demand functions used as primitive concepts [24]. Property of boundedness from below (B) is obviously satisfied for consumption sets that are bounded from below. It was introduced for consumption sets equal to the full commodity space by Balasko [16].

CHAPTER 4

The Exchange Model

4.1 INTRODUCTION

The exchange model is the simplest of all general equilibrium models. The study of its properties is already interesting for its own sake because it is the typical model of a market. It will also show us the directions to follow when studying more complex models like those that include production or take explicitly into account time and uncertainty. Even more remarkably, many properties of the more complex models often exploit those of the exchange model.

Consumers are modeled by way of their demand functions. These functions satisfy some or all of the properties identified in the previous chapters but do not necessarily result from the budget constrained maximization of standard utility functions. In particular, consumers' preferences are not necessarily transitive and the Slutsky matrices not necessarily symmetric.

This higher level of generality enhances the economic relevance and usefulness of the exchange model. Increasing numbers of econometric studies point to the lack of symmetry of Slutsky matrices. Similarly, the non-transitivity of preferences (which is equivalent to the lack of symmetry of Slutsky matrices) has now been identified in a significant number of experiments. Another important motivation for dropping the utility maximization assumption is that this more general version of the exchange model where consumers' demand functions do not result from utility maximization is apt to represent some forms of financial markets. It is therefore remarkable that the marginal cost of this higher level of generality is nil.

This chapter is an introduction to the exchange model defined by the equilibrium manifold and the natural projection. One can recognize in the equilibrium manifold and the natural projection approach an extension of the scope of comparative statics, i.e., the study of the dependence of competitive equilibrium on the parameters defining the economy. Classical comparative statics has been mostly limited to the local aspects of this dependence. The equilibrium manifold and the natural projection put this dependence in a global setup.

The main result of this chapter is the proof that the equilibrium manifold is indeed a smooth manifold. The smooth manifold structure implies that the natural projection is a smooth map. In terms of comparative statics, this tells us that equilibrium prices can be considered as depending linearly on the fundamentals defining an economy in sufficiently small neighborhoods of regular equilibria.

4.2 THE SETS $\mathcal{E}$, $\mathcal{E}_r$, AND $\mathcal{E}_c$ OF m-TUPLES OF DEMAND FUNCTIONS DEFINING THE EXCHANGE MODEL

We now define three sets of m-tuples of demand functions (f_i):

4.2.1 The Set $\mathcal{E}$

Definition 4.1. *The set $\mathcal{E} = \mathcal{F}^m$ consists of m-tuples (f_i) where the demand functions f_i are smooth (S) and satisfy Walras law (W) for every i.*

We will see that it suffices that the m-tuple of demand functions (f_i) belongs to $\mathcal{E}$ to get the main properties regarding the local and global structures of the equilibrium manifold of the exchange model when the parameter space is $\Omega = (\mathbb{R}^\ell)^m$.

4.2.2 The Set $\mathcal{E}_r$

Definition 4.2. *The set $\mathcal{E}_r$ consists of m-tuples (f_i) where $f_i \in \mathcal{F}_B$ for all i and $f_i \in \mathcal{F}_A$ for at least one i.*

With the same parameter space $\Omega = (\mathbb{R}^\ell)^m$, we will see that it suffices that the m-tuple of demand functions (f_i) belongs to $\mathcal{E}_r$ to develop the theory of regular economies up to the generic finiteness of equilibria and continuity of equilibrium allocations, and also an index theory. The r in $\mathcal{E}_r$ stands for "regular."

4.2.3 The Set $\mathcal{E}_c$

Definition 4.3. *The set $\mathcal{E}_c$ is the subset of $\mathcal{E}_r$ that consists of the m-tuples (f_i) such that $f_i \in \mathcal{F}_{B \wedge \mathrm{WARP}}$ for all i and $f_i \in \mathcal{F}_{B \wedge A \wedge \mathrm{ND}}$ for at least one i.*

Again with the parameter space $\Omega = (\mathbb{R}^\ell)^m$, we will see that it suffices that m-tuples of demand functions (f_i) belong to $\mathcal{E}_c$ to get stronger properties of the exchange model such as the genericity of regular equilibria, the regularity of no-trade equilibria, the uniqueness of equilibrium at equilibrium allocations, and the inclusion of the set of equilibrium allocations in one pathconnected component of the set of regular economies. The c in $\mathcal{E}_c$ stands for "convex" since all these properties do require the implicit form of convexity of preferences that is conveyed by (WARP) and (ND).

4.3 THE EXCHANGE MODEL

Consumer i is characterized by the pair (f_i, ω_i) where f_i is a demand function $S \times \mathbb{R} \to \mathbb{R}^\ell$ belonging to the set $\mathcal{F}$ or to some subsets (like $\mathcal{F}_{A \wedge B}$ or $\mathcal{F}_{NSD}$), and $\omega_i \in \mathbb{R}^\ell$ represents consumer i's endowments.

4.3.1 The Exchange Model: Definition

The *exchange model* with m consumers is defined by the m-tuple made of the m consumers' demand functions $(f_i) = (f_1, \ldots, f_m) \in \mathcal{E}$. This exchange model is denoted by $\mathcal{E}\big((f_i)\big)$.

Its properties depend on the choice of the parameter space Ω and on the properties of the m-tuple of demand functions (f_i). By default, the parameter space Ω, also known as the *endowment set*, is the Cartesian product of the commodity space $\mathbb{R}^\ell$ taken m times: $\Omega = (\mathbb{R}^\ell)^m$.

4.3.2 The Exchange Economy: Definition

An *exchange economy* of the exchange model $\mathcal{E}\big((f_i)\big)$ is identified to its *endowment vector* $\boldsymbol{\omega} = (\omega_i) = (\omega_1, \ldots, \omega_m) \in \Omega$. It is denoted by $\mathcal{E}\big((f_i)\big)(\boldsymbol{\omega})$ or, more simply, by $\boldsymbol{\omega}$ when there is no risk of confusion.

4.4 EQUILIBRIUM EQUATION

4.4.1 Aggregate Demand and Supply

Let $p \in S$ be some price vector. Consumer i's wealth is, for the price vector $p \in S$, equal to $w_i = p \cdot \omega_i$. Consumer i's demand is equal to $f_i(p, p \cdot \omega_i)$.

The aggregate demand for the price vector $p \in S$ is the sum of the m consumers' demands $\sum_i f_i(p, p \cdot \omega_i)$.

The aggregate supply does not depend on the price vector $p \in S$ and is equal to sum of the individual resources $\sum_i \omega_i$.

Aggregate excess demand for the price vector $p \in S$ is equal to

$$z(p, \omega) = \sum_i f_i(p, p \cdot \omega_i) - \sum_i \omega_i.$$

The aggregate excess demand function is the map $z(\,\cdot\,, \omega) : S \to \mathbb{R}^\ell$.

4.4.2 Walras Law for Aggregate Excess Demand

The next proposition is going to show us that the ℓ coordinates of $z(p, \omega)$ are not independent, a remark that will play an important role in subsequent developments.

Proposition 4.4. *For* $(f_i) \in \mathcal{E}$, *the aggregate excess demand function satisfies the identity* $p \cdot z(p, \omega) = 0$.

Proof. It suffices to write

$$z(p, \omega) = \sum_i \big(f_i(p, p \cdot \omega_i) - \omega_i \big)$$

which yields, after taking the inner product with the price vector $p \in S$,

$$p \cdot z(p, \omega) = \sum_i \big(p \cdot f_i(p, p \cdot \omega_i) - p \cdot \omega_i \big),$$

$$p \cdot z(p, \omega) = \sum_i (p \cdot \omega_i - p \cdot \omega_i) = 0$$

by Walras law (W) applied to each demand function $f_i \in \mathcal{F}$. □

This identity satisfied by the aggregate demand function is often known as *Walras law for aggregate excess demand*.

The fact that the ℓ coordinates of the aggregate excess demand function are not independent will lead us to consider $\bar{z}(p, \omega) \in \mathbb{R}^{\ell-1}$, the vector defined by the first $\ell - 1$ coordinates of $z(p, \omega)$.

4.4.3 Equilibrium Price Vector of an Economy

We now define the equilibrium price vector of an economy by the equality of aggregate supply and demand.

Definition 4.5. *The price vector* $p \in S$ *is an equilibrium price vector of the economy* $\omega \in \Omega$ *of the exchange model* $(f_i) \in \mathcal{E}$ *if there is equality of aggregate demand and supply:*

$$\sum_i f_i(p, p \cdot \omega_i) = \sum_i \omega_i. \tag{1}$$

Remark 2. The equilibrium equation (1) is equivalent to $z(p, \omega) = 0$. It follows from Walras law for aggregate excess demand that the ℓ coordinates of this equation system are not independent. In fact, the equality $z(p, \omega) = 0$ is equivalent to $\bar{z}(p, \omega) = 0$.

4.5 The Equilibrium Manifold and the Natural Projection

The program of the theory of general equilibrium, what is also known as equilibrium analysis, is the study of the properties of equation system (1). This leads us to introduce the concepts of equilibrium (not to be confused with the equilibrium price vector of an economy), of equilibrium manifold, and of natural projection.

4.5.1 Equilibrium: Definition

Definition 4.6. *The pair* $(p, \omega) \in S \times \Omega$ *is an* equilibrium *of the exchange model* $\mathcal{E}((f_i))$ *if the price vector* $p \in S$ *is an equilibrium price vector of the economy* ω *in the sense of Definition 4.5.*

The pair (p, ω) is therefore an equilibrium if and only if $\bar{z}(p, \omega) = 0$.

4.5.2 Equilibrium Manifold: Definition

The equilibrium analysis of the exchange model can be reformulated as the study of the properties of the equilibria $(p, \omega) \in S \times \Omega$ as a function of the parameter $\omega \in \Omega$ for given (f_i). This leads us to consider the:

Definition 4.7. *The* equilibrium manifold E *of the exchange model* $\mathcal{E}((f_i))$ *is the subset of* $S \times \Omega$ *consisting of the price-endowment vectors* $(p, \omega) \in S \times \Omega$ *that satisfy the equilibrium equation (1). The* natural projection *is the map* $\pi : E \to \Omega$ *defined by the formula* $(p, \omega) \to \omega$.

At this stage, it is by no means obvious that the "equilibrium manifold" is indeed a smooth manifold. Establishing this smooth manifold structure will be one of the first properties of the exchange model that we will prove. Let us start by proving the following easy property of the equilibrium manifold:

Proposition 4.8. *The equilibrium manifold* E *of the exchange model* $\mathcal{E}((f_i))$ *is a closed subset of* $S \times \Omega$.

Proof. The map $(p, \omega) \to z(p, \omega)$ is continuous. Therefore, the equilibrium manifold E is closed in $S \times \Omega$ as the preimage of the closed subset $\{0\}$ of $\mathbb{R}^\ell$ by a continuous map. $\qquad \square$

Remark 3. Note that Proposition 4.8 requires only the continuity of the individual demand functions f_i. Walras law (W) is not even necessary.

4.6 The Smooth Equilibrium Manifold

In this section, the m-tuple (f_i) belongs to $\mathcal{E}$, i.e., every demand function f_i is only assumed to be smooth (S) and to satisfy Walras law (W).

4.6.1 *The Local Structure*

The equilibrium manifold is a topological space as being a closed subset of the Cartesian product $S \times \Omega$. The local structure problem deals with the characterization of the small open neighborhoods of the points of E. This question leads us readily to the mathematical concepts of smooth manifolds and of diffeomorphisms. The heuristic presentation that follows is aimed at showing to the non-mathematically oriented reader how the smooth manifold concept fits naturally both mathematically and economically in the local structure problem.

4.6.2 *Smooth Manifolds*

As a first approximation, a smooth manifold is a topological space that locally can be identified with a Euclidean space, i.e., a finite dimensional real vector space. This means that, at every point, it is always possible to find at least one open neighborhood of this point that is homeomorphic to a Euclidean space. Such an open set is called a chart. The inverse of the homeomorphism between the open set and the Euclidean space defines a parameterization of the chart. This parameterization is also said to define a local coordinate system.

Two distinct charts U_h and U_k may have a non-empty intersection. Then, we have at least two ways of parameterizing the points of this intersection, either through U_h or U_k. It is crucial to the smooth manifold concept that none of these local coordinate systems is privileged with regard to the differentiability property. Consequently, the smooth manifold structure requires that the change of local coordinates from the parameterization through U_h to the parameterization through U_k is smooth, i.e., is a map that is differentiable up to any order. The dimension of a smooth manifold at a point is simply the number of local coordinates at that point. If the dimension is the same for all the points of the manifold, which is the case when the manifold is connected as a topological space, this common dimension is the dimension of the manifold.

4.6.3 *The Equilibrium Manifold: A Smooth Manifold*

Proposition 4.9. *The equilibrium manifold E is a smooth submanifold of $S \times \Omega$ of dimension ℓm for $(f_i) \in \mathcal{E}$.*

Proof. The proof will follow from the *regular value theorem* (Appendix, Proposition D.7) applied to the map $(p, \omega) \to \bar{z}(p, \omega)$ defined by the first $\ell - 1$ coordinates of the aggregate excess demand $z(p, \omega)$.

The equilibrium manifold E is defined by equation $\bar{z}(p, \omega) = 0$. It is therefore the preimage of $0 \in \mathbb{R}^{\ell-1}$ by the map $\bar{z} : S \times \Omega \to \mathbb{R}^{\ell-1}$. The *regular value theorem* tells us that a sufficient condition for E to be a smooth submanifold of $S \times \Omega$ is that the element $0 \in \mathbb{R}^{\ell-1}$ is a regular value of the map $\bar{z}$. This is equivalent to the map $\bar{z}$ having no critical point that would be an equilibrium. In fact, we are going to show that the map $\bar{z}$ has no critical point. This is equivalent to the Jacobian matrix of $\bar{z}$ at $(p, \omega) \in S \times \Omega$ having rank $\ell - 1$ since that matrix has $\ell - 1$ rows and $m\ell + \ell - 1$ columns.

To prove the rank property, it suffices to extract from the Jacobian matrix a submatrix that has rank $\ell - 1$. Pick arbitrarily some consumer i. Let us look at the block made of the ℓ columns (and $\ell - 1$ rows) made of the derivatives of $\bar{z}$ with respect to the coordinates $\omega_i^1, \ldots, \omega_i^\ell$ of ω_i, the endowment of consumer i. In the computation, we apply the chain rule. Given the fact that consumer i's demand does not depend on consumer j's wealth, with $j \neq i$, this yields for the Jacobian matrix the rather simple expression

$$
\begin{bmatrix}
\dfrac{\partial z^1}{\partial \omega_i^1} & \cdots & \dfrac{\partial z^1}{\partial \omega_i^\ell} \\[2mm]
\dfrac{\partial z^2}{\partial \omega_i^1} & \cdots & \dfrac{\partial z^2}{\partial \omega_i^\ell} \\[2mm]
\vdots & \ddots & \vdots \\[2mm]
\dfrac{\partial z^{\ell-1}}{\partial \omega_i^1} & \cdots & \dfrac{\partial z^{\ell-1}}{\partial \omega_i^\ell}
\end{bmatrix}
$$

$$
= \begin{bmatrix}
p_1 \dfrac{\partial f_i^1}{\partial w_i} - 1 & \cdots & p_{\ell-1} \dfrac{\partial f_i^1}{\partial w_i} & \dfrac{\partial f_i^1}{\partial w_i} \\[2mm]
p_1 \dfrac{\partial f_i^2}{\partial w_i} & \cdots & p_{\ell-1} \dfrac{\partial f_i^2}{\partial w_i} & \dfrac{\partial f_i^2}{\partial w_i} \\[2mm]
\vdots & & \vdots & \vdots \\[2mm]
p_1 \dfrac{\partial f_i^{\ell-1}}{\partial w_i} & \cdots & p_{\ell-1} \dfrac{\partial f_i^{\ell-1}}{\partial w_i} - 1 & \dfrac{\partial f_i^{\ell-1}}{\partial w_i}
\end{bmatrix}.
$$

In the right hand matrix, multiply the last column by p_1 and subtract from the first column, again multiply the last column by p_2 and subtract from the second column, and so on until multiplication of the last column by $p_{\ell-1}$ and subtraction from the $(\ell - 1)$th column. This yields the $\ell - 1 \times \ell$ matrix

$$
\begin{bmatrix}
-1 & 0 & \cdots & 0 & \dfrac{\partial f_i^1}{\partial w_i} \\[2ex]
0 & -1 & \cdots & 0 & \dfrac{\partial f_i^2}{\partial w_i} \\[2ex]
\vdots & \vdots & \ddots & \vdots & \vdots \\[2ex]
0 & 0 & \cdots & -1 & \dfrac{\partial f_i^{\ell-1}}{\partial w_i}
\end{bmatrix}
$$

that has the same rank. The rank of this new matrix is equal to $\ell - 1$ since the block made of its first $\ell - 1$ columns obviously has rank $\ell - 1$.

It also follows from the regular value theorem that the dimension of the equilibrium manifold E is equal to the dimension of $S \times \Omega$ minus the dimension of $\mathbb{R}^{\ell-1}$, and hence equal to $\ell - 1 + \ell m - (\ell - 1) = \ell m$. □

4.7 Smoothness of the Natural Projection

The natural projection is the restriction to the equilibrium manifold E of the projection map $(p, \omega) \to \omega$ from $S \times \Omega$ onto Ω. A very important implication of the smooth submanifold structure of the equilibrium manifold is the following:

Proposition 4.10. *The natural projection $\pi : E \to \Omega$ is smooth for* $(f_i) \in \mathcal{E}$.

Proof. It follows from the definition of a smooth submanifold that the embedding map $E \to S \times \Omega$, the restriction to the subset E of the identity map of $S \times \Omega$, is smooth.

The natural projection $\pi : E \to \Omega$ is the composition of the embedding map $E \to S \times \Omega$ and the projection map $S \times \Omega \to \Omega$. The projection map is smooth because its coordinate functions are smooth, as is the embedding map. Their composition is therefore smooth. □

4.8 Critical and Regular Points and Values

The natural projection $\pi : E \to \Omega$ being a smooth map between two smooth manifolds, we can define for that map its critical and regular points and its singular and regular values. The properties of the sets of regular points and singular and regular values play a major role in the analysis of the exchange model. Their exploitation, however, will require stronger properties of the m-tuple (f_i), properties that will be considered only in later chapters.

4.8.1 Critical Equilibria and Singular Economies

The equilibrium $(p, \omega) \in E$ is *critical* if it is a critical point of the natural projection $\pi : E \to \Omega$. This means that the derivative $D\pi_{(p,\omega)}$, which is a linear map from $\mathbb{R}^{\ell m}$ into itself, is not a bijection. Using coordinates, the determinant of the matrix of the derivative $D\pi_{(p,\omega)}$ is equal to zero at the critical equilibrium $(p, \omega) \in E$.

Definition 4.11. *The economy $\omega \in \Omega$ is* singular *if it is the image by the natural projection $\pi : E \to \Omega$ of a critical equilibrium. In other words, the economy $\omega \in \Omega$ is singular if there exists a price vector $p \in S$ such that the pair (p, ω) is not only an equilibrium, but a critical equilibrium.*

The set of critical equilibria is denoted by $\mathfrak{S}$ and the set of singular economies by $\mathcal{S}$. It follows from the definitions that we have $\pi(\mathfrak{S}) = \mathcal{S}$.

4.8.2 Regular Equilibria and Economies

Definition 4.12. *The equilibrium $(p, \omega) \in E$ is regular if it is a regular point of the natural projection $\pi : E \to \Omega$. Similarly, the economy $\omega \in \Omega$ is regular if it is a regular value of the natural projection $\pi : E \to \Omega$.*

Let $\mathfrak{R}$ and $\mathcal{R}$ denote the set of regular equilibria and economies respectively. It follows from the definitions that we have $\mathfrak{R} = E \setminus \mathfrak{S}$ and $\mathcal{R} = \Omega \setminus \mathcal{S}$.

4.8.3 Economic Interpretations

The concepts of regular equilibria and regular economies may seem to come out of the blue. The same remark applies to the related concepts of critical equilibria and singular economies. Nevertheless, all these concepts play crucial roles in the mathematical study of smooth mappings between smooth manifolds. (See Appendix D for example.) Therefore, these concepts are going to play an important role in the next chapters in our study of the natural projection.

In addition to their mathematical utility, these concepts have also very interesting economic implications. For example, the exchange model is structurally stable at regular economies, a result that we will prove only in Section 7.4.3. The important concept of regular equilibrium requires little more than a good understanding of the implicit function theorem (Theorem C.1 of Appendix C) because we will see shortly in Proposition 6.4 that an equilibrium is regular if and only if it is possible to apply the implicit function theorem to the aggregate demand function at that point. This implies that the equilibrium price vector at a regular equilibrium is locally a smooth function of the fundamentals defining the economy. It is therefore important from a purely economic perspective to know whether the set of regular equilibria is a large subset of the equilibrium manifold or not. Proposition 8.10 tells us that, under suitable assumptions regarding demand functions, the set of regular equilibria is indeed a very large subset because it is an open subset with full measure (which implies open and dense) of the equilibrium manifold. Additional economic implications and interpretation of these concepts of regularity and singularity will be seen in the next chapters.

4.9 NOTES AND COMMENTS

The formulation of the equilibrium equation is independently due to Jevons and Walras. Jevons limits himself to the two-good case [38]. Walras' formulation is similar to the one in this chapter [67].

The importance of discontinuities in a variety of fields ranging from biology to sociology is underlined by Thom and Zeeman in the early 1970s in what they call catastrophe theory [62], [63]. The mathematical setup of catastrophe theory is formally identical to the one of the natural projection, namely a map $\pi : E \to \Omega$. In the original version of catastrophe theory, the issue is the determination of the map π (for example, the determination of a local set of coordinates) from the qualitative picture of some local singularity of the map. Catastrophe theory has gradually evolved from a modeling tool into a theory of discontinuous phenomena within differentiable models [2]. The formulation of the general equilibrium model within the setup of the natural projection $\pi : E \to \Omega$ and, therefore, its identification with the mathematical model underlying catastrophe theory is due to Balasko in 1975 [11]. The economic importance of the discontinuities that occur at critical equilibria is highlighted in [13] and [16]. The question remains of a rigorous identification of the discontinuities predicted by the general equilibrium model with real world phenomena.

The proof of the smooth manifold structure of the equilibrium manifold appears in Delbaen's doctoral dissertation [27].

CHAPTER 5

The Equilibrium Manifold

5.1 INTRODUCTION

We now address the global structure of the equilibrium manifold E. We first start by motivating these global properties for their economic interest. These global properties can be of a topological nature like pathconnectedness, simple connectedness, and contractibility. They can also take a more practical form like the existence of global coordinate systems for the points of the equilibrium manifold in the same way the points at the surface of the earth can be located through their longitude and latitude. We continue by identifying an important subset of the equilibrium manifold, the set of no-trade equilibria. This enables us to uncover the remarkable structure of the equilibrium manifold as a collection of linear spaces parameterized by the no-trade equilibria. We apply this remarkable structure to define a global coordinate system for the equilibrium manifold. As in the previous chapter, the m-tuple of demand functions (f_i) characterizing the exchange model is assumed all throughout this chapter to belong to $\mathcal{E}$, i.e., the only assumptions are smoothness (S) and Walras law (W).

5.2 GLOBAL PROPERTIES AND THEIR INTEREST

5.2.1 Pathconnectedness

A topological space is pathconnected if it is always possible to link two arbitrarily chosen points of this space by a continuous path. For example, every convex set is pathconnected. Indeed, the segment linking two arbitrary points is, because of the convexity assumption, contained in the set and therefore defines a continuous path linking these two points. What is the economic meaning for the equilibrium manifold to be pathconnected? Let us consider the two equilibria (p, ω) and (p', ω'). We could assume that (p, ω) describes a current equilibrium of the economy while (p', ω') is an equilibrium that is aimed for a later date. But how is the economy going to move from the first to the second equilibrium? Of particular interest are continuous trajectories that belong to the equilibrium manifold. The existence or non-existence of such continuous trajectories amounts to whether the points (p, ω) and (p', ω') belong to the same pathconnected component of the equilibrium manifold. Lack of pathconnectedness implies that two equilibria that do not belong to the same pathconnected component cannot be linked by a continuous path. Discontinuities are unavoidable. "Reform" can only reach the points of the same pathconnected component. Going from one pathconnected component to another one necessitates "revolution."

We will see that the equilibrium manifold E is pathconnected.

5.2.2 Simple Connectedness

Assume now that the topological space E is pathconnected. Therefore, there exists at least one continuous path linking any point of E to any other. But generally there is more than one path. It is therefore natural to try to compare these paths. In particular, is it possible to deform continuously one of the paths into the other and is there an economically appealing interpretation of this deformation property?

A continuous path in the equilibrium manifold can be considered as the mathematical expression of some economic policy. The determination of any economic policy is often the outcome of arbitration and compromises, and the latter can easily be interpreted as more or less continuous changes of the policies. The possibility of deforming any continuous path into another one with the same end points is known as simple connectedness.

We will see that the equilibrium manifold E is simply connected.

5.2.3 Contractibility

The two important properties of pathconnectedness and simple connectedness are found in an important class of topological spaces, the contractible spaces. A topological space X is contractible if it can be continuously deformed to being just one point $\{x\}$. Let a and b be two arbitrary points. In the deformation from X to the set $\{x\}$ that consists only of the point x, the points a and b follow two continuous paths that end up at the point x. Joining them defines a continuous path linking a to b, which proves the pathconnectedness of X. Intuitively, in the deformation from X to $\{x\}$, we see that the topological space X cannot feature any "hole" that would prevent deforming one continuous path linking a to b into another continuous path with the same end points.

An important class of contractible spaces consists of the star-shaped sets, a class that includes the convex sets. In particular, every Euclidean space is contractible. We will see that the equilibrium manifold E is contractible.

5.2.4 Global Coordinate Systems

Let $\mathfrak{P}(p, \omega)$ denote a property of the equilibrium (p, ω). Let $E(\mathfrak{P})$ denote the subset of the equilibrium manifold E that consists of the equilibria for which the property $\mathfrak{P}(p, \omega)$ is satisfied. The study of $\mathfrak{P}(p, \omega)$ then reduces to the study of the set $E(\mathfrak{P})$ as a subset of the equilibrium manifold E.

A smooth manifold has a set of local coordinates associated with every chart and, in general, more than one chart is necessary to cover the whole manifold. Since local coordinates change with every chart, it is not possible to describe a smooth manifold E with a unique coordinate system unless it can be covered by a unique chart. The existence of a unique chart is therefore a very strong global property that turns the study of subsets like $E(\mathfrak{P})$ into the study of systems of equalities and inequalities. In addition, the study of subsets of the equilibrium manifold E, sets like $E(\mathfrak{P})$, often takes advantage of the structure of the set E, a structure that we will find to be quite remarkable.

We will see that the equilibrium manifold E is diffeomorphic to a Euclidean space, which will provide us with a global coordinate system.

5.3 THE NO-TRADE EQUILIBRIA

The idea of a no-trade equilibrium is that no consumer trades at such an equilibrium. In practice, this means that consumer i, who is endowed with the commodity bundle $\omega_i \in \mathbb{R}^\ell$, observes that, for the price vector $p \in S$, the demand $f_i(p, p \cdot \omega_i)$ is equal to the endowment vector ω_i. Consumer i therefore does not need to buy or sell any goods. This is reflected in the following definition:

Definition 5.1. *The price-endowment vector $(p, \omega) \in S \times \Omega$ is a no-trade equilibrium if the equality $f_i(p, p \cdot \omega_i) = \omega_i$ is satisfied for $i = 1, 2, \ldots, m$.*

Obviously, a no-trade equilibrium is an equilibrium. Let T denote the set of no-trade equilibria. This set T is a subset of the equilibrium manifold E and its structure is remarkable:

Proposition 5.2. *For the m-tuple of demand functions $(f_i) \in \mathcal{E}$, the set of no-trade equilibria T is a smooth submanifold of E and is diffeomorphic to $B = S \times \mathbb{R}^m_{++}$.*

Proof. We define the map $f : S \times \mathbb{R}^m \to S \times (\mathbb{R}^\ell)^m$ by the formula

$$f(p, w_1, \ldots.w_m) = \big(p, f_1(p, w_1), \ldots, f_m(p, w_m)\big).$$

Let us show that its image $f(S \times \mathbb{R}^m)$ is contained in the equilibrium manifold E. It suffices to check that the equality

$$\sum_i f_i\big(p, p \cdot f_i(p, w_i)\big) = \sum_i f_i(p, w_i)$$

is satisfied, which readily follows from Walras law (W). Let us still denote by f the map from $S \times \mathbb{R}^m$ into E defined by the same formula. It follows from E being a smooth submanifold of $S \times \Omega$ that this map $f : S \times \mathbb{R}^m \to E$ is smooth.

Let us define the price-income map $\phi : S \times \Omega \to B$ by the formula $\phi\big(p, (\omega_1, \ldots, \omega_m)\big) = (p, p \cdot \omega_1, \ldots, p \cdot \omega_m)$. It suffices that we show that the assumptions of Lemma C.6 are satisfied by the restriction of the wealth map $\phi : S \times \Omega \to S \times \mathbb{R}^m$ to E, a map denoted by $\phi_E : E \to S \times \Omega$.

We have $\phi_E \circ f(p, w_1, \ldots, w_m) = (p, p \cdot f_1(p, w_1), \ldots, p \cdot f_m(p, w_m))$, which is equal to $(p, w_1, \ldots, w_m)$ by (W). This proves that $\phi_E \circ f = \mathrm{id}_{S \times \mathbb{R}^m}$.

Finally, let us prove that $T = f(S \times \mathbb{R}^m)$. The equality $(p, \omega_1, \ldots, \omega_m) = f(p, w_1, \ldots, w_m)$ means that $\omega_i = f_i(p, w_i)$ for $i = 1, \ldots, m$. Walras law (W) implies that $w_i = p \cdot \omega_i$, from which follows the equality $\omega_i = f_i(p, p \cdot \omega_i)$ for $i = 1, \ldots, m$. This shows the inclusion $f(S \times \mathbb{R}^m) \subset T$.

To prove the opposite inclusion, let $(p, \omega_1, \ldots, \omega_m) \in T$. Define $w_i = p \cdot \omega_i$ for $i = 1, \ldots, m$. By assumption, $\omega_i = f_i(p, p \cdot \omega_i) = f_i(p, w_i)$, which implies

$$(p, \omega_1, \ldots, \omega_m) = f(p, w_1, \ldots, w_m),$$

and proves the inclusion $T \subset f(S \times \mathbb{R}^m)$. $\qquad\square$

5.4 THE FIBERS OF THE EQUILIBRIUM MANIFOLD

The set of no-trade equilibria T has dimension $\ell + m - 1$ in the equilibrium manifold E that has dimension ℓm. From a measure theoretic sense, the set of no-trade equilibria T is therefore very small in the equilibrium manifold E. In particular, the probability of randomly selecting a no-trade equilibrium is zero. This section is therefore devoted to the other points of the equilibrium manifold.

5.4.1 The Linear Fibers

Definition 5.3. *The fiber $F(b)$ associated with $b = (p, w_1, \ldots, w_m) \in S \times \mathbb{R}^m$ is the set of pairs $(p, \omega) \in S \times \Omega$ that satisfy the following equations:*

$$p \cdot \omega_i = w_i \quad for \; i = 1, \ldots, m;$$

$$\sum_i \omega_i = \sum_i f_i(p, w_i).$$

Proposition 5.4. *The fiber $F(b)$ is a subset of the equilibrium manifold E.*

Proof. Let $(p, \omega) \in F(b)$. It suffices to substitute $p \cdot \omega_i$ to w_i in the equality $\sum_i \omega_i = \sum_i f_i(p, w_i)$ to see that (p, ω) satisfies the equilibrium equation (1) in section 4.4.3. $\square$

Proposition 5.5. *The fiber $F(b)$ is a linear manifold of dimension $(\ell - 1)(m - 1)$ embedded in E for every $b \in S \times \mathbb{R}^m$.*

Proof. The equations defining the fiber $F(b)$ are linear with a constant term, which proves that the fiber is a linear manifold. To obtain the dimensionality property, it suffices to find a suitable coordinate system. Given the equality $\sum_i \omega_i = r$ where $r = \sum_i f_i(p, w_i)$, it is sufficient to know $\omega_1, \ldots, \omega_{m-1}$ to get ω_m. From $p \cdot \omega_i = w_i$, it suffices to know the first $\ell - 1$ coordinates $\omega_i^1, \ldots, \omega_i^{\ell-1}$ of the endowment vector ω_i to determine the quantity ω_i^ℓ of the ℓ-th good. This has to be done just for the first $m - 1$ consumers. $\square$

5.4.2 Coordinates for the Equilibria in a Given Fiber

With $\bar{\omega}_i = (\omega_i^1, \ldots, \omega_i^{\ell-1})$ representing the first $\ell - 1$ coordinates of the endowment vector $\omega_i \in \mathbb{R}^\ell$, we have therefore shown that $(\bar{\omega}_1, \ldots, \bar{\omega}_{m-1}) \in \mathbb{R}^{(\ell-1)(m-1)}$ defines a set of coordinates for the points of the fiber $F(b)$ associated with $b = (p, w_1, \ldots, w_m) \in S \times \mathbb{R}^m$.

Incidentally, Proposition 5.5 implies that no fiber is empty. We shall see in a moment that each fiber contains indeed one and only one no-trade equilibrium.

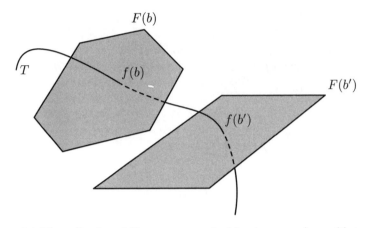

Figure 5.1 The collection of fibers parameterized by the no-trade equilibria

5.5 THE EQUILIBRIUM MANIFOLD AS A COLLECTION OF LINEAR FIBERS PARAMETERIZED BY THE NO-TRADE EQUILIBRIA

Proposition 5.6. *Every equilibrium* $(p, \omega) \in E$ *belongs to one and only one fiber.*

Proof. Let $(p, \omega) \in E$. The unique fiber containing the equilibrium $(p, \omega) \in E$ is the fiber $F(b)$ associated with $b = \phi_E(p, \omega)$, where ϕ_E is the price-income map restricted to the equilibrium manifold. $\square$

Proposition 5.7. *Every fiber contains one and only one no-trade equilibrium.*

Proof. Let $b = (p, w_1, \ldots, w_m) \in S \times \mathbb{R}^m$ and define

$$f(b) = \big(p, f_1(p, w_1), \cdots, f_m(p, w_m)\big).$$

Then, $f(b)$ is a no-trade equilibrium and belongs to the fiber $F(b)$. This no-trade equilibrium is unique in the fiber because the map $f : S \times \mathbb{R}^m \to T$ is a bijection whose inverse map is the price-income map $\phi_E : E \to S \times \mathbb{R}^m$. $\square$

5.6 A PICTURE OF THE EQUILIBRIUM MANIFOLD

It is now possible to provide a better geometric picture of the equilibrium manifold E as the disjoint union of fibers themselves parameterized by the no-trade equilibria belonging to the set T. The fibers being linear manifolds, the non-linearities involved in the equilibrium equation are captured by the parameterization of the linear fibers by the no-trade equilibria.

5.7 DIFFEOMORPHISM WITH $\mathbb{R}^{\ell m}$

Before stating the main result of this section, let us introduce the map

$$\Phi : S \times \Omega \to S \times \mathbb{R}^m \times \mathbb{R}^{(\ell-1)(m-1)}$$

defined by the formula

$$\Phi(p, \omega_1, \ldots, \omega_m) = (p, p \cdot \omega_1, \ldots, p \cdot \omega_m, \bar{\omega}_1, \ldots, \bar{\omega}_{m-1})$$

where $\bar{x}$ denotes the vector defined by the first $\ell - 1$ coordinates of $x \in \mathbb{R}^\ell$.

Proposition 5.8. *For the m-tuple of demand functions $(f_i) \in \mathcal{E}$, the restriction of the map Φ to the equilibrium manifold E is a diffeomorphism between E and $S \times \mathbb{R}^m \times \mathbb{R}^{(\ell-1)(m-1)}$.*

Proof. Let $\theta : S \times \mathbb{R}^m \times \mathbb{R}^{(\ell-1)(m-1)} \to S \times \Omega$ be defined by the formula

$$\theta(p, w_1, \ldots, w_m, \bar{\omega}_1, \ldots, \bar{\omega}_{m-1}) = (p, \bar{\omega}_1, \omega_1^\ell, \bar{\omega}_2, \omega_2^\ell, \ldots, \bar{\omega}_{m-1}, \omega_{m-1}^\ell, \omega_m)$$

where

$$\omega_i^\ell = w_i - \bar{p} \cdot \bar{\omega}_i \qquad \text{for } i = 1, 2, \ldots, m - 1, \tag{1}$$

and

$$\omega_m = \sum_{i=1}^{m} f_i(p, w_i) - \sum_{i=1}^{m-1} \omega_i. \tag{2}$$

The strategy of this proof is to show that the equilibrium manifold E is the image of the map θ, i.e., $E = \theta(S \times \mathbb{R}^m \times \mathbb{R}^{(\ell-1)(m-1)})$ and then to apply Lemma C.6 to the maps Φ and θ.

The maps Φ and θ are smooth as defined by smooth formulas. Straightforward computations yield the equality

$$\Phi \circ \theta = \mathrm{id}_{S \times \mathbb{R}^m \times \mathbb{R}^{(\ell-1)(m-1)}}.$$

In order to apply the Lemma, we have to show that the equilibrium manifold E is the image of θ, i.e., $\theta(S \times \mathbb{R}^m \times \mathbb{R}^{(\ell-1)(m-1)}) = E$. The argument requires two simple computations. One computation is to prove the inclusion $\mathrm{im}(\theta) \subset E$, the other the inclusion $E \subset \mathrm{im}(\theta)$.

Let $x = (p, w_1, \ldots, w_m, \bar{\omega}_1, \ldots, \bar{\omega}_{m-1})$. The inner product of equality (2) with the price vector $p \in S$ combined with Walras law (W) implies $w_m = p \cdot \omega_m$. Then, equality (2) can be reformulated as

$$\sum_i f_i(p, p \cdot \omega_i) = \sum_i \omega_i,$$

which is the equilibrium equation. In other words, this proves the inclusion $\mathrm{im}(\theta) \subset E$.

Let $(p, \omega) \in E$. A straightforward computation proves the equality

$$\theta \circ \Phi(p, \omega) = (p, \omega),$$

which implies the inclusion $E \subset \mathrm{im}(\theta)$. $\qquad\qquad\square$

Lemma C.6 used in the proof of Proposition 5.8 offers us as, icing on the cake, an alternative proof of Proposition 4.9, namely that the "equilibrium manifold" E is indeed a smooth submanifold of $S \times \Omega$.

Corollary 5.9. *The equilibrium manifold E is diffeomorphic to $\mathbb{R}^{\ell m}$.*

5.8 CONCLUSION

The equilibrium manifold, the domain of the natural projection, is not different from a Euclidean space. The natural projection can therefore be identified to a vector-valued map of a finite number of real variables. At this point, we could pursue the study of the exchange model without making any reference to smooth manifolds and submanifolds.

More importantly from an economic perspective, the very nice global structure of the equilibrium manifold is interesting by the wealth of economic phenomena simply excluded because the equilibrium manifold is diffeomorphic to a Euclidean space. For example, equilibria cannot belong to two different pathconnected components. Similarly, it is always possible to deform continuously one path on the equilibrium manifold to another one with the same endpoints. Many issues in the political debate depend in fact on the global structure of the equilibrium manifold.

5.9 NOTES AND COMMENTS

The study of the global structure of the equilibrium manifold E is due to Balasko with the proofs of the pathconnectedness [10], simple connectedness and contractibility for the endowment set $\Omega = (\mathbb{R}^\ell_{++})^m$ [12], and the homeomorphism and diffeomorphism with a Euclidean space in [11]. An alternative proof of the diffeomorphism property is given by Schecter [59]. With the endowment set $\Omega = (\mathbb{R}^\ell)^m$ considered here, the same proofs work except for the diffeomorphism property, which is much easier [16].

CHAPTER 6

Applications of the Global Coordinate System

6.1 INTRODUCTION

A global coordinate system for the equilibrium manifold follows from: 1) The determination of the unique fiber $F(b)$ through the equilibrium (p, ω) where $b = \phi(p, \omega) = (p, p \cdot \omega_1, \ldots, p \cdot \omega_m)$; 2) The determination of the location of the equilibrium (p, ω) within the fiber $F(b)$ viewed as a linear space of dimension $(\ell - 1)(m - 1)$ and, therefore, parameterized by $(\ell - 1)(m - 1)$ coordinates. If there is little leeway in determining the fiber $F(b)$ through the equilibrium (p, ω), there are different ways of representing the equilibrium (p, ω) within its fiber $F(b)$. This leads us to define coordinate systems (A) and (B) for the equilibrium manifold.

After having defined these two coordinate systems, we apply them to get an analytical characterization of the critical equilibria, i.e., the critical points of the natural projection. These coordinate systems and the computations based on them do not require of the m-tuple (f_i) more than being an element of $\mathcal{E}$. But the full implications will become apparent only in later chapters where more assumptions on the m-tuple (f_i) will be made.

6.2 COORDINATE SYSTEM (A)

It follows from Proposition 5.8 that the equilibrium $(p, \omega) \in E$ is determined by the price income vector $b = \phi(p, \omega) \in S \times \mathbb{R}^m$ that determines the fiber $F(b)$ that contains the equilibrium, and by the location of the equilibrium in the fiber $F(b)$, the location determined by the coordinates $(\bar{\omega}_1, \ldots, \bar{\omega}_{m-1})$.

Coordinate system (A) has the advantage of simplicity. This will be particularly useful when writing the coordinates of the natural projection map. The drawback is that the coordinates of the no-trade equilibrium $(p, \omega) \in T$ in system (A) are

$$\left(p, w_1, \ldots, w_m, \bar{f}_1(p, w_1), \ldots, \bar{f}_{m-1}(p, w_{m-1})\right),$$

coordinates that do not lend themselves to an easy identification of the lack of trade at equilibrium, and by extension, of the proximity of a given equilibrium to the no-trade equilibrium of the corresponding fiber.

6.3 COORDINATE SYSTEM (B)

This alternative coordinate system is particularly well-suited to the analysis of properties of equilibria in relation to the trade vector.

Define $-\bar{y}_i = f_i(p, w_i) - \bar{\omega}_i \in \mathbb{R}^{\ell-1}$, the first $\ell - 1$ coordinates of the net trade vector of consumer i, with i varying from 1 to $m - 1$. The $(m - 1) \times (\ell - 1)$ matrix Y^T (the transpose of matrix Y) is by definition the matrix

$$Y^T = (\bar{y}_1, \bar{y}_2, \ldots, \bar{y}_{m-1}).$$

Matrix Y parameterizes the equilibria of the fiber $F(b)$.

Coordinate system (B) for the equilibrium manifold is then defined by the pair (b, Y) with $b \in S \times \mathbb{R}^m$ and Y a $(m - 1) \times (\ell - 1)$ matrix.

One nice feature of coordinate system (B) is that the coordinate $(b, 0)$ now corresponds to the no-trade equilibrium $f(b)$ of the fiber $F(b)$.

6.4 FORMULAS OF THE NATURAL PROJECTION

The equilibrium manifold E and the endowment set Ω being both diffeomorphic to $\mathbb{R}^{\ell m}$, the natural projection can be identified to a map from $\mathbb{R}^{\ell m}$ into itself. It is therefore interesting to use the coordinate systems of E and Ω to get some explicit formulation of the natural projection.

We use coordinate system (A) for the equilibrium manifold E based on the diffeomorphism with $S \times \mathbb{R}^m \times \mathbb{R}^{(\ell-1)(m-1)}$. For $\Omega = (\mathbb{R}^\ell)^m$, we use the coordinates $\omega_1, \omega_2, \ldots, \omega_{m-1}$ and $r = \omega_1 + \omega_2 + \cdots + \omega_m$ instead of ω_m.

By definition, we have $\pi(p, \omega) = \omega$. In coordinate system (A), the equilibrium (p, ω) has coordinates $(p, w_1, \ldots, w_m, \bar{\omega}_1, \ldots, \bar{\omega}_{m-1})$. Since we already know the components $(\bar{\omega}_1, \ldots, \bar{\omega}_{m-1})$ of ω, we only need to express the $\omega_1^\ell, \ldots, \omega_{m-1}^\ell$ and r as functions of $(p, w_1, \ldots, w_m, \bar{\omega}_1, \ldots, \bar{\omega}_{m-1})$.

Proposition 6.1. *The analytic expression of the natural projection π takes the form:*

$$r^1 = \sum_{i=1}^{m} f_i^1(p, w_i);$$

$$\cdots = \cdots$$

$$r^{\ell-1} = \sum_{i=1}^{m} f_i^{\ell-1}(p, w_i);$$

$$\omega_1^\ell = w_1 - p_1\omega_1^1 - \cdots - p_{\ell-1}\omega_1^{\ell-1};$$

$$\cdots = \cdots$$

$$\omega_{m-1}^\ell = w_{m-1} - p_1\omega_{m-1}^1 - \cdots - p_{\ell-1}\omega_{m-1}^{\ell-1};$$

$$r^\ell = w_1 + w_2 + \cdots + w_m - p_1 r^1 - p_2 r^2 - \cdots - p_{\ell-1} r^{\ell-1}.$$

Proof. This expression follows readily from the definition of the map $\pi : E \to \Omega$. □

It follows from Proposition 6.1 that the natural projection $\pi : E \to \Omega$ can be identified to a smooth map from $\mathbb{R}^{\ell m}$ into itself for an m-tuple of demand functions (f_i) that belongs to $\mathcal{E}$.

6.5 THE JACOBIAN MATRIX OF AGGREGATE EXCESS DEMAND

In this section, we use the analytic expression of the natural projection to express the Jacobian matrix of aggregate excess demand in function of the coordinates of the equilibrium $(p, \omega) \in E$ in system (B). Prices follow the numeraire normalization $p_\ell = 1$.

6.5.1 Characterization of Critical Equilibria

Let us define matrices $M(p, \omega)$ and $N(p, \omega)$ as follows:

$$M(p, \omega) = \begin{bmatrix}
\sum_i \dfrac{\partial f_i^1(p, w_i)}{\partial p_1} & \cdots & \sum_i \dfrac{\partial f_i^1(p, w_i)}{\partial p_{\ell-1}} & \dfrac{\partial f_1^1(p, w_1)}{\partial w_1} & \cdots & \dfrac{\partial f_m^1(p, w_m)}{\partial w_m} \\
\vdots & \ddots & \vdots & \vdots & \ddots & \vdots \\
\sum_i \dfrac{\partial f_i^{\ell-1}(p, w_i)}{\partial p_1} & \cdots & \sum_i \dfrac{\partial f_i^{\ell-1}(p, w_i)}{\partial p_{\ell-1}} & \dfrac{\partial f_1^{\ell-1}(p, w_1)}{\partial w_1} & \cdots & \dfrac{\partial f_m^{\ell-1}(p, w_m)}{\partial w_m} \\
-\omega_1^1 & \cdots & -\omega_1^{\ell-1} & 1 & \cdots & 0 \\
-\omega_2^1 & \cdots & -\omega_2^{\ell-1} & 0 & \cdots & 0 \\
\vdots & \ddots & \vdots & \vdots & \ddots & \vdots \\
-\omega_{m-1}^1 & \cdots & -\omega_{m-1}^{\ell-1} & 0 & \cdots & 0 \\
-\omega_m^1 & \cdots & -\omega_m^{\ell-1} & 0 & \cdots & 1
\end{bmatrix}.$$

Matrix $N(p, \omega)$ is identical to $M(p, \omega)$ except for its last row, which is equal to

$$(-r^1, \ldots, -r^{\ell-1}, 1, \ldots, 1, 1).$$

We define matrix $J_{\ell\ell}(p, \omega)$ as the Jacobian matrix of the aggregate excess demand map $\bar{z}(., \omega) : p \to \bar{z}(p, \omega) \in \mathbb{R}^{\ell-1}$.

Lemma 6.2. *We have* $\det N(p, \omega) = \det M(p, \omega) = \det J_{\ell\ell}(p, \omega)$.

Proof. In $N(p, \omega)$, subtract the rows ℓ to $\ell + m - 1$ from the last row. We thus obtain the last row of $M(p, \omega)$. This proves $\det N(p, \omega) = \det M(p, \omega)$.

Matrix $M(p, \omega)$ is made of four blocks

$$M(p, \omega) = \begin{bmatrix} A & B \\ C & I \end{bmatrix}$$

with I denoting the identity matrix. The coefficient $-\omega_i^j$ belonging to row i and column j of matrix C is "killed" by multiplying column $((\ell - 1) + i)$ of $M(p, \omega)$ by ω_i^j and adding the result to column j of $M(p, \omega)$. Performing this operation for every element of C yields matrix

$$\begin{bmatrix} J_{\ell\ell}(p, \omega) & B \\ 0 & I \end{bmatrix}$$

whose determinant is equal to $\det J_{\ell\ell}(p, \omega)$. □

Proposition 6.3. *The equilibrium* (p, ω) *is critical if and only if*

$$\det N(p, \omega) = 0.$$

Proof. With the analytical expression of the map π given in Proposition 6.1, the Jacobian matrix $D\pi_{(p,\omega)}$ of π at (p, ω) is seen to be equal to

$$\begin{bmatrix} N(p, \omega) & * \\ 0 & I \end{bmatrix}$$

where I is the $(\ell - 1)(m - 1)$ identity matrix. We therefore have $\det D\pi_{(p,\omega)} = \det N(p, \omega)$. □

Proposition 6.4. *The equilibrium* $(p, \omega) \in E$ *is critical if and only if*

$$\det J_{\ell\ell}(p, \omega) = 0.$$

Proof. The equilibrium $(p, \omega) \in E$ is critical if and only if $\det N(p, \omega)$ is equal to 0. It then suffices to apply the equality $\det N(p, \omega) = \det M(p, \omega) = \det J_{\ell\ell}(p, \omega)$ of Lemma 6.2. □

Proposition 6.5. *The economy $\omega \in \Omega$ is regular if and only if the vector $0 \in \mathbb{R}^{\ell-1}$ is a regular value of the aggregate excess demand map $\bar{z}(.\,,\omega) : S \to \mathbb{R}^{\ell-1}$.*

Proof. By definition, the vector $0 \in \mathbb{R}^{\ell-1}$ is a regular value of the excess demand map $\bar{z}(.,\omega) : S \to \mathbb{R}^{\ell-1}$ associated with the economy $\omega \in \Omega$ if and only if for every equilibrium $(p, \omega) \in E$, $\det J_{\ell\ell}(p, \omega)$ is not equal to 0. This condition is equivalent to having (p, ω) not a critical point of the natural projection π, which also means that ω is a regular value of the natural projection. □

6.5.2 Matrix $J_{\ell\ell}(p, \omega)$ and Coordinate System (B)

Matrix $J_{\ell\ell}(p, \omega)$ takes a remarkably simple form in coordinate system (B) where the equilibrium (p, ω) is represented by its coordinates (b, Y).

Let $S_{\ell\ell}(b) = \sum_{i=1}^{m} S_{\ell\ell} f_i(p, w_i)$ be the sum of the Slutsky matrices $S_{\ell\ell} f_i(p, w_i)$ for the m consumers and $(\ell - 1) \times (m - 1)$ matrix $K(b)$ be with (h, i) coefficient equal to

$$k_{(h,i)} = \frac{\partial f_i^h(p, w_i)}{\partial w_i} - \frac{\partial f_m^h(p, w_m)}{\partial w_m}.$$

Proposition 6.6.

$$J_{\ell\ell}(b, Y) = S_{\ell\ell}(b) + K(b)\, Y.$$

Proof. This formula follows readily from the chain rule applied to the aggregate excess demand map $p \to \bar{z}(p, \omega)$. Note that the only assumption for this to hold true is that the m-tuple (f_i) belongs to $\mathcal{E}$, i.e., only smoothness (S) and Walras law (W) are needed. □

Corollary 6.7. *The Jacobian matrix of aggregate excess demand at the no-trade equilibrium $(p, \omega) = (b, 0)$ is equal to*

$$J_{\ell\ell}(b, 0) = S_{\ell\ell} f_1(p, w_1) + \cdots + S_{\ell\ell} f_m(p, w_m).$$

Proof. It suffices to have $Y = 0$ in Proposition 6.6. □

EXERCISE

6.1. Prices are not normalized. Let (p, ω) be equilibrium. Prove the equality $p \cdot (\partial z / \partial p_j) = 0$ for $j = 1, 2, \ldots, \ell$. Show that if $\partial z^j / \partial p_k > 0$ for $j \neq k$ (gross substitutability), then $\partial z^j / \partial p_j < 0$ for $j = 1, 2, \ldots, \ell$.

6.6 CONCLUSION

The explicit use of coordinate systems for the equilibrium manifold and the natural projection may give the impression that the study of the exchange model has been liberated from the yoke of smooth manifolds and submanifolds. This impression is technically correct. However, we will see in the next chapter that the powerful tools and ideas of differential topology that play such an important role in the study of the natural projection do not really depend on the explicit formulation of that natural projection provided the latter satisfies the right topological properties, namely properness.

Having an explicit formula for the natural projection is very useful when it comes to determining whether some specific equilibria are critical for example. It is also very likely that such explicit formulas will prove useful in applications of the general equilibrium model.

6.7 NOTES AND COMMENTS

A global coordinate system for the equilibrium manifold is implicit in Balasko's proof of the regularity of the no-trade equilibria and in the diffeomorphism between the equilibrium manifold and a Euclidean space [12]. However, the first explicit formulation of such a global coordinate system and its application to an explicit set of equations for the natural projection appears for the first time in [16].

CHAPTER 7

The Broad Picture

7.1 INTRODUCTION

In this chapter, the m-tuple (f_i) of demand functions defining the exchange model belongs to $\mathcal{E}_r$, i.e., the demand function f_i is bounded from below (B) for every consumer and satisfies desirability (A) for at least one consumer. These additional properties will give to the natural projection the very important property of properness. The combination of smoothness and properness will suffice to yield what is now known as the theory of regular economies following [24].

7.2 PROPERNESS

By definition, the continuous map $\pi : E \to \Omega$ is proper if the preimage of every compact set is compact. A set is compact if every sequence in this set contains a convergent subsequence. Furthermore, all compact sets in a Euclidean space are closed and bounded.

Proposition 7.1. *The natural projection* $\pi : E \to \Omega$ *is proper for* $(f_i) \in \mathcal{E}_r$.

Proof. In this proof, we use the simplex normalization $p_1 + \cdots + p_\ell = 1$ for the price vector $p = (p_1, \ldots, p_\ell)$. Recall that S_Σ denotes the open price simplex and $\overline{S_\Sigma} = \{p \in \mathbb{R}_+^\ell \mid p_1 + \cdots + p_\ell = 1\}$ the closed price simplex. Note that $\overline{S_\Sigma}$ is compact.

Let K be a compact subset of Ω. Let us show that the preimage $\pi^{-1}(K)$ is compact. It follows from the continuity of π that $\pi^{-1}(K)$ is closed in E.

Let (p^q, ω^q) be an infinite sequence in $\pi^{-1}(K)$. The Cartesian product $\overline{S_\Sigma} \times K$ is compact as the Cartesian product of two compact sets. The preimage $\pi^{-1}(K)$ is a subset of $\overline{S_\Sigma} \times K$. By the compactness of $\overline{S_\Sigma} \times K$ and by considering a suitable subsequence, we can assume without loss of generality that the sequence (p^q, ω^q) is converging to some $(p^0, \omega^0) \in \overline{S_\Sigma} \times K$.

The projection map $\omega = (\omega_1, \ldots, \omega_m) \to \omega_i$ being continuous, the projection K_i of the compact set K is therefore compact. It follows from boundedness from below (B) satisfied by the demand function f_i that, for the compact set K_i, there exists $B_i \in \mathbb{R}^\ell$ such that the inequality $B_i \leq f_i(p^q, p^q \cdot \omega_i^q)$ is satisfied for every i.

The map $\omega = (\omega_1, \ldots, \omega_m) \to \omega_1 + \cdots + \omega_m$ is also continuous. The image of the compact set K is then a compact subset of $\mathbb{R}^\ell$ and, therefore, is bounded. There exists $A \in \mathbb{R}^\ell$ such that $\omega_1^q + \cdots + \omega_m^q \leq A$ is satisfied for all q.

The inequality

$$B_1 \leq f_1(p^q, p^q \cdot \omega_1^q) \leq A - (B_2 + \cdots + B_m) \tag{1}$$

then follows from the equilibrium equation satisfied by (p^q, ω^q).

Let us show that the limit p^0 of the sequence (p^q) belongs to the open price simplex S_Σ. Assume the contrary. This means that p^0 belongs to $\overline{S_\Sigma} \setminus S_\Sigma$.

There is no loss of generality in assuming that consumer 1's demand function satisfies (A). It then follows from (A) that the sequence $\|f_1(p^q, p^q \cdot \omega_1^q)\|$ is not bounded, which contradicts inequality (1).

It then follows from the closedness of $\pi^{-1}(K)$ that the limit (p^0, ω^0) belongs to $\pi^{-1}(K)$. $\qquad\square$

7.3 SMOOTH SELECTION AT A REGULAR EQUILIBRIUM

Proposition 7.2. *There exists an open neighborhood $U \subset E$ of the regular equilibrium $(p, \omega) \in \mathfrak{R}$ such that $V = \pi(U)$ is open in Ω and the restriction $\pi \mid U : U \to V$ is a diffeomorphism.*

Proof. This follows from the application of the inverse mapping theorem at the regular point (p, ω) for the natural projection $\pi : E \to \Omega$. See Proposition D.8 in the Appendix D. $\qquad\square$

Note that Proposition 7.2 is simply a reformulation of the inverse mapping theorem.

SMOOTH EQUILIBRIUM PRICE SELECTIONS

The inverse map $(\pi \mid U)^{-1} : V \to U$ is a map $\omega' \to (s(\omega'), \omega')$ where the map $s : V \to S$ is smooth. The map s is known as an equilibrium price selection map. Therefore, Proposition 7.2 tells us that smooth equilibrium price selections exist at regular equilibria.

7.4 THE EQUILIBRIUM MANIFOLD OVER REGULAR ECONOMIES

The following proposition gives us a fairly accurate image of the equilibrium manifold E over the set of regular economies $\mathcal{R}$. This image is only partial, however, because the proposition holds true only for sufficiently small open subsets V of the set of regular economies $\mathcal{R}$.

Proposition 7.3. *Let $(f_i) \in \mathcal{E}_r$. Then, there exists an open neighborhood $U \subset \mathcal{R}$ of the regular economy $\omega \in \mathcal{R}$ such that the preimage $\pi^{-1}(U)$ is the union of a finite number of pairwise disjoint open sets V_k such that the restriction $\pi_k : V_k \to U$ of the map $\pi : E \to \Omega$ is a diffeomorphism for all k.*

Proof. Let $(p, \omega) \in \pi^{-1}(\omega)$. By Proposition 7.2, there exists an open subset U of E such that $(p, \omega) = \pi^{-1}(\omega) \cap U$. Every subset of $\pi^{-1}(\omega)$ reduced to a point is therefore open. The collection of points of $\pi^{-1}(\omega)$ defines an open covering of the set $\pi^{-1}(\omega)$. Since that set is also compact by the properness of the map $\pi : E \to \Omega$, that set can be covered by a finite number of points or, in other words, is a finite union of its elements, hence is finite.

Let n be the (finite) number of elements of $\pi^{-1}(\omega)$. If $n = 0$, there is nothing to prove. Assume $n \geq 1$. Let $x_1, \ldots, x_n$ be all the elements of $\pi^{-1}(\omega)$. By Proposition 7.2, there exist (small enough) open pairwise disjoint neighborhoods $U'_1, U'_2, \ldots, U'_k, \ldots, U'_n$ in E of $x_1, x_2, \ldots, x_k, \ldots, x_n$ such that the restriction of π to U'_k is a diffeomorphism with $U_k = \pi(U'_k)$.

The set $E \setminus (U'_1 \cup \cdots \cup U'_k \cup \cdots \cup U'_n)$ is closed in E. Its image by the natural projection π is closed in Ω because π is proper. Let us define the set U as $U = (U_1 \cap U_2 \cap \cdots \cap U_k \cap \cdots \cap U_n) \setminus \pi(E \setminus (U'_1 \cup \cdots \cup U'_k \cup \cdots \cup U'_n))$, i.e., U is the intersection of the sets U_k for k varying from 1 to n and of the complement in Ω of the set $\pi(E \setminus (U'_1 \cup \cdots \cup U'_k \cup \cdots \cup U'_n))$. Clearly, U is open in Ω. Let us show that ω belongs to U. All we have to check is that ω does not belong to $\pi(E \setminus (U'_1 \cup \cdots \cup U'_k \cup \cdots \cup U'_n))$, which follows from the inclusion

$$\pi^{-1}(\omega) \subset U'_1 \cup \cdots \cup U'_k \cup \cdots \cup U'_n.$$

Let $V_k = U'_k \cap \pi^{-1}(U)$. The restriction $\pi_k = \pi \mid V_k$ is by construction a diffeomorphism between V_k, and $\pi(V_k)$.

Let us check that $\pi^{-1}(U)$ is the union of $V_1 \cup \cdots \cup V_k \cup \cdots \cup V_n$. Let $x \in \pi^{-1}(U)$. Assume that x does not belong to any V_k. Then, it belongs to the set $E \setminus (U_1' \cup \cdots \cup U_k' \cup \cdots \cup U_n')$, which implies

$$\omega = \pi(x) \in \pi\left(E \setminus (U_1' \cup \cdots \cup U_k' \cup \cdots U_n')\right).$$

Therefore, ω belongs to the open set U, hence a contradiction. $\qquad\square$

Corollary 7.4. *Let $(f_i) \in \mathcal{E}_r$. The equilibria associated with $\omega \in \mathcal{R}$ are locally unique and their number finite.*

Proof. Local uniqueness means that, for $(p, \omega) \in \pi^{-1}(\omega)$, there exists an open set U of $(p, \omega) \in E$ such that the intersection $U \cap \pi^{-1}(\omega) = (p, \omega)$. Local uniqueness therefore follows from the first part of the proof of Proposition 7.2. $\qquad\square$

The property described by Corollary 7.4 is known as the local uniqueness of equilibrium. More generally, the mathematical structure described by Proposition 7.3 is known as the property that the restriction of the map π to $\pi^{-1}(\mathcal{R})$ is an open finite covering of the set of regular economies $\mathcal{R}$. What follows are just ways of rephrasing that covering property.

7.4.1 Selections of Equilibrium Prices

Proposition 7.5. *Assume $(f_i) \in \mathcal{E}_r$. Let $\omega \in \mathcal{R}$. There exists an open neighborhood U of ω with $U \subset \mathcal{R}$ and a finite number n of smooth maps $s_k : U \to S$ such that the union $\cup_k s_k(\omega')$ is identical to the set $W(\omega')$ of equilibrium price vectors associated with every $\omega' \in U$.*

Proof. If $n = 0$, there is nothing to prove. Assume $n \geq 1$. In Proposition 7.3, let us compose the map $\pi_k^{-1} : U \to V_k$ with the projection map $S \times \Omega \to S$ to define the map $s_k : U \to S$. We then have

$$\pi^{-1}(\omega') = \bigcup_{1 \leq k \leq n} \{(s_k(\omega'), \omega')\}$$

for $\omega' \in U$. $\qquad\square$

Proposition 7.5 enables us to express all the equilibrium prices associated with a regular economy as functions of the parameter ω describing these economies.

7.4.2 Constant Number of Equilibria at Regular Economies

Proposition 7.6. *Assume* $(f_i) \in \mathcal{E}_r$. *Let* $\omega \in \mathcal{R}$ *be a regular economy. There exists an open neighborhood* U *of* ω *with* $U \subset \mathcal{R}$ *such that the number of equilibria is constant all over* U.

Proof. Let $\omega \in \mathcal{R}$ be a regular economy. It then suffices to pick U as in Proposition 7.5. □

Proposition 7.6 is often stated as the local constancy of the number of equilibria.

7.4.3 Structural Stability

Proposition 7.5 implies that infinitesimal variations of the (regular) endowment vector $\omega \in \mathcal{R}$ entail only infinitesimal variations of the corresponding equilibrium prices. This "stability" property (though a better word would be robustness) is satisfied by the full equilibrium set $\pi^{-1}(\omega)$. This property is known as *structural stability*.

Structural stability explains the relative constancy of market prices in competitive economies. Nevertheless, discontinuities of equilibrium price selections are likely to occur when the equilibrium (p, ω) moves through the set of critical equilibria $\mathfrak{S}$ (and the endowment vector ω through the set of singular economies $\mathcal{S}$).

7.4.4 Constant Number of Equilibria over the Connected Components of $\mathcal{R}$

By definition, the *connected component of a point* in a topological space is the largest connected set containing that point. (See, for example [28], (3.1.9).) The *connected components* of a set are the various connected components of the points of this set. It follows from this definition that the set of regular economies $\mathcal{R}$ is partitioned into its connected components. By partitioned, it is meant that the connected components are pairwise disjoint and their union is equal to the full set $\mathcal{R}$.

We have:

Proposition 7.7. *Assume* $(f_i) \in \mathcal{E}_r$. *The number of equilibria is constant over each connected component of the set of regular economies* $\mathcal{R}$.

Proof. Let $N(\omega) = \#\pi^{-1}(\omega)$ denote the number of equilibria of the regular economy $\omega \in \mathcal{R}$. This defines a function $N : \mathcal{R} \to \mathbb{N}$, where $\mathbb{N}$ is the set of natural integers. Let us equip this set with the discrete topology, the topology where each subset is open (and also closed).

Proposition 7.6 tells us for $\omega \in \mathcal{R}$, there exists an open neighborhood U of ω contained in $\mathcal{R}$ over which the number of equilibria $N(\omega)$ is constant. The function N is said to be *locally constant*.

Let us show that a locally constant function is necessarily constant on every connected component of its domain. First, let us show that the locally constant function N is continuous.

Continuity is established if we can show that the preimage by the function N of every open subset of $\mathbb{N}$ is open in $\mathcal{R}$. Since the topology of $\mathbb{N}$ is discrete, open subsets of $\mathbb{N}$ are the union of open subsets reduced to just one point. The preimage of a union of sets being also the union of the preimages of the sets and the union of open sets being open, it therefore suffices to show that the preimage $N^{-1}(k)$ of the set $\{k\}$ (reduced to the element k) by the map $N : \mathcal{R} \to \mathbb{N}$ is open. This set consists of the economies $\omega \in \mathcal{R}$ that have k equilibria. If this set is empty (i.e., there are no such economies), then it is open since an empty set is open by definition. If $N^{-1}(k)$ is nonempty, let $\omega \in N^{-1}(k)$. It follows from Proposition 7.6 that there exists an open neighborhood U of ω where the number of equilibria is equal to k, hence the inclusion $U \subset N^{-1}(k)$. This shows that the set $N^{-1}(k)$ is an open neighborhood of each of its elements. This property characterizes open sets and implies that $N^{-1}(k)$ is open. This proves the continuity of the map $N : \mathcal{R} \to \mathbb{N}$.

Let C be a connected component of $\mathcal{R}$. The image of a connected set by a continuous map is connected. Therefore, the image $N(C)$ is a connected subset of the set $\mathbb{N}$ (equipped with the discrete topology). It follows from the definition of a connected set combined with the definition of the discrete topology that the only connected sets of $\mathbb{N}$ (equipped with the discrete topology) are the sets that consist of only one element. This implies that the set $N(C)$ consists of just one element $k \in \mathbb{N}$, which is just another way of saying that the map N is constant on C. □

7.5 GENERICITY OF REGULAR ECONOMIES

The importance of regular economies comes from the fact that all their equilibria are regular and, therefore, "well-behaved" in the sense that all equilibrium prices are defined by smooth maps on sufficiently small neighborhoods. Regular economies feature the nicest possible form of dependence of the equilibrium price vectors on the fundamentals of the economy. The following property tells us that there are many regular economies. If economies are picked at random, the probability that an economy is regular is equal to one.

7.5.1 Full Measure

We already know that the set $\mathcal{R}$ is open. The following proposition tells us that this set is really "big" in the sense that its complement has Lebesgue measure zero in Ω.

Proposition 7.8. *Assume* $(f_i) \in \mathcal{E}_r$. *The set of regular economies* $\mathcal{R}$ *is open with full measure in* Ω.

Proof. Sard's theorem tells us that the set of singular values of a smooth map between two smooth manifolds has Lebesgue measure zero. This implies that the set $S = \pi(\mathfrak{S})$, the set of singular values of the natural projection $\pi : E \to \Omega$ has measure zero in Ω and its complement $\mathcal{R} = \Omega \setminus S$ full measure. $\qquad\square$

The full measure property of the set of regular values of the natural projection $\pi : E \to \Omega$ would be satisfied even with $(f_i) \in \mathcal{E}$, i.e., without the properness of the natural projection. But then it cannot be proved that the set of regular economies is open.

7.5.2 Density

The full measure property implies an interesting topological property, density, as follows from the following corollary:

Corollary 7.9. *Assume* $(f_i) \in \mathcal{E}_r$. *The set of regular economies* $\mathcal{R}$ *is open and dense in* Ω.

Proof. All we have to show is that $\mathcal{R}$ is dense. Assume the contrary. Then there exists a non-empty open cube U, such that the intersection $\mathcal{R} \cap U$ is empty. This means that the non-empty open set U is contained in S. Therefore, the measure of S must be larger than or at least equal to the measure of U. But the measure of the non-empty cube U is the product of the lengths of its sides and, as such, is strictly positive. This yields a contradiction. $\qquad\square$

Density means that the set $\mathcal{R}$ is "big" from a topological perspective. Note, however, that the set of rational numbers $\mathbb{Q}$ is dense in the set of real numbers $\mathbb{R}$. Nevertheless, its Lebesgue measure is equal to 0 as the measure of a countable set. Here, we have much more than just density since the set $\mathcal{R}$ is also open.

7.6 THE DEGREES OF THE NATURAL PROJECTION

7.6.1 Degrees of Smooth Proper Maps

As a smooth proper map from $\mathbb{R}^{\ell m}$ into itself (through the diffeomorphism of Corollary 5.9), the modulo 2 and the topological degrees can be defined for the natural projection $\pi : E \to \Omega$. .

It follows from Corollary 7.4 that the number of equilibria, i.e., the number of elements of the set $\pi^{-1}(\omega)$, is finite for the regular value $\omega \in \mathcal{R}$. Though this number may depend on the choice of $\omega \in \mathcal{R}$, it is possible to "count" the finite number of elements of $\pi^{-1}(\omega)$ in ways such that this "count" becomes independent of the choice of $\omega \in \mathcal{R}$.

For example, the remainder after division by two of the number of elements of the set $\pi^{-1}(\omega)$ can be shown not to depend on the choice of the regular value $\omega \in \mathcal{R}$. This remainder defines the modulo 2 degree of the smooth proper map $\pi : E \to \Omega$. In addition, the modulo 2 degree can be shown to be invariant through proper homotopy, a concept rigorously defined in the appendix. Roughly speaking, two smooth proper maps π and π' are properly homotopic if there is a continuous path in the set of smooth proper maps linking π to π'. Then, we have $\deg_2(\pi) = \deg_2(\pi')$.

The definition of the topological degree requires that the two manifolds E and Ω are orientable, which they are since they are both diffeomorphic to $\mathbb{R}^{\ell m}$, and the Euclidean space $\mathbb{R}^n$ possesses two orientations, one defined by the canonical base $(e_1, \ldots, e_k, \ldots, e_n)$ where the vector $e_k = (0, \ldots, 0, 1, 0, \ldots, 0)$ has all its coordinates equal to 0 except for the k-th one that is equal to one. The opposite orientation is defined by the base $(e_1, \ldots, e_{n-1}, -e_n)$.

These diffeomorphisms define two (global) coordinate systems for E and Ω respectively and we can calculate the Jacobian determinant of the natural projection π at the regular equilibrium $(p, \omega) \in \mathfrak{R}$ for these coordinates. We associate with the regular equilibrium $(p, \omega) \in \mathfrak{R}$ the number $+1$ or -1 depending on whether the sign of this Jacobian determinant is positive or negative. It can be shown that the sum of these $+1$'s and -1's over all the elements of $\pi^{-1}(\omega)$ does not depend on the choice of the regular value $\omega \in \mathcal{R}$. The value of this sum is by definition the topological degree of the map $\pi : E \to \Omega$ for the orientations of E and Ω defined by these diffeomorphisms with $\mathbb{R}^{\ell m}$. See for example [48].

Like the modulo 2 degree, the topological degree depends only on the proper homotopy class of the natural projection $\pi : E \to \Omega$ and not on the map π itself.

7.6.2 Invariance of the Proper Homotopy Class of the Natural Projection

In order to compute the degrees of the natural projection $\pi : E \to \Omega$, we are going to use their invariance by proper homotopy. But changing the demand functions (f_i) also changes the equilibrium manifold. This leads us to use the diffeomorphism $\Phi \mid E : E \to S \times \mathbb{R}^m \times \mathbb{R}^{(\ell-1)(m-1)}$ of Proposition 5.8 and to define $\rho_{(f_i)} = \pi \circ (\Phi \mid E)^{-1} : S \times \mathbb{R}^m \times \mathbb{R}^{(\ell-1)(m-1)} \to \Omega$. Obviously, the maps $\pi : E \to \Omega$ and $\rho_{(f_i)}$ have the same degrees, whether modulo 2 or topological.

Lemma 7.10. *Let (f_i) and (f_i') be two m-tuples of demand functions in $\mathcal{E}_r$. Then, the maps $\rho_{(f_i)}$ and $\rho_{(f_i')}$ are properly homotopic.*

Proof. To say that the two maps $\rho_{(f_i)}$ and $\rho_{(f_i')}$ are properly homotopic means that there exists a continuous proper map $R : S \times \mathbb{R}^m \times \mathbb{R}^{(\ell-1)(m-1)} \times [0, 1] \to \Omega$ such that $R(.,0) = \rho_{(f_i)}$ and $R(.,1) = \rho_{(f_i')}$.

Define $F_i(p, w_i, t) = (1 - t)f_i(p, w_i) + tf_i'(p, w_i)$ for $i = 1, \ldots, m$ and let $R(.,t) = \rho_{(F_i(.,t))}$.

Clearly, the map R is continuous and we have $R(.,0) = \rho_{(f_i)}$ and $R(.,1) = \rho_{(f_i')}$. Let us show that

$$R : S \times \mathbb{R}^m \times \mathbb{R}^{(\ell-1)(m-1)} \times [0, 1] \to \Omega$$

is proper.

In this part of the proof, we use the price simplex normalization. Let K be some compact subset of Ω. It follows from the continuity of R that the preimage $R^{-1}(K)$ is closed. To prove compactness, it suffices that we show that any sequence $(p^q, w_1^q, \ldots, w_m^q, z^q, t^q)$ in $R^{-1}(K)$ has a convergent subsequence. The proof parallels very much the one of Proposition 7.1. By considering suitable subsequences as in the proof of Proposition 7.1, there is no loss in generality in assuming that the sequence $(p^q, w_1^q, \ldots, w_m^q, z^q, t^q)$ converges to $(p^0, w_1^0, \ldots, w_m^0, z^0, t^0)$ where p^0 belongs to the closed price simplex $\overline{S_\Sigma}$. To prove compactness, we only need to show that the limit p^0 does not belong to the boundary $\overline{S_\Sigma} \setminus S_\Sigma$.

It follows from the boundedness from below (B) applied to both f_i and f_i' that there exist B_i and B_i' in $\mathbb{R}^\ell$ such that $B_i \leq f_i(p^q, w_i^q)$ and $B_i' \leq f_i'(p^q, w_i^q)$. Let $B_i'' = \inf(B_i, B_i')$. It follows that $B_i'' \leq (1-t)f_i(p^q, w_i^q) + tf_i'(p^q, w_i^q)$ for all i and q.

As in the proof of Proposition 7.1, there exists $A \in \mathbb{R}^\ell$ such that the inequality

$$B_i'' \leq F_i(p^q, w_i^q, t^q) \leq A - \sum_{j \neq i} B_j'' \tag{2}$$

is satisfied for all q.

Let i_0 and i_1 be such that f_{i_0} and f_{i_1}' satisfy desirability (A). (Note that we do not impose $i_0 \neq i_1$.) If $t^0 = 0$, pick $i = i_0$ in inequality (2) to get a contradiction with (A) satisfied by f_{i_0}. Similarly, if $t^0 \neq 0$, pick $i = i_1$ to get a contradiction with (A) satisfied by f_{i_1}' while $f_{i_0}(p^q, w_i^q)$ is bounded from below. $\qquad\square$

Proposition 7.11. *The modulo 2 (resp. topological) degree of the natural projection $\pi : E \to \Omega$ does not depend on the m-tuple $(f_i) \in \mathcal{E}_r$.*

Proof. This follows readily from Lemma 7.10 $\qquad\square$

7.6.3 The Modulo 2 Degree of the Natural Projection

Proposition 7.12. *Assume $(f_i) \in \mathcal{E}_r$. The modulo 2 degree of the natural projection $\pi : E \to \Omega$ is defined and equal to 1.*

Proof. It follows from Proposition 7.11 that this degree is the same for an *m*-tuple of demand functions $(f_i) \in \mathcal{E}_c$. It suffices then to apply Proposition 8.4 that is proved in the next chapter. $\qquad\square$

Note that despite the fact we use a result that is proved in the next chapter, there will be no circular reasoning.

7.6.4 An Existence Theorem

The following proposition is the equivalent for the setup of the exchange model of the celebrated existence theorems of Arrow, Debreu, and McKenzie. Here this result becomes a direct byproduct of the equilibrium manifold and the natural projection approach and requires nothing more than the set of demand functions (f_i) belonging to $\mathcal{E}_r$.

Proposition 7.13. (Existence theorem) *The natural projection $\pi : E \to \Omega$ is surjective for $(f_i) \in \mathcal{E}_r$.*

Proof. Assume that $\pi : E \to \Omega$ is not surjective. There exists some $\omega \in \Omega$ that does not belong to $\pi(E)$ and, therefore, that cannot be the image of some critical equilibrium $(p, \omega) \in \mathfrak{S}$ of π. This element ω is therefore a "regular value" of the map π even if it is not a "value" of that map. The number of elements of the preimage $\pi^{-1}(\omega)$ is zero since this set is empty. This contradicts a modulo 2 degree being equal to one. □

Surjectivity of the natural projection means that we have $\pi(E) = \Omega$. In other words, for every $\omega \in \Omega$, there exists a price vector $p \in S$ such that (p, ω) is an equilibrium and, therefore, $p \in S$ an equilibrium price vector associated with the economy ω. Surjectivity of $\pi : E \to \Omega$ is therefore equivalent to the existence of equilibrium for all economies $\omega \in \Omega$.

7.6.5 The Topological Degree of the Natural Projection

Proposition 7.14. *Assume $(f_i) \in \mathcal{E}_r$. The topological degree of the natural projection $\pi : E \to \Omega$ is defined and equal to $+1$ for suitable orientations of E and Ω.*

Proof. It suffices to reproduce the proof of Proposition 7.12. □

7.7 CONCLUSION

Here is a short summary of the main properties of the exchange model under the rather weak assumptions that the natural projection $\pi : E \to \Omega$ is smooth and proper, a sufficient condition for this being that m-tuple (f_i) of demand functions belongs to $\mathcal{E}_r$.

 i) The set of no-trade equilibria T is a smooth submanifold of the equilibrium manifold E.
 ii) The set of regular economies (a.k.a., the regular values of the natural projection) $\omega \in \mathcal{R}$ is open with full measure in $\Omega = (\mathbb{R}^\ell)^m$.
 iii) The equilibria associated with a regular economy $\omega \in \mathcal{R}$ are locally unique.
 iv) The set of equilibria $\pi^{-1}(\omega)$ of the regular economy $\omega \in \mathcal{R}$ is finite.
 v) For $\omega \in \mathcal{R}$, there exists an open set V containing ω such that the preimage $\pi^{-1}(V)$ is the union of a disjoint family of open sets $U_1, \dots, U_n$ such that the restriction of π to each of these subsets is a diffeomorphism with V.

vi) The modulo 2 degree of the natural projection $\pi : E \to \Omega$ is equal to one.

vii) The natural projection $\pi : E \to \Omega$ is onto, i.e., equilibrium exists for all ω.

The properties in this list are probably the most important ones. Nevertheless, there are other properties, possibly less interesting ones, of the exchange model that also require only the smoothness and properness of the natural projection. This is the case of the upper bound in A/n on the size of economies with more than n equilibria when n tends to ∞ [14].

7.8 NOTES AND COMMENTS

The ideas developed in this chapter appeared for the first time in 1970 in a paper by Debreu that marked the introduction of the methods of differential topology for the study of the general equilibrium model [24]. In that paper, Debreu used the aggregate excess demand map. The property of local uniqueness of equilibrium at regular economies was then hailed as the best result possible towards a solution to the long-standing problem of characterizing economies with a unique equilibrium [6].

The first rigorous proof of the existence of an equilibrium for the exchange model is given by Wald in 1936 under the additional assumption of gross substitutability at all prices [66]. The first existence proofs that are general enough not to assume gross substitutability are given in 1954 by Arrow and Debreu [5] and McKenzie [47].

CHAPTER 8

The Fine Picture

8.1 INTRODUCTION

In the previous chapter, we have seen that, for m-tuples of demand functions $(f_i) \in \mathcal{E}_r$, the natural projection $\pi : E \to \Omega$ is a smooth proper map and the properties that we have developed so far are essentially properties of any smooth proper map.

In this chapter, the m-tuple (f_i) of demand functions defining the exchange model is restricted to belong to $\mathcal{E}_c$. In addition to the assumptions made in the previous chapters (recall that $\mathcal{E}_c$ is a subset of $\mathcal{E}_r$), the demand function f_i satisfies the weak axiom of revealed preferences (WARP) for every consumer, and the slightly stronger negative definiteness of the Slutsky matrix (ND) for the consumer whose demand function satisfies desirability (A). These stronger assumptions are aimed at giving more economic flesh to the exchange model. As a consequence, the natural projection inherits much stronger properties that give a specificity of its own to the exchange model.

The most important properties of the exchange model with $(f_i) \in \mathcal{E}_c$ are the regularity of the no-trade equilibria, the openness and full measure (a.k.a., the genericity) of the set of regular equilibria as a subset of the equilibrium manifold, the inclusion of the set of equilibrium allocations in one and only one connected component of the set of regular economies, the uniqueness of equilibrium for all economies belonging to that component, and the interpretation of that property in terms of trade intensity.

8.2 AGGREGATE DEMAND AT A NO-TRADE EQUILIBRIUM

Using the coordinate system (B) for the equilibrium manifold, recall that the matrix $S_{\ell\ell}(b)$ has been defined in section 6.5.2 for $b = (p, w_1, \ldots, w_m)$ as the sum of the individual Slutsky matrices $S_{\ell\ell}f_i(p, w_i)$:

$$S_{\ell\ell}(b) = \sum_{i=1}^{m} S_{\ell\ell}f_i(p, w_i).$$

Proposition 8.1. *For $(f_i) \in \mathcal{E}_c$, we have $\det S_{\ell\ell}(b) \neq 0$.*

Proof. Matrix $S_{\ell\ell}(b)$ is equal to the sum of the individual Slutsky matrices. Therefore, it defines a quadratic form that is the sum of the quadratic forms defined by the individual Slutsky matrices. It follows from $(f_i) \in \mathcal{E}_c$ that all these quadratic forms are negative semidefinite and one of them is negative definite. Their sum is a negative definite quadratic form. We conclude by observing that the determinant of a definite quadratic form is necessarily different from zero. □

8.3 REGULARITY OF THE NO-TRADE EQUILIBRIA

Proposition 8.2. *Assume $(f_i) \in \mathcal{E}_c$. Then, every no-trade equilibrium $(p, \omega) \in T$ is regular.*

Proof. Using coordinate system (B), we identify the no-trade equilibrium (p, ω) with its coordinates $(b, 0)$ where $b = (p, p \cdot \omega_1, \ldots, p \cdot \omega_m)$.
From Corollary 6.7, we have

$$J_{\ell\ell}(b, 0) = S_{\ell\ell}(b)$$

where $J_{\ell\ell}(b, 0)$ is the numeraire normalized Jacobian matrix of aggregate excess demand at the no-trade equilibrium $(p, \omega) = (b, 0)$.
It then suffices to combine Proposition 6.4 and Proposition 8.1. □

Proposition 8.2 can be restated as the inclusion $T \subset \mathfrak{R}$.

Proposition 8.3. *Assume $(f_i) \in \mathcal{E}_c$. The set of no-trade equilibria is contained in one connected component of the set of regular equilibria $\mathfrak{R}$.*

Proof. This follows from the pathconnectedness of the set of no-trade equilibria T. □

8.4 THE SET OF EQUILIBRIUM ALLOCATIONS

The set of equilibrium allocation $\pi(T)$ consists of the allocations that result from the operation of the market mechanism. Not every allocation $x = (x_1, \ldots, x_m) \in \Omega$ can be the equilibrium allocation of some economy $\omega = (\omega_1, \ldots, \omega_m) \in \Omega$. It is therefore important to get a better understanding of this set. Our first result is the following proposition that is quite elementary within the setup of budget constrained utility maximizing demand functions.

Proposition 8.4. *Assume $(f_i) \in \mathcal{E}_c$. The set of equilibrium allocations $\pi(T)$ is diffeomorphic to $B = S \times \mathbb{R}^m$.*

Proof. By construction, the map $\pi : T \to \pi(T)$ is a surjection. Let us show that it is a bijection. Otherwise, there would be two price vectors p and p' such (p, ω) and (p', ω) would be no-trade equilibria. For the consumer i_0 whose demand function belongs to $\mathcal{F}_{B \wedge A \wedge ND}$, the equality

$$f_{i_0}(p, p \cdot \omega_{i_0}) = f_{i_0}(p', p' \cdot \omega_{i_0}) = \omega_{i_0}$$

contradicts the property that the demand function f_{i_0} is a diffeomorphism between $S \times \mathbb{R}$ and $\mathbb{R}^\ell$. □

Corollary 8.5. *The set of equilibrium allocations $\pi(T)$ is pathconnected.*

THE SET OF EQUILIBRIUM ALLOCATIONS AND THE TWO THEOREMS
OF WELFARE ECONOMICS

Since we do not have utility functions but just preferences, the two theorems of welfare economics have no equivalent in our more general setup. It is interesting, however, to state them within the setup of the natural projection. Therefore, assume for a moment that demand functions result from the budget constrained maximization of standard utility functions. The allocation $x = (x_i)$ is a Pareto optimum if there is there is no $x' = (x_i')$ for which $u_i(x_i) \leq u_i(x_i')$, with a strict inequality for at least one i, and $\sum_i x_i = \sum_i x_i'$. Let P denote the subset of Ω consisting of Pareto optima. It is an easy exercise to show that, for standard utility functions at least, the allocation $x = (x_i)$ is a Pareto optimum if and only if there exists a price vector $p \in S$ that supports that allocation. This is equivalent to having $x_i = f_i(p, p \cdot x_i)$ for $i = 1, \ldots, m$. The two theorems of welfare economics are therefore equivalent to the equality $\pi(T) = P$.

8.4.1 Uniqueness of Equilibrium at Equilibrium Allocations

Proposition 8.4 about the diffeomorphism between the set of no-trade equilibria and the set of equilibrium allocations is in fact a special case of a much stronger property that we now address.

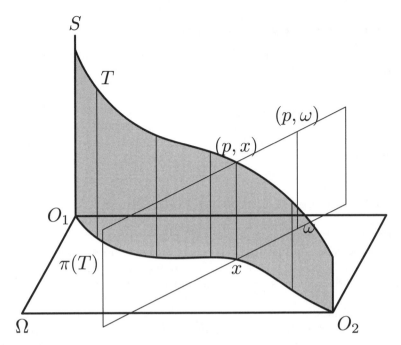

Figure 8.1 The set of no-trade equilibria and the set of equilibrium allocations $\pi(T)$

Proposition 8.6. *Assume $(f_i) \in \mathcal{E}_c$. Then, equilibrium is unique for any $\omega \in \pi(T)$.*

Proof. Let $\omega \in \pi(T)$. There exists some price vector $p \in S$ such that $(p, \omega) \in T$ and we also have $\omega_i = f_i(p, p \cdot \omega_i)$ for $i = 1, \ldots, m$.

The proof proceeds by contradiction. Assume that there exists another equilibrium $(p', \omega) \in E$ with $p' \neq p \in S$. For consumer i_0 that satisfies (A) and (ND), the demand function $f_{i_0} : S \times \mathbb{R} \to \mathbb{R}^\ell$ is a bijection by Proposition 3.29, which implies $f_{i_0}(p, p \cdot \omega_{i_0}) \neq f_{i_0}(p', p' \cdot \omega_{i_0})$.

Let $x_i' = f_i(p', p' \cdot \omega_i)$ for $i = 1, \ldots, m$. By Walras law (W), we have $p' \cdot (\omega_i - x_i') = 0$. The application of (WARP) yields the inequality $p \cdot (x_i' - \omega_i) \geq 0$ for every i, an inequality that is strict for consumer i_0 since $f_{i_0}(p, p \cdot \omega_{i_0}) \neq f_{i_0}(p', p' \cdot \omega_{i_0})$.

It suffices to add up all these inequalities to get a contradiction with the equilibrium condition $\sum_i x_i' = \sum_i \omega_i$. $\qquad\square$

Proposition 8.6 can be reformulated as the equality

$$\pi^{-1}(\pi(T)) = T.$$

8.4.2 *Regularity of Equilibrium Allocations*

Proposition 8.7. *Assume* $(f_i) \in \mathcal{E}_c$. *Then, every equilibrium allocation is regular:* $\pi(T) \subset \mathcal{R}$.

Proof. Let $x \in \pi(T)$ be an equilibrium allocation. The set $\pi^{-1}(x)$ contains as its unique element the no-trade equilibrium $(p, x) \in T$, with $T \subset E$. Therefore the equilibrium (p, x) is regular. This implies that the economy x is regular. $\qquad\square$

8.5 ECONOMIES WITH A UNIQUE EQUILIBRIUM

The results of the previous sections enable us to get a much better picture of the natural projection. Essentially, the equilibrium manifold E has just one layer over the pathconnected component of the set of regular economies that contains the set of equilibrium allocations $\pi(T)$.

Proposition 8.8. *Assume* $(f_i) \in \mathcal{E}_c$. *The set of equilibrium allocations* $\pi(T)$ *is contained in a single pathconnected component of the set of regular economies* $\mathcal{R}$. *Equilibrium is unique for all endowment vectors* ω *in that component.*

Proof. The pathconnectedness of $\pi(T)$, which is a subset of $\mathcal{R}$, implies that $\pi(T)$ is contained in just one pathconnected component of $\mathcal{R}$. The uniqueness of equilibrium for $\omega \in \pi(T)$ implies the uniqueness of equilibrium for all economies ω in that component. $\qquad\square$

The condition for ω to belong to that component where equilibrium is unique is simply that the trade vector $(f_i(p, p \cdot \omega_i) - \omega_i)_{i=1,\ldots,m}$ (where $p \in S$ is some equilibrium price vector associated with ω) is sufficiently small.

The economic implication is therefore that for "relatively small" trade vectors, equilibrium is unique. In that case, the equilibrium price vector and the equilibrium allocation depend smoothly and, therefore, continuously on the fundamentals of the economy defined by the endowment vector ω.

An interesting problem is whether the number of equilibria is necessarily larger than one for economies ω in the other pathconnected components of the set $\mathcal{R}$ of regular economies. This property is true for the case of two consumers. It is an open problem in the case of more than two consumers.

8.6 DEGREE OF THE NATURAL PROJECTION

For an equilibrium allocation, its regularity combined with the uniqueness of equilibrium gives us a straightforward way of computing the degree of the natural projection.

Proposition 8.9. *For* $(f_i) \in \mathcal{E}_c$, *the modulo 2 and the topological degrees are equal to one (for suitable orientations of the equilibrium manifold for the topological degree).*

Proof. Pick $\omega \in P = \pi(T)$. Then, ω is regular. It then suffices to observe that the preimage $\pi^{-1}(\omega)$ contains only one element. $\qquad\square$

8.7 THE SET OF REGULAR EQUILIBRIA

Proposition 8.10. *Assume* $(f_i) \in \mathcal{E}_c$. *The set of regular equilibria* $\mathfrak{R}$ *is an open subset of the equilibrium manifold E with full Lebesgue measure.*

Proof. Let $\mathfrak{S}$ denote the set of critical equilibria, the complement in E of the set of regular equilibria $\mathfrak{R}$. The proposition is then equivalent to showing that the set $\mathfrak{S}$ is closed with measure zero.

Using coordinate system (B), the equilibrium $(p, \omega) \in E$ is identified to its coordinates (b, Y). It follows from Proposition 6.6 that we have

$$J_{\ell\ell}(b, Y) = S_{\ell\ell}(b) + K(b)\, Y.$$

In coordinate system (B), the coefficients of matrix $J_{\ell\ell}(b, Y)$ are polynomials of degree one with respect to the coefficients of Y.

The equilibrium (b, Y) is critical if and only if $\det J_{\ell\ell}(b, Y) = 0$. Closedness of the set $\mathfrak{S}$ results from the continuity of the map $(b, Y) \to J_{\ell\ell}(b, Y)$. To prove the measure zero property, the key argument is to observe that the restriction of the map $(b, Y) \to \det J_{\ell\ell}(b, Y) = \det(S_{\ell\ell}(b) + K(b)\, Y)$ to the fiber $F(b)$ defines a function denoted by $P(Y)$, a function that is the determinant of a matrix whose coefficients are themselves polynomials of degree one in the coefficients of Y. There is no need here to do the explicit computations, the only thing that really matters is that $P(Y)$ is polynomial in the coefficients of Y.

The set of zeros of the polynomial function $Y \to P(Y)$ is by definition a (semi) algebraic subset of the fiber $F(b)$. As an algebraic subset, this set can be stratified into a collection of smooth manifolds (see

Appendix F.1 and the references that follow). In practice, this implies that the set $F(b) \cap \mathfrak{S} = P^{-1}(0)$, the preimage of $0 \in \mathbb{R}$ by the polynomial function $Y \to P(Y)$ is the union of a finite number of smooth manifolds. Let us show that none of these manifolds can have full dimension $(\ell - 1)(m - 1)$, (i.e., the dimension of the fiber $F(b)$).

Assume the contrary, i.e., that the fiber $F(b)$ contains a smooth manifold of full dimension. It follows from the definition of the dimension of a smooth manifold that the dimension $(\ell - 1)(m - 1)$ manifold contains a non empty open subset U of the fiber $F(b)$.

The polynomial function $Y \to P(Y)$ is therefore equal to zero on U. But, a polynomial that is equal to zero on some non-empty open set (of a Euclidean space) is identically equal to zero. (Use a simple induction argument on the degree of the polynomial; alternatively, make a Taylor expansion of the polynomial at some point of the open set.) This implies that the polynomial $P(Y)$ takes the value 0 all over the fiber $F(b)$. This contradicts the property that $P(0) = \det S_{\ell\ell}(b) \neq 0$ (Proposition 8.1).

This implies that the algebraic set $\mathfrak{S} \cap F(b)$ is a finite union of smooth manifolds of dimension strictly less than $(\ell - 1)(m - 1)$. Smooth submanifolds of dimension strictly less than the dimension of the ambient space have measure zero, which implies that the set $\mathfrak{S} \cap F(b)$ also has dimension zero for every $b \in S \times \mathbb{R}^m$.

It then suffices to observe that

$$\mathfrak{S} = \bigcup_{b \in S \times \mathbb{R}^m} (\mathfrak{S} \cap F(b)),$$

and to apply either Fubini's theorem or the more elementary version of Fubini's theorem for sets of measure zero. □

EXERCISES

8.1. Assume $\ell = 2$ and $(f_i) \in \mathcal{E}_c$. Show that the aggregate demand curve $p_1 \in \mathbb{R}_{++} \to \sum_i (f_i(p, p \cdot \omega_i) - \omega_i)$ has two infinite branches. Use the intermediate value theorem to show that there exists an equilibrium price vector associated with any endowment vector $\omega = (\omega_1, \omega_2, \ldots, \omega_m) \in \Omega$.

8.2. Let $E = \{(x, p, q) \in \mathbb{R}^3 \mid x^2 + px + q = 0\}$ be the equilibrium manifold associated with the polynomial equation $x^2 + px + q = 0$. Write the equation system defining the set of critical equilibria $\mathfrak{S} \subset E$. Write the equation system defining the set of singular values S of the parameter $(p, q) \in \mathbb{R}^2$. Draw a picture of the curve with singularities S in $\mathbb{R}^2$ and determine the number of solutions for the connected components of $\mathbb{R}^2 \setminus S$. Show that finding the solutions to the equation $x^2 + px + q = 0$ is equivalent to drawing from the point (p, q) the tangent lines to the curve S.

8.3. Repeat exercise 8.2 but with the polynomial equation $x^3 + px + q = 0$.

8.4. Let $E = \{(x, p, q, r) \in \mathbb{R}^4 \mid x^4 + px^2 + qx + r = 0\}$ be the equilibrium manifold associated with the polynomial equation $x^4 + px^2 + qx + r = 0$. Write the equation system defining the set of critical equilibria $\mathfrak{S} \subset E$. Write the equation system defining the set of singular values S of the parameter $(p, q, r) \in \mathbb{R}^3$. Draw a picture of the "surface" (with singularities) S in $\mathbb{R}^3$ and determine the number of equilibria for the connected components of $\mathbb{R}^3 \setminus S$.

8.8 CONCLUSION

Here is a summary of the main properties of the exchange model viewed from the perspective of the equilibrium manifold and natural projection under the stronger assumptions that the m-tuple (f_i) of demand functions belongs to $\mathcal{E}_c$:

  i) The set of regular economies $\mathcal{R}$ is open with full measure in Ω;
  ii) The set of no-trade equilibria T is contained in the set of regular equilibria $\mathfrak{R}$;
  iii) The restriction of the natural projection $\pi : E \to \Omega$ to the set of no-trade equilibria T, i.e., the map $\pi \mid T : T \to \pi(T)$, is a diffeomorphism;
  iv) The preimage of the set of equilibrium allocations by the natural projection is the set of no-trade equilibria: $\pi^{-1}(\pi(T)) = T$.

8.9 NOTES AND COMMENTS

In the early phases of the theory of smooth and regular economies, the concept of regular economy has overshadowed the one of regular equilibrium because the proof of the full measure of the set of regular economies follows from Sard's theorem and requires the m-tuple of demand functions (f_i) just to belong to $\mathcal{E}_r$. But the possibility of using the implicit function theorem to linearize the equilibrium correspondence, for example, is a property of regular equilibria. The proof that the set of regular economies $\mathfrak{R}$ is open with full measure in the equilibrium manifold is due to Balasko [17].

Walras misses the economic importance of the uniqueness vs. multiplicity issue because he wrongly believes that equilibrium is unique whenever the number of goods is greater than or equal to three [67]. For Walras, the multiplicity of equilibrium solutions he acknowledges in the case of two goods is at best a mathematical curiosity. Auspitz and Lieben are the first to fully understand the economic importance of the multiplicity issue. In their 1889 treatise [8], they circumvent this problem by assuming that equilibrium is unique, which is logically inconsistent. But it follows from their correspondence with Walras [37] and an article published in 1909 [9] that they make this assumption only for simplicity's sake, not because they think that equilibrium is always unique. At the time, there existed no theory of singularities of smooth maps in general and no model of catastrophe theory in particular. Auspitz and Lieben therefore address bare-handed the difficult multiplicity problem and, unsurprisingly, are rewarded with little success. The first rigorous study of an economy with a unique equilibrium is due to Wald who assumes gross substitutability [66].

The proof of the regularity of the no-trade equilibria, of the regularity of all equilibrium allocations, and of the uniqueness of equilibrium for economies in the pathconnected component of the set of regular economies containing the set of equilibrium allocations is due to Balasko [12].

CHAPTER 9

Production with Decreasing Returns

9.1 Introduction

This chapter is devoted to the theory of the firm. Production consists in the transformation of goods known as inputs into other goods, the outputs. The firm is the center of productive activity. Its activity is represented by a vector in the commodity space. This chapter starts with the definition of the firm's production set. This set consists of the activities that are technologically feasible for the firm. A few very general properties are satisfied by all or almost all production sets. Despite their generality, these properties simplify the analysis of production. If the firm's production set describes all activities that are feasible, not all of them are efficient. An activity is efficient when it cannot be improved upon in the sense that more outputs could be produced with less inputs. The set of efficient activities is a subset of the production set, in fact, a subset of the boundary of the production set. This set is also known as the efficient boundary of the production set. The production functions used in the classical theory of the firm are a way of expressing the equation of that efficient boundary.

In the second part of this chapter, we study the maximization of the firm's profit subject to the feasibility constraint. The properties of the solution of this maximization problem depend on the structure of the production set. For efficient boundaries of strictly convex sets, the problem of profit maximization has a unique solution. This solution is a function of the price vector and defines the firm's net supply function. In the third part of this chapter, we take the firm's net supply function as our primitive concept. As we did with consumers' demand functions, we then introduce a set of properties that are to be satisfied by these net supply functions.

9.2 Production Sets: Definitions

We consider a typical firm represented by the subscript j. In the general equilibrium model with production considered in the next chapter, there will be a finite number n of firms.

9.2.1 The Activity Vector

Inputs and outputs are differentiated by a sign convention: inputs are negative, outputs are positive. Let $y_j = (y_j^1, \ldots, y_j^\ell) \in \mathbb{R}^\ell$ be some activity vector of firm j. An interesting aspect of this sign convention is that the value $p \cdot y_j$ of the commodity bundle y_j for the price vector $p \in S$ represents the profit made by firm j for activity $y_j \in \mathbb{R}^\ell$.

DECOMPOSITION OF THE ACTIVITY VECTOR INTO ITS INPUT
AND OUTPUT COMPONENTS

Let $a \in \mathbb{R}$ be some real number. Let $a^+ = \sup(a, 0)$ and $a^- = -\inf(a, 0)$. Then, a^+ and a^- are ≥ 0 and $a = a^+ - a^-$. Now let $y_j = (y_j^1, \ldots, y_j^\ell)$ be some vector in $\mathbb{R}^\ell$. We define $y_j^+ = (y_j^{1+}, \ldots, y_j^{\ell+})$ and $y_j^- = (y_j^{1-}, \ldots, y_j^{\ell-})$. We have $y_j = y_j^+ - y_j^-$.

Proposition 9.1. *The non-zero coordinates of the vectors y_j^+ and y_j^- represent the outputs and the inputs of the activity vector $y_j \in \mathbb{R}^\ell$.*

Proof. This follows readily from the definition of y_j^+ and y_j^-. □

9.2.2 The Production Set

The activity vector $y_j \in \mathbb{R}^\ell$ is *technologically feasible* or more simply, feasible, if firm j can produce the quantities of outputs represented by the strictly positive components of y_j^+ with the quantities of inputs themselves represented by the strictly positive components of y_j^-.

Definition 9.2. *The production set Y_j of firm j consists of the activity vectors $y_j \in \mathbb{R}^\ell$ that are technologically feasible for firm j.*

Not all activity vectors are feasible for firm j. For example, it is impossible to produce goods out of nothing. In other words, no activity vector $y_j \in \mathbb{R}_{++}^\ell$ (i.e., with all coordinates strictly positive) is feasible.

One goal of an economic theory of production is to come up with properties of the production sets that are general enough to be satisfied by many production technologies and sufficiently rich to yield a meaningful theory of production and exchange. First, we see that the definition of a feasible activity vector is certainly too general to be really interesting. For example, the activity vector $y_j \in -\mathbb{R}_{++}^\ell$ (all its coordinates are strictly negative) is obviously feasible since it consists only of inputs and there is no output, but this activity vector has little economic interest. This leads us to focus on a subset of the production set, the efficient boundary.

9.2.3 The Efficient Boundary

Economically the most interesting activity vectors are those such that it is not possible to produce more outputs with the same quantity of inputs or to produce the same quantity of outputs with fewer inputs. Such activity vectors are known as the production efficient activity vectors:

Definition 9.3. *The activity* $y_j \in Y_j$ *is efficient if* $(y_j + \mathbb{R}^\ell_{++}) \cap Y_j = \{y_j\}$.

The set of efficient activities of firm j is the *efficient boundary* of the production set Y_j and is denoted by $\partial Y_j^{\text{eff}}$.

9.3 PRODUCTION SETS: MAIN PROPERTIES

The properties of the technologies available to firm j determine the characteristics of the firm's production set Y_j as a subset of the commodity space $\mathbb{R}^\ell$. In the same way that it has been possible to identify very general properties satisfied by consumers' demand functions, it is also possible to formulate very general properties satisfied by a sufficiently large number of technologies for an economic theory of the firm to make sense. Following the classical approach to the theory of the firm, we first formulate these properties in terms of firm j's production set Y_j.

9.3.1 Returns to Scale

One of the first properties of a production technology to have been investigated in the economic literature is the property of returns to scale. Let $y_j \in Y_j$ be a feasible activity vector. The technology represented by the production set Y_j features:

Constant returns to scale: $\lambda y_j \in Y_j$ for $\lambda \geq 0$;
Decreasing returns to scale: $\lambda y_j \in Y_j$ for $\lambda \leq 1$;
Increasing returns to scale: $\lambda y_j \in Y_j$ for $\lambda \geq 1$.

A widely held view is that, if all production factors and outputs are accounted for, then most production activities feature constant returns to scale. Increasing returns to scale occur when some inputs are indivisible like the production chains in the automobile industry. Decreasing returns to scale with respect to variable production factors are often observed when the production process requires additional production factors that are fixed and, as a consequence, not accounted for. This property is commonly observed in short-run models where capital is fixed. The property of decreasing (resp. constant, increasing) returns is often expressed in the literature as the property of increasing (resp. constant, decreasing) marginal costs.

Constant returns to scale is equivalent to the property that the production set Y_j is a cone with its vertex at the origin $0 \in \mathbb{R}^\ell$. In a moment we will see another assumption that also implies that the zero activity vector $0 \in \mathbb{R}^\ell$ is feasible even when the production set Y_j is not a cone.

9.3.2 Convexity of Production Sets and Decreasing Returns

The production set Y_j cannot be convex under increasing returns because there can exist some activities $y \in \mathbb{R}^\ell$ that do not belong to the production set Y_j while the activity $2y$ belongs to Y_j. This contradicts convexity when the origin $0 \in \mathbb{R}^\ell$ also belongs to the production set.

The property that the activity $y_1 + y_2$ is feasible if activities y_1 and y_2 are feasible is satisfied by many production processes. Under decreasing or constant returns, this also implies that the half-sum $y_1 + y_2/2$ is also feasible, i.e., belongs to the production set Y_j. In other words, the production set Y_j is then convex. Therefore, the properties of convexity and strict convexity not only generalize the idea of constant and decreasing returns, they are often taken as equivalent to constant and decreasing returns. The overwhelming number of convex production sets justifies the development of a general theory for these production sets.

As for preferences in consumer theory, convexity comes with various levels of strength. Two extreme forms are represented by the convex polyhedra defined as the intersection of a finite number of halfspaces and the strictly convex sets that are bounded by smooth hypersurfaces with everywhere non-zero Gaussian curvature, sets that we are going to call smooth strictly convex sets.

At this point it is worth mentioning the following approximation property for convex sets. The set of convex subsets of $\mathbb{R}^\ell$ can be equipped with a distance. This implies that it is possible to approximate a convex set by another one for this distance and there is indeed a well-developed theory of approximation convex sets. In particular, every smooth convex set can be "squeezed" in between two arbitrarily close convex polyhedra. Similarly, a convex polyhedron can be "squeezed" in between two arbitrarily close smooth convex sets. See, for example, [30]. Properties established for one category of convex sets can generally be extended to the other category of convex sets by suitable approximations. Therefore, we are going to follow the same approach here as in consumer theory and focus on the smooth version of convex production.

CONVEXITY

Definition 9.4. *The production technology is convex if the production set Y_j is convex.*

The convexity of the production set Y_j expresses the property that the activity vector $(y_j + y_j')/2$ is feasible if the two activity vectors y_j and y_j' are feasible. The property of decreasing returns to scale defined in section 9.3.1 corresponds to the special case where $y_j' = 0$. Increasing returns to scale are incompatible with the convexity of the production set Y_j. This explains that, by extension, the convexity of the production set Y_j is often identified in the literature with the property of decreasing returns even if, strictly speaking, it is an extension of that property.

STRICT CONVEXITY OF THE EFFICIENT PRODUCTION BOUNDARY

The convexity assumption is often strengthened into strict convexity under the following form:

Definition 9.5. *The production technology is strictly convex if the activity* $(y_j + y_j')/2$ *belongs to the interior* $\overset{\circ}{Y}_j$ *of the production set* Y_j *whenever* y_j *and* y_j' *are efficient activities, i.e.,* y_j *and* y_j' *in* $\partial Y_j^{\text{eff}}$.

This property is slightly weaker than the strict convexity of the production set Y_j because the production set Y_j is not strictly convex as we will see in a moment. However, the lack of strict convexity occurs for activities that have no economic interest. Only efficient activities play a role in the theory of the firm. It is therefore the efficient boundary $\partial Y_j^{\text{eff}}$ that is the boundary of some strictly convex subset of the production set.

Definition 9.5 is in practice almost equivalent, if not strictly equivalent, to having a strictly convex production set Y_j.

The strict convexity of the production technology represented by the production set Y_j excludes in particular constant returns to scale.

ON NON-CONVEX PRODUCTION SETS

We have seen that a production set may fail to be convex because of indivisibilities or, more generally, of increasing returns to scale. But there are more than these two ways for a production set to fail the mathematical definition of convexity. The study of non-convex production is therefore not an easy task. Its integration within the theory of general equilibrium is far from having reached the level of maturity of convex production. The theory of non-convex production is therefore beyond the scope of this book. Nevertheless, the tools developed here for dealing with convex productions can be adapted to handle many aspects of non-convex production.

9.3.3 Zero Activity

Inactivity, or zero activity, is represented by the vector $0 = (0, 0, \ldots, 0) \in \mathbb{R}^\ell$.

Definition 9.6. *Inactivity is feasible and efficient if the following property is satisfied:*

$$0 \in Y_j \quad and \quad Y_j \cap \mathbb{R}^\ell_{++} = \{0\}.$$

9.3.4 Free Disposals

Let y_j and y'_j be two activity vectors satisfying the inequality $y'_j \leq y_j$. The economic interpretation of this inequality is straightforward. Activity y'_j involves the production of less outputs y'^+_j with more inputs y'^-_j than activity y_j. In general, activity y'_j is technologically feasible because it is less technologically demanding than activity y_j. This property is known as free disposals because it assumes that it is possible to get rid, i.e., to dispose of any output.

Definition 9.7. *The production technology satisfies the property of free disposals if the inclusion $y_j - \mathbb{R}^\ell_+ \subset Y_j$ is satisfied for every $y_j \in Y_j$.*

The property of free disposal plays a role in the theory of production similar to the monotonicity of preferences in consumer theory.

THE NON STRICT-CONVEXITY OF THE PRODUCTION SET

The production set Y_j of a strictly convex technology satisfying the zero activity and free disposals assumptions is not strictly convex as seen from the following example. Let y_j and y'_j be two activity vectors with one common coordinate at least being equal to zero, all the non-zero coordinates being strictly negative. These two activity vectors are feasible given the assumptions of free disposals and the possibility of inactivity. In addition, these activity vectors belong to the boundary ∂Y_j of the production set Y_j (though they do not belong to the efficient boundary $\partial Y_j^{\text{eff}}$). The half-sum $(y_j + y'_j)/2$ is also feasible, belongs to the boundary ∂Y_j and, therefore, is not in the interior of the production set Y_j. This proves that the production set Y_j is not strictly convex.

9.3.5 Closedness

The following property expresses the idea of continuity for production processes.

Definition 9.8. *The production technology is continuous if the production set Y_j is closed in $\mathbb{R}^\ell$.*

This assumption is equivalent to the following property: let (y_j^q) be a sequence of feasible activity vectors converging to the vector $y_j^0 \in \mathbb{R}^\ell$; then, the activity vector y_j^0 is feasible.

9.3.6 Recession Cones of Convex Production Sets

The recession cone of a convex set plays an important role in maximization problems involving that convex set. (See Appendix E.5.) This leads us to define the *recession cone* of the production set Y_j. It is the set

$$0^+ Y_j = \{ d \in \mathbb{R}^\ell \mid Y_j + d \subset Y_j \}.$$

Proposition 9.9. *The recession cone $0^+ Y_j$ of a production set Y_j that satisfies Assumptions 9.7 and 9.4 contains the negative orthant $-\mathbb{R}^\ell_+$.*

Proof. Let $-t \in \mathbb{R}^\ell_+$. Let $y_j \in Y_j$. Then, the vector $y_j - t$ belongs to $y_j - \mathbb{R}^\ell_+$, hence to Y_j by Assumption 9.7 (free disposals). $\square$

The following property of the production technology is expressed in terms of the recession cone $0^+ Y_j$.

Definition 9.10. *The convex production technology represented by the production set Y_j is neutral if the recession cone $0^+ Y_j$ is the negative orthant $-\mathbb{R}^\ell_+$.*

This property implies that if y_j is a feasible activity vector with some positive output, then there exists a $\lambda_0 > 0$ large enough such the activity λy_j is not feasible for $\lambda > \lambda_0$. This property is therefore consistent with and in fact slightly strengthens the idea of decreasing returns to scale.

Remark 4. We will see in a moment that the "neutrality property" implies that the firm has a profit maximizing solution for any price system $p \in S$. With recession cones that are strictly bigger than $-\mathbb{R}^\ell_+$, the normal cone to the recession cone is smaller than $\mathbb{R}^\ell_{++}$ and there exist price vectors $p \in S$ (that do not belong to the normal cone to $0^+ Y_j$), and activity vectors $y_j \in Y_j$ such that the profit $p \cdot y_j$ can be arbitrarily large. This is incompatible with the price vector being at equilibrium. In other words, the firm's technology represented by the production set Y_j would directly exclude some price vectors $p \in S$ from being possible equilibrium price vectors. This justifies our terminology of "neutral technology" used to express the idea that the technology does not interfere with the determination of equilibrium prices. Though convenient, the assumption of neutral technology is not essential and could easily be dispensed.

EXERCISE

9.1 Let Y_j be a production set that, in addition to satisfying Assumptions 9.6, 9.7, and 9.8 is bounded from above. Give an economic interpretation of boundedness from above. Show that the recession cone $O^+ Y_j$ is then the non-positive orthant $-\mathbb{R}^\ell_+$ and that the technology satisfies the neutrality property.

9.4 THE FIRM'S OBJECTIVE FUNCTION

Definition 9.11. *The firm's objective function is its profit.*

The classical theory of the firm takes it as an axiom that the firm maximizes its profit. Indeed, it is necessary at this stage where the firm is considered in isolation from the rest of the economy, to impose the definition of some objective function. In that sense, profit is indeed a very natural objective function. Nevertheless, we will see that the objective function of privately owned firms embedded in the competitive environment represented by the general equilibrium model of an economy with private ownership of production can then be derived from the property that consumers maximize their preferences subject to their budget constraints. The firm's objective function is then its profit, but this is now a theorem instead of being an axiom.

9.4.1 The Firm's Maximization Problem

The main characteristic of the competitive environment is that firms, like consumers, take prices as exogenously given.

We therefore assume that, given the price vector $p \in S$, firm j maximizes its profit $p \cdot y_j$ subject to the feasibility constraint $y_j \in Y_j$.

9.4.2 Efficiency of Profit Maximization

The following property is a direct consequence of the firm's profit maximizing behavior:

Proposition 9.12. *Let y_j be a solution of the firm's profit maximization problem. Necessarily, y_j is an efficient activity.*

Proof. Assume the contrary. There exists an activity vector y'_j with $y_j < y'_j$ that is feasible. The contradiction then follows from $p \cdot y_j < p \cdot y'_j$. $\qquad\square$

9.5 THE STRICT DECREASING RETURNS TO SCALE FIRM

Definition 9.13. *The typical strict decreasing returns to scale firm j is characterized by a production set Y_j that satisfies Definitions 9.5, 9.6, 9.7, 9.8, and 9.10.*

9.5.1 Existence of a Profit Maximizing Solution

Proposition 9.14. *The maximization of profit $p \cdot y_j$ subject to the constraint $y_j \in Y_j$ for $p \in S$ given for the strict decreasing returns firm j has a unique solution.*

Proof. Existence of a maximum.

Define the set $K_j(p) = \{y_j \in Y_j \mid p \cdot y_j \geq 0\}$. Because inactivity is feasible, the maximization of $p \cdot y_j$ has the same solutions subject to the constraint $y_j \in Y_j$ or to the constraint $y_j \in K_j(p)$.

Let us show that the set $K_j(p)$ is compact. This set is closed and convex as the intersection of the two closed and convex sets Y_j and $\{y_j \in \mathbb{R}^\ell \mid p \cdot y_j \geq 0\}$. To prove that this set is bounded, we consider the recession cone $O^+ K_j(p)$ (see Appendix E.5).

Let us now show that the recession cone is reduced to the vector 0. Assume the contrary. Let $d \neq 0$ be a vector in the recession cone $O^+ K_j(p)$. The vector d also belongs to the recession cone $O^+ Y_j$ of the production set Y_j. Since the price vector $p \in S$ belongs to the normal cone to $O^+ Y_j$, this implies the strict inequality $p \cdot d < 0$. It also follows from the definition of the recession cone that, since d belongs to $K_j(p)$, the inequality $p \cdot d \geq 0$ is also satisfied by the definition of $K_j(p)$. Hence a contradiction between these two inequalities.

We now observe that the recession cone of a closed convex set is reduced to 0 if and only if this set is bounded: Appendix E.5, Proposition E.12. The set $K_j(p) = \{y_j \in Y_j \mid p \cdot y_j \geq 0\}$ is therefore bounded. Since it is also closed, it is compact.

The profit function $y_j \to p \cdot y_j$ being continuous, it reaches a maximum on the compact set $K_j(p)$.

Uniqueness of a profit maximizing solution. Assume that there are at least two distinct solutions $y_j \neq y_j'$. Then $(y_j + y_j')/2$ is feasible but not efficient. Therefore, there exists some $y_j'' > (y_j + y_j')/2$ that is feasible and the profit for this activity vector satisfies $p \cdot y_j'' > p \cdot (y_j + y_j')/2 = p \cdot y_j$, which contradicts the definition of y_j (and also the definition of y_j') as solutions of the profit maximization problem. $\square$

9.5.2 *The Net Supply Function*

Definition 9.15. *The net supply function of the strict decreasing returns to scale firm j is the map $g_j : S \to \mathbb{R}^\ell$ that associates with every price vector $p \in S$ the unique solution to the firm's profit maximization problem.*

The terminology of the net supply function is justified by the sign convention where outputs are positive and inputs negative.

Our goal in this section is to establish a few properties of the net supply function of a typical strictly convex firm. These properties will then be taken as axioms satisfied by the net supply functions of abstract firms.

Proposition 9.16. *The net supply function $g_j : S \to \mathbb{R}^\ell$ of a strict decreasing returns firm is continuous.*

Proof. See for example [53]. □

Proposition 9.17. *The net supply function $g_j : S \to \mathbb{R}^\ell$ of a strict decreasing returns firm satisfies the following condition;*

$$p \cdot g_j(p) > p \cdot g_j(p') \qquad for \ p' \neq p \in S.$$

Proof. This follows from the uniqueness of the profit maximizing solution. □

Proposition 9.18. *The net supply function $g_j : S \to \mathbb{R}^\ell$ of a strict decreasing returns convex firm satisfies the following condition;*

$$p \cdot g_j(p) \geq 0 \qquad for \ any \ p \in S.$$

Proof. This follows from the feasibility of no activity $0 \in Y_j$. □

Proposition 9.19. *The profit function $s_j : p \to s_j(p) = p \cdot g_j(p)$ of the strict decreasing returns firm j is strictly convex.*

Proof. Let $p \neq p'$ in S. The inequalities $p \cdot g_j((p+p')/2) < p \cdot g_j(p)$ and $p' \cdot g_j((p+p')/2) < p' \cdot g_j(p')$ follow from the definition of g_j as profit maximizing. Adding up these two inequalities yields $(p+p') \cdot g_j((p+p')/2) < p \cdot g_j(p) + p' \cdot g_j(p')$ from which follows $s_j((p+p')/2) < (s_j(p) + s_j(p'))/2$. □

9.5.3 Summary: Properties of the Strictly Convex Firm

The following properties are therefore satisfied by strictly convex firms:
1) For every price vector $p \in S$, there exists a unique activity $y_j = g_j(p)$ that maximizes the profit $p \cdot y_j$ subject to the production constraint $y_j \in Y_j$; 2) The net supply function $g_j : S \to X$ is continuous, injective, and its image $g_j(S)$ is the efficient boundary: $g_j(S) = \partial Y_j^{\text{eff}}$; 3) The profit function $s_j : S \to \mathbb{R}$ defined by $s_j(p) = p \cdot g_j(p)$ is continuous.

9.6 THE NET SUPPLY FUNCTION AS A PRIMITIVE CONCEPT

We now continue the theory of the firm with the net supply function $g_j : S \to \mathbb{R}^\ell$ used as primitive concept. We are essentially going to add smoothness to several properties of the net supply functions of strictly convex firms established in the previous section for profit maximizing strict decreasing returns firms.

9.6.1 The Net Supply Functions

NOTATION

Let $\gamma : \mathbb{R}^\ell_{++} \to \mathbb{R}^\ell$ be some arbitrary function. This function is going to be at some point the net supply function of some firm. Note also that we are going to use non-normalized prices in a few places. The same notation will then be used for normalized and non-normalized prices. In the case of non-normalized prices, $\gamma(p)$ is then homogenous of degree zero, i.e., $\gamma(\lambda p) = \gamma(p)$ for any $\lambda > 0$.

In the case where γ is differentiable, we denote by $D\gamma(p)$ the $\ell \times \ell$ Jacobian matrix of the map γ for the non-normalized price vector $p = (p_1, \ldots, p_\ell)$.

PROPERTIES OF THE NET SUPPLY FUNCTIONS

We define the following properties for the maps $\gamma : \mathbb{R}^\ell_{++} \to \mathbb{R}^\ell$.

- (PS) (Production smoothness) γ is smooth.
- (PM) (Profit maximization) $p \cdot \gamma(p) > p \cdot \gamma(p')$ for $p' \neq p \in S$.
- (PP) (Profit positivity) $p \cdot \gamma(p) \geq 0$ for any $p \in S$.
- (PC) (Profit convexity) Assuming (PS), the restriction of the quadratic form $z \to z^T D\gamma(p) z$ to the hyperplane $H(p) = \{z \in \mathbb{R}^\ell \mid p^T z = 0\}$ is positive definite for every p.

Definition 9.20. *The set $\mathcal{P}$ consists of the functions $\gamma : \mathbb{R}^\ell_{++} \to \mathbb{R}^\ell$ that are homogenous of degree zero and satisfy (PS), (PM), (PP), and (PC).*

Because there is no serious risk of confusion, we also denote by the same letter $\mathcal{P}$ the set of the maps in $\mathcal{P}$ restricted to the set of numeraire normalized prices $S = \{p = (p_1, \ldots, p_\ell) \in \mathbb{R}^\ell_{++} \mid p_\ell = 1\}$.

It follows from Propositions 9.17 and 9.18 that (PM) and (PP) are satisfied by the supply functions of typical strictly convex firms while (PS) and (PC) are the smooth versions of Propositions 9.16 and 9.19.

Proposition 9.21. *Let $\gamma \in \mathcal{P}$. We have*

$$p \cdot \frac{\partial \gamma}{\partial p_k}(p) = 0$$

for $1 \leq k \leq \ell$ (non-normalized price vector).

Proof. This follows from the necessary first order conditions applied to the function $p' \to p \cdot \gamma(p')$ that reaches its maximum at $p' = p$ by (PM). $\square$

The following proposition where prices are numeraire normalized expresses a form of monotonicity of the supply functions.

Proposition 9.22. *The supply function $\gamma \in \mathcal{P}$ is increasing, i.e., it satisfies the inequality*

$$(p - p') \cdot (\gamma(p) - \gamma(p')) \geq 0$$

for $p \neq p'$ in S.

Proof. It follows from the definition of the supply function $\gamma \in \mathcal{P}$ that, for p and p' in S, we have $p \cdot \gamma(p) - p \cdot \gamma(p') \geq 0$ and $p' \cdot \gamma(p) - p' \cdot \gamma(p') \leq 0$. This implies the inequality $(p - p') \cdot (\gamma(p) - \gamma(p')) \geq 0$. $\square$

9.6.2 The Profit Function of Smooth Production

We now associate with the net supply function $\gamma \in \mathcal{P}$ the "profit function" defined by $s(p) = p \cdot \gamma(p)$. Let $Ds = \left(\dfrac{\partial s}{\partial p_1}, \ldots, \dfrac{\partial s}{\partial p_\ell} \right)$ denote the gradient vector of s with respect to the non-normalized price vector $p = (p_1, \ldots, p_\ell)$.

Proposition 9.23. *We have* $\gamma = Ds$.

Proof. The derivative of $s(p) = p \cdot \gamma(p)$ with respect to p_k (non-normalized price vector) is equal to

$$\frac{\partial s}{\partial p_k} = \gamma^k(p) + p \cdot \frac{\partial \gamma}{\partial p_k}(p) = \gamma^k(p)$$

by Proposition 9.21. □

We now restrict the "profit function" $s(p) = p \cdot \gamma(p)$ to *numeraire* normalized prices $p \in S$. Let $(D^2s)_{\ell\ell}$ then denote the $(\ell-1) \times (\ell-1)$ Hessian matrix of second order derivatives with respect to $p_1, \ldots, p_{\ell-1}$.

Proposition 9.24. *Property (PC) is equivalent to matrix* $(D^2s)_{\ell\ell}$ *being positive definite.*

Proof. From Proposition 9.23 comes $\gamma = Ds$, which implies $D\gamma = D^2s$ computed with non-normalized prices. Let $(D\gamma)_{\ell\ell}$ denote the $(\ell-1) \times (\ell-1)$ matrix obtained from the $(\ell \times \ell)$ matrix $D\gamma$ by deleting the ℓ-th row and column. It follows from the homogeneity of degree zero of γ with respect to non-normalized prices that (PC) is equivalent to $(D\gamma)_{\ell\ell}$ being positive definite and, therefore, to $(D^2s)_{\ell\ell}$ also positive definite. □

The following corollary is essentially the smooth version of Proposition 9.19.

Corollary 9.25. *Assume (PC). The "profit function"* $p \to s(p) = p \cdot \gamma(p)$ *is a smooth strictly convex function of the numeraire normalized prices* $p \in S$.

Proof. Proposition 9.24 states a sufficient condition for the function s to be strictly convex. □

9.7 CONCLUSION

In this chapter, we have gone from the standard formulation of the firm through its production set and profit maximization to the net supply function. This parallels our approach of the consumer, from preference maximization subject to a budget constraint to the demand functions.

The typical firm subject to decreasing returns to scale is from now on characterized by a net supply function that satisfies the four properties (PS), (PM), (PP), and (PC). These properties will enable us to study in the next chapter the general equilibrium model with private ownership of production in the case of decreasing returns.

9.8 NOTES AND COMMENTS

The first two parts of this chapter on production sets and profit maximization are standard. An early exposition focusing on activity analysis is due to Koopmans [44]. Nice presentations in book forms of the production set approach are to be found in Debreu [23], Koopmans[43] and Nikaido [49]. The third part on net supply functions is certainly not new. Unfortunately, no easily accessible references seem to exist.

CHAPTER 10

Equilibrium with Decreasing Returns

10.1 INTRODUCTION

The approach to the study of the general equilibrium model with private ownership of smooth production with decreasing returns is to adjust consumers' individual demand functions for production. The "exchange model" defined by these production adjusted demand functions is then shown to be equivalent to the original general equilibrium model with private ownership of production.

The production adjusted demand functions are very close to satisfy the properties considered in the first part of this book, properties that guarantee that the main properties of the exchange model are satisfied. As a result, the general equilibrium model with private ownership of smooth production with decreasing returns features exactly the same properties as the standard smooth exchange model.

10.2 THE GENERAL EQUILIBRIUM MODEL WITH PRIVATE OWNERSHIP OF DECREASING RETURNS TO SCALE FIRMS

10.2.1 Firms and Their Supply Functions

There is a finite number n of firms. The activity of firm j is represented by a vector $y_j \in \mathbb{R}^\ell$. Outputs and inputs are represented by the positive and negative coordinates respectively of the activity vector y_j.

The activity of firm j is a function $g_j(p)$ of the price vector $p = (p_1, \dots, p_\ell) \in \mathbb{R}^\ell_{++}$ and is known as the firm's net supply function. The same notation is used when prices are not normalized, or simplex normalized, or numeraire normalized. In the case of non-normalized prices, the supply function $g_j(p)$ is homogenous of degree zero, i.e., $g_i(\lambda p) = g_i(p)$ for any $\lambda > 0$.

From now on in this chapter, we assume that the net supply function $g_j : \mathbb{R}^\ell_{++} \to \mathbb{R}^\ell$ of firm j satisfies the four properties (PS), (PM), (PP), and (PC) and, therefore, belongs to the set $\mathcal{P}$ of Definition 9.20.

10.2.2 Consumers and Their Ownership Rights

There is a finite number m of consumers. Consumer i is endowed with the resources represented by the vector $\omega_i \in \mathbb{R}^\ell$ and the ownership of the fraction θ_{ij} of firm j, with $0 \leq \theta_{ij} \leq 1$. Let $\Theta = \{\theta = (\theta_{ij}) \in (\mathbb{R}_+^n)^m \mid \sum_j \theta_{ij} = 1$ for $1 \leq i \leq m\}$. An economy with private ownership of production is therefore represented by the pair $(\omega, \theta) \in \Omega \times \Theta$ where $\omega = (\omega_i) \in \Omega$ and $\theta = (\theta_{ij}) \in \Theta$. The collection of all economies with private ownership of production define the *exchange and production with decreasing returns model*.

10.2.3 The Exchange and Production with Decreasing Returns Model

The exchange and production with decreasing returns model can then be identified to the element $((f_i), (g_j), \theta)$ of the Cartesian product $\mathcal{F}^m \times \mathcal{P}^n \times \Theta$. As in the exchange model, the variable parameter is the endowment vector $\omega = (\omega_i) \in \Omega$.

10.2.4 Equilibrium Equation

Let $p \in S$. Consumer i's wealth is equal to $w_i = p \cdot \omega_i + \sum_j \theta_{ij}\, p \cdot g_j(p)$. Consumer i's demand is equal to $f_i(p,\, p \cdot \omega_i + (\sum_j \theta_{ij}\, p \cdot g_j(p)))$. Aggregate demand is the sum of the m consumers' demands.

Aggregate supply consists of two terms: 1) The sum of the individual endowments $\sum_i \omega_i$; 2) The aggregate supply of the m firms, namely the vector $\sum_j g_j(p)$.

Definition 10.1. *The price vector $p \in S$ is an equilibrium price vector of the economy with private ownership of production represented by the endowment vector ω for the exchange and production model $((f_i), (g_j), \theta)$ if there is equality of aggregate demand and supply:*

$$\sum_i f_i\left(p,\, p \cdot \omega_i + \sum_j \theta_{ij}\, p \cdot g_j(p)\right) = \sum_i \omega_i + \sum_j g_j(p). \qquad (1)$$

The pair (p, ω) is then called an equilibrium *of the exchange and production model defined by the demand functions f_i and supply function g_j for $1 \leq i \leq m$ and $1 \leq j \leq n$ and ownership structure $\theta = (\theta_{ij})$.*

The equilibrium analysis of the exchange and production model consists of the study of the properties of the equilibria (p, ω) as a function of the parameter $\omega \in \Omega$.

The set of all those equilibria is known as the "equilibrium manifold" though, at this stage, it is by no means obvious that this set is indeed a smooth manifold and this will require a proof.

10.2.5 Private Ownership of Production and the Firm's Objective Function

In the previous chapter, the firm's objective function was set to be profit. We can now show that this property is a straightforward consequence of private ownership of production. To make matters simple, assume that consumer i's preferences are represented by the utility function u_i. With the (normalized) price vector $p \in S$ exogenously given, the maximization of consumer i's utility is equivalent to the maximization of consumer i's wealth w_i. This wealth is equal to $w_i = p \cdot \omega_i + \sum_j \theta_{ij} p \cdot y_j$ where y_j belongs to the production set Y_j. The maximum of w_i is therefore reached with each term $p \cdot y_j$ being maximal, which is equivalent to every firm j maximizing its profit.

10.3 PRODUCTION ADJUSTED DEMAND FUNCTIONS

In this section, we are going to adjust the demand function $f_i : S \times \mathbb{R} \to \mathbb{R}^\ell$ of consumer i to account for the impact of production on consumer's wealth and on the resources in the economy. We assume from now on that the ownership structure represented by $\theta = (\theta_{ij}) \in \Theta$ is given and fixed. We also assume that all firms' net supply functions $g_j : S \to \mathbb{R}^\ell$ belong to $\mathcal{P}$.

10.3.1 The Consumer as a Virtual Producer

The idea is to substitute to an economy where production takes place in firms that are owned by a collection of consumers a virtual economy where consumers are also producers. Each consumer would then come equipped with a suitable production set. Since we have adopted the formulation of production by way of net supply functions, we define:

Definition 10.2. *Consumer i's virtual production activity is defined by the function $\gamma_i : S \to \mathbb{R}^\ell$ where*

$$\gamma_i(p) = \sum_j \theta_{ij} g_j(p).$$

This function is known as the equivalent consumer's virtual production supply function.

The economic interpretation of $\gamma_i(p)$ is straightforward. Consumer i receives a wealth amount equal to $\theta_{ij}p \cdot g_j(p)$ from the firm j of which he owns the fraction θ_{ij}. He therefore receives from all the firms he owns the wealth quantity equal to $\sum_j \theta_{ij} p \cdot g_j(p)$. This expression is equal to $p \cdot \gamma_i(p)$.

The function γ_i can be interpreted as the net supply function of a virtual or fictitious firm that would be owned entirely by consumer i. Unsurprisingly, the function γ_i satisfies the following property:

Proposition 10.3. *Consumer i's virtual production supply function $\gamma_i : S \to \mathbb{R}^\ell$ associated with (θ_{ij}) given belongs to $\mathcal{P}$.*

Proof. This follows readily from the fact that properties (PS) (resp. (PM), (PP), and (PC)) are invariant by non-negative linear combinations. $\square$

10.3.2 Production Adjusted Demand Functions: Definition

Definition 10.4. *The* production adjusted demand function *of consumer i associated with (θ_{ij}) given is the map $h_i : S \times \mathbb{R} \to \mathbb{R}^\ell$ where*

$$h_i(p, w_i) = f_i\big(p,\ w_i + p \cdot \gamma_i(p)\big) - \gamma_i(p).$$

Note that the demand function h_i is adjusted both for wealth and for demand. With the interpretation that γ_i is the net supply function of a firm entirely owned by consumer i, $h_i(p, w_i)$ represents the net demand of consumer i after taking into account the full activity $\gamma_i(p)$ of the fictitious firm that consumer i now owns entirely.

Let us now check that the production adjusted demand function $h_i : S \times \mathbb{R} \to \mathbb{R}^\ell$ behaves as well or almost as well as a standard demand function.

10.3.3 Production Adjusted Demand Functions: Smoothness (S) and Walras Law (W)

The following proposition tells us that the production adjusted demand functions h_i are smooth and satisfy Walras law if the original demand functions f_i are themselves smooth and satisfy Walras law. Note that we assume that all net production supply functions belong to the set $\mathcal{P}$.

Proposition 10.5. *We have*

$$(f_i) \in \mathcal{E} \implies (h_i) \in \mathcal{E}.$$

Proof. We have to show that each production adjusted demand function h_i is smooth and satisfies Walras law. Smoothness is obvious. Walras law (W) for h_i follows readily from Walras law (W) for f_i by

$$p \cdot h_i(p, w_i) = p \cdot \left(f_i(p, w_i + p \cdot \gamma_i(p)) - \gamma_i(p) \right),$$

$$p \cdot h_i(p, w_i) = w_i + p \cdot \gamma_i(p) - p \cdot \gamma_i(p),$$

$$p \cdot h_i(p, w_i) = w_i.$$

$\square$

10.3.4 Production Adjusted Demand Functions: Negative Definiteness (ND)

Our goal is now to show that if the demand function f_i satisfies (NSD), then the production adjusted demand function satisfies (ND). Since (WARP) also implies (NSD), we will then have that, for all demand functions $(f_i) \in \mathcal{E}_c$, the production adjusted demand functions (h_i) belong also to $\mathcal{E}_c$.

We begin with a useful lemma:

Lemma 10.6. *The Jacobian matrix at $p' = p$ of the map*

$$p' \to f_i\big(p', p' \cdot (\omega_i + \gamma_i(p'))\big) - f_i\big(p', p' \cdot (\omega_i + \gamma_i(p))\big)$$

is equal to 0.

Proof. The only term of row j and column k that is not obviously equal to zero in the computation of this Jacobian matrix is

$$\frac{\partial f_i^j}{\partial w_i}\big(p, p \cdot (\omega_i + \gamma_i(p))\big) \, p \cdot \frac{\partial \gamma_i}{\partial p_k}(p) \cdot$$

This term is also equal to zero because $p \cdot \dfrac{\partial \gamma_i}{\partial p_k}(p) = 0$ by Proposition 9.21.

$\square$

We now address (ND). As above, all net supply functions $g_j : S \to \mathbb{R}^\ell$ belong to $\mathcal{P}$.

Proposition 10.7. *The production adjusted demand function $h_i : S \times \mathbb{R} \to \mathbb{R}^\ell$ satisfies (ND) if the demand function $f_i : S \times \mathbb{R} \to \mathbb{R}^\ell$ satisfies (NSD).*

Proof. In this proof, prices are not normalized.

Let $\omega_i = h_i(p, w_i)$. The Slutsky matrix $Sh_i(p, w_i)$ of the (production adjusted) demand function h_i at (p, w_i) is the Jacobian matrix at $p' = p$ of the map

$$p' \to h_i(p', p' \cdot \omega_i) = f_i(p', p' \cdot (\omega_i + \gamma_i(p'))) - \gamma_i(p').$$

By writing

$$
\begin{aligned}
f_i(p', p' \cdot (\omega_i + \gamma_i(p'))) - \gamma_i(p') = {}& f_i(p', p' \cdot (\omega_i + \gamma_i(p))) - \gamma_i(p') \\
& + f_i(p', p' \cdot (\omega_i + \gamma_i(p'))) \\
& - f_i(p', p' \cdot (\omega_i + \gamma_i(p))),
\end{aligned}
$$

this Jacobian matrix is the sum of the Jacobian matrices of the maps $p' \to f_i(p', p' \cdot (\omega_i + \gamma_i(p)) - \gamma_i(p'))$ and $p' \to f_i(p', p' \cdot (\omega_i + \gamma_i(p'))) - f_i(p', p' \cdot (\omega_i + \gamma_i(p)))$.

The Jacobian matrix of the second map at $p' = p$ is equal to zero by Lemma 10.6. The Jacobian matrix of the first map is itself the sum of two matrices, the Jacobian matrix of the map $p' \to f_i(p', p' \cdot (\omega_i + \gamma_i(p)))$ and of the map $p' \to -\gamma_i(p')$. The restriction to the hyperplane $H(p)$ of $\mathbb{R}^\ell$ perpendicular to $p \in S$ of the quadratic form defined by the second matrix is negative definite by (PC). The first matrix is a standard Slutsky matrix since $\omega_i + \gamma_i(p) = f_i(p, p \cdot (\omega_i + \gamma_i(p)))$. The restriction of the quadratic form it defines to the hyperplane perpendicular to the price vector p is again negative semidefinite by (NSD). The sum of two quadratic forms, one negative semidefinite and the other one negative definite is negative definite. $\qquad\square$

10.4 THE EQUIVALENT EXCHANGE MODEL

We now associate with the m production adjusted demand functions $h_i : S \times \mathbb{R} \to \mathbb{R}^\ell$ the "exchange model" defined by these m consumers characterized by their "demand functions" equal to h_i and an endowment vector equal to ω_i, for i varying from 1 to m. We then have:

Proposition 10.8. *The pair $(p, \omega) \in S \times \Omega$ is an equilibrium of the production model $((f_i), (g_j), \theta)$ if and only if it is an equilibrium of the exchange model $\mathcal{E}(h_i)$ defined by the m (production adjusted) demand functions $h_i : S \times \mathbb{R} \to \mathbb{R}^\ell$.*

Proof. Let us write the equilibrium equation (1) as

$$\sum_i f_i\big(p,\, p \cdot (\omega_i + \gamma_i(p))\big) = \sum_i \omega_i + \sum_j g_j(p),$$

$$\sum_i f_i\big(p,\, p \cdot (\omega_i + \gamma_i(p))\big) = \sum_i \omega_i + \sum_i \Big(\sum_j \theta_{ij} g_j(p)\Big),$$

$$\sum_i f_i\big(p,\, p \cdot (\omega_i + \gamma_i(p))\big) = \sum_i \omega_i + \sum_i \gamma_i(p),$$

from which follows

$$\sum_i \Big(f_i\big(p,\, p \cdot (\omega_i + \gamma_i(p))\big) - \gamma_i(p)\Big) = \sum_i \omega_i,$$

$$\sum_i h_i(p,\, p \cdot \omega_i) = \sum_i \omega_i,$$

the equilibrium equation of the exchange model defined by the m demand functions $h_i : S \times \mathbb{R} \to \mathbb{R}^\ell$. □

The properties of the exchange model for the (production adjusted) demand functions h_i, with $i = 1, \ldots, m$, obviously depend on the properties of these "demand functions." We will see shortly that these properties are very close (when they are not identical) to those developed in the first part of this book.

10.4.1 *Applications to the Global Structure of the Equilibrium Manifold*

Recall that it is not readily obvious from the definition of the equilibrium manifold by equation (1) that this set is indeed a smooth manifold and, even more, a smooth submanifold of $S \times \Omega$.

Nevertheless, it follows from Proposition 10.5 that the exchange model $\mathcal{E}(h_i)$ defined by the m-tuple of production adjusted demand functions (h_i) satisfies the properties listed in Chapter 4 whenever the m-tuple of consumer demand function (f_i) belongs to $\mathcal{E}$.

Proposition 10.9. *The equilibrium manifold E and the set of no-trade equilibria T for the m-tuple of production adjusted demand functions (h_i) satisfy the following properties:*

  i) *The equilibrium manifold E is a smooth submanifold of S × Ω of dimension ℓm.*

ii) The set of no-trade equilibria T is diffeomorphic to $S \times \mathbb{R}^m$ and, therefore, to $\mathbb{R}^{\ell+m-1}$.

iii) The equilibrium manifold E is diffeomorphic to $T \times \mathbb{R}^{(\ell-1)(m-1)}$.

Proof. These are Propositions 4.9, 5.2, and 5.8 for the m-tuple of (production adjusted) demand functions (h_i). □

10.5 PROPERNESS OF THE NATURAL PROJECTION

The production adjusted demand functions h_i do not satisfy desirability (A) or boundedness from below (B) under economically realistic assumptions on the firms' supply functions g_j. These two properties would require significantly stronger assumptions than those that are generally accepted.

The main role of desirability (A) for at least one demand function f_i and (B) for all demand functions (f_i) in the exchange model is to imply the properness of the natural projection $\pi : E \to \Omega$. A solution is to substitute to (A) and (B) a weaker property that would make more economic sense in the production environment and still imply the properness of the natural projection. Such property exists and involves the aggregate production sector instead of individual firms.

10.5.1 The Aggregate Supply Function

The aggregate net supply function $g : S \to \mathbb{R}^\ell$ is the sum $\sum_j g_j$ of all net supply functions. We then have:

Proposition 10.10. *Assume that the m supply functions $g_j : S \to \mathbb{R}^\ell$ satisfy (PS) (resp. (PM), (PP), and (PC)). The aggregate supply function $g = \sum_j g_j : S \to \mathbb{R}^\ell$ satisfies (PS) (resp. (PM),(PP), and (PC)).*

Proof. This is the same as for Proposition 10.3. □

Corollary 10.11. *In a production economy where the net supply function g_j belongs to $\mathcal{P}$ for $1 \leq j \leq n$, the aggregate net supply function $g = \sum_j g_j$ also belongs to $\mathcal{P}$.*

Let us denote by $g^+(p)$ and $g^-(p)$ the positive and the opposite of the negative components of $g(p)$. This definition implies $g(p) = g^+(p) - g^-(p)$. The vector $g^-(p)$ represents the quantities of inputs (measured positively) while $g^+(p)$ represents the quantities of outputs. We then define the following property:

Definition 10.12. *(BIBO) (Bounded Inputs Bounded Outputs) For any $A \in \mathbb{R}^\ell_{++}$, there exists $B \in \mathbb{R}^\ell_{++}$ such that the inequality $g^-(p) \leq A$ implies the inequality $g^+(p) \leq B$.*

10.5.2 BIBO for Production Sets

Property (BIBO) for net supply functions simply states the impossibility of producing infinite quantities of some goods with only finite quantities of inputs. However natural this property can be, it is worth relating (BIBO) for net supply functions to the production sets. This will enable us to assess its relevance more easily. The formulation of (BIBO) for production sets expresses the idea that outputs are bounded once inputs are bounded. It takes the form:

Definition 10.13. *((BIBO) for production sets). The production set Y satisfies (BIBO) if, for any $A \in \mathbb{R}^\ell_{++}$, there exists $B \in \mathbb{R}^\ell_{++}$ such that any activity $y = (y^+, -y^-) \in Y$ with $y^- \leq A$ is such that the inequality $y^+ \leq B$ is satisfied.*

Proposition 10.14. *Property (BIBO) for the production set Y implies (BIBO) for the associated net supply function $g : S \to \mathbb{R}^\ell$ when the latter is defined.*

Proof. It is obvious. $\square$

Recall that Proposition 9.14 gives sufficient conditions for the existence of a net supply function defined on the full price set S. These conditions fail to be satisfied by production sets that are not strictly convex.

Property (BIBO) for the production set Y is a very weak requirement as follows from:

Proposition 10.15. *Property (BIBO) for the production set Y is satisfied whenever there exists a price vector $p^* \in S$ such that the maximization of the profit $p^* \cdot y$ subject to the constraint $y \in Y$ has a solution.*

Proof. Let y^* be a profit maximizing solution. The inequality $p^* \cdot y \leq p^* \cdot y^*$ is satisfied for every $y \in Y$. Let $y = y^+ - y^-$ be the decomposition of the activity vector y in its inputs and outputs by Proposition 9.1. The inequality $p^* \cdot y^+ - p^* \cdot y^- \leq p^* \cdot y^*$ then implies the inequality

$$p^* \cdot y^+ \leq p^* \cdot y^* + p^* \cdot y^-.$$

If all components of the input vector y^- are bounded by some real number A, then

$$p^* \cdot y^+ \leq p^* \cdot y^* + A\, p^* \cdot (1, 1, \ldots, 1)$$

from which follows for coordinate k

$$p_k^* \cdot y^{+k} \leq p^* \cdot y^* + A\, p^* \cdot (1, 1, \ldots, 1).$$

This implies that (BIBO) is satisfied by

$$B = \sup_{1 \leq k \leq \ell} \frac{p^* \cdot y^* + A\, p^* \cdot (1, 1, \ldots, 1)}{p_k^*}. \qquad \square$$

In practice, (BIBO) for production sets is satisfied whenever a **profit maximizing** net supply function exists. Since we will be mostly using net supply functions in our analysis of the equilibrium equation, assuming (BIBO) may seem redundant. We refer explicitly to (BIBO) because the model with production can be generalized to non-profit maximizing firms, i.e., to firms having net supply functions that do not result from profit maximization. In such a case (BIBO) cannot be derived from the existence of these net supply functions.

10.5.3 Properness of the Natural Projection

Proposition 10.16. Let $(f_i) \in \mathcal{E}_c$ and $g_j \in \mathcal{P}$ for $1 \leq j \leq n$. Let the aggregate net supply function $g = \sum_j g_j \in \mathcal{P}$ satisfy (BIBO). The natural projection $\pi : E \to \Omega$ for the exchange model $\mathcal{E}(h_i)$ defined by the production adjusted demand functions (h_i) is a proper map.

Proof. Let K be a compact subset of Ω. Let us show that the preimage $\pi^{-1}(K)$ is a compact subset of the equilibrium manifold E. First, the set $\pi^{-1}(K)$ is closed in E as the preimage of a closed set by a continuous map.

The image of the compact set K by the map $\omega \to \omega_1 + \omega_2 + \cdots + \omega_m$ is a compact set and, therefore, is bounded from above by some $A \in \mathbb{R}^\ell$. In other words, we have $\omega_1 + \omega_2 + \cdots + \omega_m \leq A$ for any $\omega \in K$.

The compactness of $\pi^{-1}(K)$ will be proved by showing that every infinite sequence (p^q, ω^q) in $\pi^{-1}(K)$ has a convergent subsequence. It follows from the compactness of K that the sequence ω^q has a subsequence that converges to $\omega^0 \in K$. There is no loss in generality in considering directly this subsequence (p^q, ω^q).

Let $\tilde{p}^q$ be the simplex normalized price vector corresponding to the numeraire normalized price vector p^q. It follows from the compactness of the closed price simplex $\overline{S_\Sigma}$ that there is a subsequence of the sequence $\tilde{p}^q$ that converges to some $\tilde{p}^0 \in \overline{S_\Sigma}$.

If $\tilde{p}^0$ belongs to the interior S_Σ, then p^0, the numeraire normalized price vector corresponding to $\tilde{p}^0$ belongs to S and is the limit of the (sub)sequence p^q and there is nothing more to prove.

Let us show that the limit $\tilde{p}^0$ cannot belong to the boundary $\partial S_\Sigma = \overline{S_\Sigma} \setminus S_\Sigma$. The proof proceeds by contradiction. Assume the contrary. The equilibrium equation satisfied by (p^q, ω^q) is

$$f_1(p^q, p^q \cdot \omega_1^q + p^q \cdot \gamma_1(p^q)) + \cdots + f_m(p^q, p^q \cdot \omega_m^q + p^q \cdot \gamma_m(p^q))$$
$$= \sum_i \omega_i^q + g(p^q)$$

for any $q \geq 0$. It follows from $p^q \cdot \gamma_i(p^q) \geq 0$ (PP) combined with (B) that $f_i(p^q, p^q \cdot \omega^q + p^q \cdot \gamma_i(p^q))$ is bounded from below for every i. There exists therefore $B_i \in \mathbb{R}^\ell$ such that

$$B_i \leq f_i(p^q, p^q \cdot (\omega_i^q + \gamma_i(p^q))),$$

for $1 \leq i \leq m$ and any integer $q \geq 0$. This implies the inequality

$$B_1 + \cdots + B_m \leq f_1(p^q, p^q \cdot (\omega_1^q + \gamma_1(p^q))) + \ldots$$
$$+ f_m(p^q, p^q \cdot (\omega_m^q + \gamma_m(p^q)))$$

for any $q \geq 0$, from which we get the following inequality because (p^q, ω^q) is an equilibrium:

$$B_1 + \cdots + B_m \leq A + g(p^q).$$

The sequence $g(p^q)$ is therefore bounded from below. This implies that it is also bounded from above by the definition of (BIBO): 10.12. We can find a subsequence of p^q such that the corresponding subsequence $g(p^q)$ converges to some limit $g^0 \in \mathbb{R}^\ell$. Then, the inner product $p^q \cdot g(p^q)$ tends to the limit $p^0 \cdot g^0$ and is finite. It follows from the positivity of profit (PP) that the inequality $0 \leq p^q \cdot \gamma_1(p^q) \leq p^q \cdot g(p^q)$ implies that the sequence $p^q \cdot \gamma_1(p^q)$ belongs to a compact interval and, by considering a subsequence, converges to some finite limit.

There is no loss in generality in assuming that the demand function of consumer 1 satisfies (A). We have seen that the sequence $f_1(p^q, p^q \cdot (\omega_1^q + \gamma_1(p^q)))$ is bounded. We have also seen that $p^q \cdot (\omega_1^q + \gamma_1(p^q))$ tends to a finite limit. These two conditions are incompatible with (A) if the limit $\bar{p}^0$ belongs to the boundary $\partial S_\Sigma = \overline{S_\Sigma} \setminus S_\Sigma$. □

EXERCISE

10.1. Let $Y = \sum_j Y_j$ be the sum of the n convex production sets Y_j. Let $p \in S$ be given. Assume that the problem of maximizing $p \cdot y$ subject to the constraint $y \in Y$ has a solution y^*. Show that there exists $y_j^* \in Y_j$ for $1 \leq j \leq n$ such that $y^* = \sum_j y_j^*$ where y_j^* maximizes $p \cdot y_j$ subject to the constraint $y_j \in Y_j$.

10.6 CONCLUSION

It follows from this chapter that the general picture for the production model, i.e., the model of an economy with private ownership of production, is exactly the same as for the exchange model.

This implies far more than the generic finiteness and continuity of equilibria or the homeomorphism of the equilibrium manifold with a Euclidean space. For example, this approach underlines the remarkable role played by the quantity of trade as a cause for discontinuities of equilibrium price selections, a phenomenon that is therefore not limited to pure exchange economies. The identification of that phenomenon for production economies is new.

10.7 NOTES AND COMMENTS

The generic finiteness and generic continuity of equilibria for smooth production economies is proved by Fuchs and Smale [31, 61]. Dierker's index number for exchange economies is extended to smooth production economies by T. Kehoe [41]. The extension to smooth production economies of the properties of pathconnectedness and simple connectedness of the equilibrium manifold is due to Jouini [39].

Property (BIBO) is essentially (A7) in [31].

The proof of the equivalence between the exchange model and the smooth production model (with private ownership of production) is new, as are the implications of this equivalence in terms of the equilibrium manifold and of the natural projection.

CHAPTER 11

Production with Constant Returns

11.1 INTRODUCTION

The assumption of decreasing returns to scale is often justified by the fact that the quantities of some factors used in the production process are fixed and cannot be increased in order to produce more outputs. The latter are then produced with less efficient use of resources. This is typically the case in short-run models where, by definition, capacity and, more generally, capital is not variable. The situation is totally different in long-run models where all production factors, including capital, can be varied. In growth models for example, the output is a homogenous function of degree one of the capital and labor inputs, hence the expression of constant returns to scale. The importance of these models more than justifies the study of the properties of the general equilibrium model when some firms feature constant returns to scale.

As in the previous chapters, we start by formulating constant returns to scale production by way of production sets with arbitrary numbers of inputs and outputs.

We then address the profit maximization problem of a constant returns to scale firm. That problem does not always have a solution. More accurately, if some feasible activity yields a strictly positive profit at some given prices, then it suffices to consider an arbitrarily large multiple of that activity vector to get a feasible activity that yields an arbitrarily large profit at the same prices. The firm can then make an arbitrarily large profit. Mathematicians then say that the maximization problem has no solution and they would exclude from the analysis the prices at which profit would be arbitrarily large or, in short, infinite. The exclusion of those prices would be an artifact of the mathematical approach if these prices could be observed in economically relevant situations. A view of the broader picture will show us that this is not the case. A firm may try to maximize profit while taking prices as exogenously given. But, in doing so, the firm is not alone in the economy. There are other economic agents, firms, and consumers. Resources being limited, prices depend on aggregate supply and demand through the market mechanism. A firm that can make an arbitrarily large profit when facing some price system will then buy arbitrarily large quantities of inputs and sell on the market arbitrarily large quantities of outputs to realize that potential profit.

The intuition is that this will drive the prices of the inputs towards infinity and those of the outputs towards zero. This will not only reduce the firm's profit, it will let it tend to zero or even to a negative value. In other words, prices such that the firm's profit maximization problem has no solution (because the firm's profit would be infinite at such prices) are ruled out by the market mechanism in which the firm is operating. This intuition will be sustained by a rigorous mathematical argument. But the latter has to wait until the next chapter because this argument can be developed only within the general equilibrium setup made of firms and consumers.

The production set of a constant returns to scale firm being a cone, no activity vector can give a strictly positive profit at prices compatible with the existence of a profit maximizing solution. The possibility of inactivity then implies that the maximum of the firm's profit is, when it exists, necessarily equal to zero.

Another complicating factor of the profit maximization problem for a constant returns to scale firm is that, when that problem has a solution that is different from the inactivity vector, any multiple of that activity by some strictly positive real number is also a profit maximizing solution. We have seen in the previous chapters how to represent the activity of a strictly decreasing returns to scale firm by its net supply function, a function defined over the full price set. In the case of a constant returns to scale firm, the net supply function becomes a correspondence and differs from the net supply functions of the preceding chapters on two accounts: 1) It associates the empty set with prices such that the profit maximization problem has no solution; 2) It associates a set that contains more than one element, in fact a full ray of activities, at prices such that profit maximization has a solution different from inactivity.

The main focus of this chapter is therefore the study of the net supply correspondence of a constant returns to scale firm under suitable convexity and smoothness assumptions. These assumptions are comparable to those used in the previous chapters for consumers and production with decreasing returns to scale. The graph of the net supply correspondence in particular will play an important role in the next chapter because it will be substituted to the price system in the definition of an equilibrium between aggregate supply and demand.

11.2 PRODUCTION SETS

11.2.1 General Properties

We start with general properties of production sets of firms that operate under constant returns to scale.

Definition 11.1. *The production set* Y *of a firm operating under constant returns to scale satisfies the following properties:*

(i) **Constant returns:** *The set* Y *is a pointed cone with vertex at the origin* $0 \in \mathbb{R}^\ell$;

(ii) **Free disposals:** *The set* Y *contains the subset* $y - \mathbb{R}^\ell_+$ *for any* $y \in Y$;

(iii) **Closedness:** *The set* Y *is closed;*

(iv) **Convexity:** *The set* Y *is convex;*

(v) **BIBO (bounded inputs, bounded outputs):** *There exists a price vector* $p \in S$ *such that* $p \cdot y \le 0$ *for all* $y \in Y$.

The first four assumptions are standard in the literature on constant returns to scale. They result from the direct application to convex cones of the assumptions made in chapter 8 for general convex production sets. The fifth property is simply the statement that there exists a price vector for which the firm has a profit maximizing solution. As we have seen in chapter 9, this assumption is slightly stronger than (BIBO).

EXERCISES

11.1. Irreversibility of production is defined as $Y \cap -Y = \{0\}$. Show that irreversibility of production implies (BIBO) if Y is a production set satisfying the first four properties of Definition 11.1.

In the following exercises, the first k *goods are inputs and the remaining* $\ell - k$ *goods outputs.*

11.2. The production set Y satisfies the properties of Definition 11.1. The set of feasible outputs $(y^{k+1}, \ldots, y^\ell)$ for the input vector $(y^1, \ldots, y^k) \in -\mathbb{R}^k_+$ is the set

$$P(y^1, \ldots, y^k) = \{(y^{k+1}, \ldots, y^\ell) \in \mathbb{R}^{\ell-k}_+ \mid (y^1, \ldots, y^k, y^{k+1}, \ldots, y^\ell) \in Y\}.$$

1) Show that $P(y^1, \ldots, y^k)$ is closed and convex for $(y^1, \ldots, y^k) \in -\mathbb{R}^k_+$.

2) Show that the vector $0 = (0, \ldots, 0) \in \mathbb{R}^{\ell-k}$ belongs to $P(y^1, \ldots, y^k)$ for $(y^1, \ldots, y^k) \in -\mathbb{R}^k_+$.

3) Show that the interior of $P(y^1, \ldots, y^k)$ is not empty for $(y^1, \ldots, y^k) \in -\mathbb{R}^k_{++}$ (all inputs are different from zero).

11.3. We assume that the production set Y satisfied irreversibility: $Y \cap -Y = \{0\}$. Show that the set $P(y^1, \ldots, y^k)$ is compact for $(y^1, \ldots, y^k) \in -\mathbb{R}^k_{++}$. (Hint: Prove that $P(y^1, \ldots, y^k)$ is bounded by showing that there is no direction of recession different from zero.)

11.4. Let h denote some output good: $k + 1 \le h \le \ell$. We denote by $pr_h : \mathbb{R}^\ell \to \mathbb{R}^{\ell-1}$ the projection map that associates with $y = (y^1, \ldots, y^{h-1}, y^h, y^{h+1}, \ldots, y^\ell)$ the vector $pr_h(y) = y^{-h} = (y^1, \ldots, y^{h-1}, y^{h+1}, \ldots, y^\ell)$. We simplify the notation by writing $y = (y^{-h}, y^h)$ though this is incorrect except in the case $h = \ell$. The set Y^{-h} is the image $pr_h(Y)$. 1) Show that the set Y^{-h} is a convex cone of $\mathbb{R}^{\ell-1}$ with vertex at the origin. 2) For every $y^{-h} = (y^1, \ldots, y^{h-1}, y^{h+1}, \ldots, y^\ell) \in Y^{-h}$, there exists a unique $y^h \ge 0$ such that $y = (y^{-h}, y^h)$ is efficient. (The h-th *good production function* $H_h : Y^{-h} \to \mathbb{R}$ of the firm with production set Y is defined by $H_h(y^{-h}) = y^h$.)

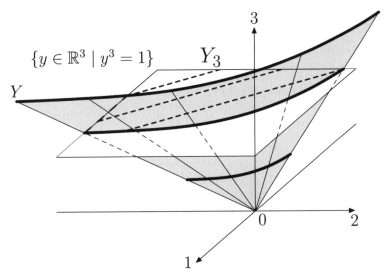

Figure 11.1 The production set of a constant returns firm with two inputs and one output

11.2.2 Vertex and Base of Production Sets

The production set Y is generated by its vertex and a base. The vertex of Y is the origin $0 \in \mathbb{R}^\ell$. The base of the cone Y can be any subset contained in a hyperplane that does not go through its vertex.

In practice, we arbitrarily pick some output good of the production process. There is no loss of generality in assuming that this good is the ℓ-th one which, incidentally, is also the numeraire though this plays no role here.

Definition 11.2. (Base of the production cone). *The base Y_ℓ of the cone Y is the set defined by the intersection*

$$Y_\ell = Y \cap \{y \in \mathbb{R}^\ell \mid y^\ell = 1\}$$

of the production cone Y with the hyperplane $\{y \in \mathbb{R}^\ell \mid y^\ell = 1\}$.

The cone Y consists of the points of the half-lines that go through the origin and the points of the base Y_ℓ. The cone Y is convex if and only if its base Y_ℓ is convex. In addition, the base Y_ℓ can be squeezed like all convex sets between two strictly convex (or even smoothly strictly) convex sets that are arbitrarily close, one set containing the set Y_ℓ and the other one contained in the set Y_ℓ. That very strong approximation property justifies making directly the assumption of smooth strict convexity for the base Y_ℓ. This parallels the assumptions made in the preceding chapters for the convex production sets of decreasing returns to scale firms.

11.3 THE NET SUPPLY CORRESPONDENCE

11.3.1 Definition

As in the previous chapters, we assume that the objective of the constant returns to scale firm is profit maximization subject to the technological feasibility constraint $y \in Y$. At variance with strict decreasing returns firms, the problem of profit maximization does not have a solution for all normalized price vectors $p \in S$. A simple reason is that the recession cone of the production set Y is the cone Y itself, a set that is strictly larger than $-\mathbb{R}_+^\ell$. (See remark 4, in section 9.3.6.)

In addition, we have also seen that the profit maximizing solution is not necessarily unique when it exists. It is therefore necessary to widen the definition of the net supply function to allow for the non existence or multiplicity of the profit maximizing solutions. This leads us to start by defining for arbitrary production sets Y the net supply correspondence:

Definition 11.3. *The firm's net supply correspondence* $\Gamma : S \to \mathbb{R}^\ell$ *associates with the price vector* $p \in S$ *the subset of* Y *consisting of the profit maximizing solutions.*

A correspondence is almost like a function except that it is not necessarily single-valued. A correspondence associates with every element of its domain a subset of its range. Here, the domain is the set of numeraire normalized prices S while the range is the production set Y. The value set of a correspondence may be empty or may contain more than one element. A function with the same domain and range would associate with every element of its domain **one and only one** element of the range.

Note that the range of the net supply correspondence Γ is the production set Y, itself a subset of the commodity space $\mathbb{R}^\ell$. It is possible to use $\mathbb{R}^\ell$ instead of Y for the range of the net supply correspondence. This may be convenient in a few instances. We then use the same notation for the net supply correspondence, whether its range is the production set Y or the commodity space $\mathbb{R}^\ell$.

11.3.2 The Normal Cone $Y^\perp$ to the Production Set Y

The introduction of the normal cone $Y^\perp$ to the cone Y will enable us to get much a clearer picture of the net supply correspondence of a firm operating under constant returns to scale.

Definition 11.4. *The normal cone $Y^\perp$ to the cone Y consists of the (non-normalized) vectors $p \in \mathbb{R}^\ell$ that satisfy the inequality $p \cdot y \leq 0$ for all $y \in Y$.*

Note that, in this definition, we use the same notation for an element of the normal cone and for price vectors. Nevertheless, at this stage, we impose no sign restrictions on the coordinates of that vector p in the normal cone $Y^\perp$ since that vector is not necessarily a price vector.

We have seen that a profit maximizing solution for a given a price vector p can exist only if there are no activities y giving a strictly positive profit $p \cdot y$. This means that the price vector p must then belong to the normal cone $Y^\perp$. Of particular interest for the net supply correspondence is the nature of the normal cone and of its boundary because, as we might expect, profit maximizing activities different from zero will exist only for prices at the boundary of the normal cone, not in its interior.

Proposition 11.5. *The normal cone $Y^\perp$ is convex.*

Proof. Let p and p' be in $Y^\perp$. For every $y \in Y$, we have $p \cdot y \leq 0$ and $p' \cdot y \leq 0$, from which follows $(p + p') \cdot y \leq 0$ and, therefore, $(p + p')/2 \cdot y \leq 0$ for any $y \in Y$. $\qquad\square$

Note that the normal cone $Y^\perp$ is convex even if the cone Y is not convex.

Proposition 11.6. *The normal cone $Y^\perp$ of the production set Y of a firm operating under constant returns to scale is a subset of $\mathbb{R}_+^\ell$.*

Proof. This follows from the inclusion $-\mathbb{R}_+^\ell \subset Y$. $\qquad\square$

11.3.3 The Interior of the Normal Cone $Y^\perp$

Proposition 11.7. *The vector $p \in Y^\perp$ belongs to the interior $\overset{o}{Y^\perp}$ of the normal cone $Y^\perp$ if and only if the strict inequality $p \cdot y < 0$ is satisfied for every $y \neq 0$ in Y.*

The condition is necessary. Let $p \in \overset{o}{Y^\perp}$ and assume that there exists $y \neq 0$ in Y with $p \cdot y = 0$. It then suffices to reduce (even slightly) the coordinate of the vector p (i.e., the price) of one input to get a vector

$p' \in \overset{\scriptstyle o}{\overset{\smile}{Y^{\perp}}}$ that makes the inner product $p' \cdot y$ strictly larger than $p \cdot y = 0$, a contradiction.

The condition is sufficient. Let $d(p, p')$ denote the Euclidean distance in $\mathbb{R}^{\ell}$. Let $S^{\ell} = \{y \in \mathbb{R}^{\ell} \mid d(y, 0) = 1\}$ denote the unit sphere of $\mathbb{R}^{\ell}$ centered at the origin. (Do not confuse the unit sphere S^{ℓ} with the price set S.) The unit sphere S^{ℓ} is a compact set as being a closed and bounded subset of $\mathbb{R}^{\ell}$. The intersection $Y \cap S^{\ell}$ is a closed subset of the compact sphere S^{ℓ} and is also compact. Assume that we have $p \cdot y < 0$ for all $y \neq 0$ in Y. By simply taking the vector $\frac{y}{d(y,0)}$, we can assume without loss of generality that the vector y belongs to the unit sphere S^{ℓ}.

Let us show that the strict inequality $p' \cdot y < 0$ is satisfied for all $y \in Y$ with p' in some open ball centered at p. We argue by contradiction. For any integer n, there exists a price vector $p^{(n)}$ and $y^{(n)} \in S^{\ell}$ such that $d(p, p^{(n)}) < 1/n$ and $p^{(n)} \cdot y^{(n)} \geq 0$. The sequence $y^{(n)}$ belongs to the compact $Y \cap S^{\ell}$. It has a subsequence that converges to a limit $y^* \neq 0$. It follows from the continuity of the inner product $(p, y) \to p \cdot y$ that at the limit we have $p \cdot y^* \geq 0$. This contradicts the assumption $p \cdot y^* < 0$. □

It follows from the proposition that the boundary $\partial Y^{\perp}$ consists of the price vectors $p \in S \cap Y^{\perp}$ for which there exists at least one activity vector $y \neq 0$ with $y \in Y$ such that $p \cdot y = 0$.

11.3.4 The Normal Base $Y_{\ell}^{\perp}$

With price vectors normalized by the numeraire convention $p_{\ell} = 1$, we define the base of the normal cone $Y^{\perp}$, or the **normal base**, as the set $Y_{\ell}^{\perp} = Y^{\perp} \cap S$. It consists of the numeraire normalized price vectors that belong to the normal cone $Y^{\perp}$. The nature of the profit maximizing solution depends on the location of the numeraire normalized price vector $p \in S$ relative to the normal base $Y_{\ell}^{\perp}$. The following characterization of the interior of the normal base $Y_{\ell}^{\perp}$ will be useful.

Proposition 11.8. *The price vector $p \in S$ belongs to the interior $\overset{\scriptstyle o}{\overset{\smile}{Y_{\ell}^{\perp}}}$ of the normal base $Y_{\ell}^{\perp}$ if the strict inequality $p \cdot y < 0$ is satisfied for every $y \neq 0$ in Y.*

Proof. It suffices to apply Proposition 11.7. □

11.3.5 Application to the Net Supply Correspondence

Proposition 11.9. *Let* $\Gamma : S \to \mathbb{R}^\ell$ *be the net supply correspondence of a smooth constant returns to scale firm. We have:*

- $\Gamma(p) = \emptyset$ *for* $p \notin Y_\ell^\perp$;
- $\Gamma(p) = \{0\}$, *the zero activity vector, for* $p \in \overset{o}{Y_\ell^\perp}$, *the interior of* $Y_\ell^\perp$;
- *The set* $\Gamma(p)$ *contains more than the zero element for* $p \in \partial Y_\ell^\perp$.

Proof. Let $p \in S$ that is not in the normal cone $Y^\perp$. Then, there exists $y \in Y$ such that $p \cdot y > 0$. Then, $p \cdot (\lambda y) = \lambda(p \cdot y)$ is strictly greater than $p \cdot y$ for $\lambda > 1$. This implies that the maximization problem cannot have a solution for that price vector $p \in S$, hence $\Gamma(p) = \emptyset$.

Let now $p \in \overset{o}{Y_\ell^\perp}$ be in the interior of the normal cone. The strict inequality $p \cdot y < 0$ is satisfied for any $y \neq 0$ in Y. This implies that the maximum of profit is reached only for the zero activity vector $y = 0 \in \mathbb{R}^\ell$, hence $\Gamma(p) = \{0\}$.

Now let p be in the boundary $\partial Y^\perp$ of the normal cone $Y^\perp$. By definition, there exists some activity vector $y \neq 0$ such that $p \cdot y = 0$. This activity vector y therefore maximizes the profit $p \cdot y$ as does the activity vector λy for $\lambda \geq 0$. ☐

11.4 THREE EXAMPLES

The goal of the following three examples is to give the reader some intuition for the net supply correspondence $\Gamma : S \to \mathbb{R}^\ell$ of Definition 11.13. The graph of that correspondence is a subset of $S \times \mathbb{R}^\ell$ denoted by Z.

11.4.1 Example 1

Assume $\ell = 2$. The production set Y consists of the activities $\{y = (y^1, y^2) \in \mathbb{R}^2 \mid y^1 \leq 0, y^2 \leq -\alpha y^1\}$ with $\alpha > 0$. Prices are normalized by the numeraire convention $p_2 = 1$. The base Y_2 of the production set Y consists of the activity vectors $y = (y^1, y^2)$ such that $y^2 = 1$ and $y^1 \leq -\frac{1}{\alpha}$. The boundary ∂Y_2 consists of the activity $y = (y^1, y^2) = (-\frac{1}{\alpha}, 1)$.

For $p_1 = \alpha$, all profit maximizing activities are of the form $\lambda(-\frac{1}{\alpha}, 1)$ for $\lambda \geq 0$. For $p_1 > \alpha$, the only profit maximizing activity is the zero activity.

The graph Z can therefore be identified to the set of pairs $(p_1, \lambda) \subset \mathbb{R}^2$ where $p_1 \geq \alpha$, $\lambda \geq 0$ and $(p_1 - \alpha)\lambda = 0$. This set is homeomorphic to $\mathbb{R}$.

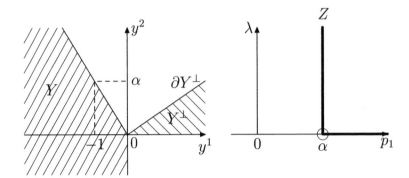

Figure 11.2 Case $\ell = 2$

11.4.2 Example 2

Assume $\ell = 3$. Goods 1 and 2 are inputs while 3 is the output. The production set Y is defined by

$$Y = \{y = (y^1, y^2, y^3) \in \mathbb{R}^3 \mid y^3 \leq \sqrt{y^1 y^2}, y^1 \leq 0, y^2 \leq 0\}.$$

The base Y_3 of the production set Y consists of the activity vectors $y = (y^1, y^2, y^3)$ such that $y^3 = 1$ and $y^1 y^2 \geq 1$ and y^1 and $y^2 \leq 0$. The boundary ∂Y_3 satisfies equation $\{y \in \mathbb{R}^3 \mid y^1 y^2 = 1, y^3 = 1, y^1 \leq 0, y^2 \leq 0\}$. It is a piece of the hyperbola $y^1 y^2 = 1$.

The normal cone $Y^\perp$ consists of the vectors $p = (p_1, p_2, p_3)$ in $\mathbb{R}^3_+$ that satisfy $4p_1 p_2 - p_3^2 \geq 0$. The normal base $Y_3^\perp$ consists of the (numeraire normalized) prices $p = (p_1, p_2, 1)$ that satisfy $4p_1 p_2 \geq 1$. The boundary $\partial Y_3^\perp$ is defined by equation $4p_1 p_2 = 1$ (and $p_3 = 1$). Associated with $p = (p_1, p_2, 1) \in \partial Y_3^\perp$ is the unique (normalized) profit maximizing activity $n_3(p_1, p_2, 1)$ equal to

$$n_3(p_1, p_2, 1) = (-2p_1, -2p_2, 1).$$

The graph Z can then be identified to the subset of $\mathbb{R}^2 \times \mathbb{R}$ consisting of the points (p_1, p_2, λ) satisfying

$$\begin{cases} \lambda(4p_1 p_2 - 1) = 0; \\ 4p_1 p_2 - 1 \geq 0; \\ p_1 > 0, p_2 > 0, \lambda \geq 0. \end{cases}$$

The set Z is not a smooth submanifold of $\mathbb{R}^3$. It is made of two smooth pieces: the vertical half-cylinder over the boundary $\partial Y_3^\perp$, that is, the

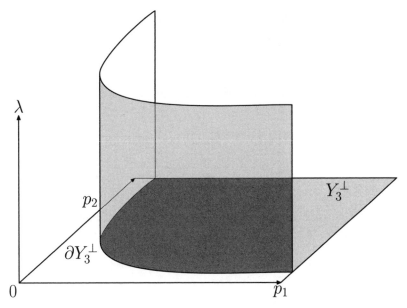

Figure 11.3 Graph Z of the supply function

branch of the hyperbola $4p_1p_2 = 1$ with $p_1 \geq 0$ and $p_2 \geq 0$ and the interior of that hyperbolic branch, the set $\{(p_1, p_2) \mid 4p_1p_2 \geq 1, p_1 > 0, p_2 > 0\}$. The set Z is homeomorphic (though not diffeomorphic) to $\mathbb{R}^2$.

11.4.3 Example 3

Assume $\ell = 3$. Good 1 is the only input while goods 2 and 3 are outputs. The production set Y is defined by

$$Y = \{y = (y^1, y^2, y^3) \in \mathbb{R}^3 \mid (y^2)^2 + (y^3)^2 \leq (y^1)^2, y^1 \leq 0, y^2 \geq 0, y^3 \geq 0\}.$$

The base Y_3 of the production set Y consists of the activity vectors $y = (y^1, y^2, y^3)$ such that $y^3 = 1$ and $(y^1)^2 - (y^2)^2 \geq 1$, $y^1 \leq 0$ and $y^2 \geq 0$. The boundary ∂Y_3 is defined by equation $y^2 = \sqrt{(y^1)^2 - 1}$ for $y^1 \leq 0$. This is a piece of the hyperbola defined by equation $(y^1 + y^2)(y^1 - y^2) = 1$.

The base $Y_3^\perp$ of the normal cone $Y^\perp$ is the set

$$Y_3^\perp = \left\{ (p_1, p_2, 1) \mid (p_2)^2 \leq \sqrt{(p_1)^2 - 1}, p_1 > 0, p_2 > 0 \right\}.$$

The boundary $\partial Y_3^\perp$ is defined by equation $p_2 = \sqrt{(p_1)^2 - 1}$, with $p_1 > 0$.

Associated with $p = (p_1, p_2, 1) \in \partial Y_3^{\perp}$ is the unique (normalized) profit maximizing activity $n_3(p_1, p_2, 1)$ equal to

$$n_3(p_1, p_2, 1) = (-p_1, p_2, 1).$$

The graph Z can then be identified to the subset of $\mathbb{R}^2 \times \mathbb{R}$ consisting of the points (p_1, p_2, λ) that satisfy

$$\begin{cases} \lambda((p_1)^2 - (p_2)^2 - 1) = 0; \\ (p_1)^2 - (p_2)^2 - 1 \geq 0; \\ p_1 > 0, p_2 > 0, \lambda \geq 0. \end{cases}$$

The set Z is made of two smooth pieces: the vertical half-cylinder over the boundary $\partial Y_3^{\perp}$ that is a piece of the hyperbola $(p_1)^2 = (p_2)^2 + 1$ and the interior of the convex set bounded by $\partial Y_3^{\perp}$. The set Z is again homeomorphic, but not diffeomorphic, to $\mathbb{R}^2$.

EXERCISES

11.5. Do the computations that underlie the three examples above.

11.6. Let Y be the production set of a firm with strict decreasing returns to scale. Show that the graph of the net supply function is homeomorphic to the price set S. Show that this homeomorphism is in fact a diffeomorphism for a firm with smooth decreasing returns.

11.5 NET SUPPLY CORRESPONDENCE OF A SMOOTH CONSTANT RETURNS TO SCALE FIRM

We can see in the three examples, and it is not difficult to prove in general, that the set $\Gamma(p) \cap Y_{\ell}$, the set of numeraire normalized profit maximizing activities, contains a unique element if the set $\partial Y_{\ell} = Y \cap \{y \in \mathbb{R}^{\ell} \mid y^{\ell} = 1\}$ bounds a strictly convex set.

Definition 11.10. *The normalized net supply function is the map $n_{\ell} : \partial Y_{\ell}^{\perp} \to \partial Y_{\ell}$ that associates with the price vector $p \in \partial Y_{\ell}^{\perp}$ the unique numeraire normalized profit maximizing activity $n_{\ell}(p)$ when the set ∂Y_{ℓ} bounds a strictly convex set.*

We now introduce simplifying assumptions about the boundary $\partial Y_{\ell}^{\perp}$ and the existence of normalized profit maximizing solutions $\{y \in Y \mid y^{\ell} = 1\}$ for prices belonging to this boundary.

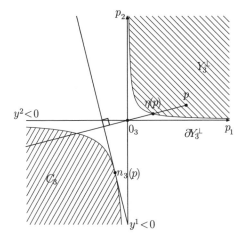

Figure 11.4 The normalized net supply function n_3 in example 2

Definition 11.11. *The firm operates under **strict** constant returns to scale if, in addition to previous properties regarding the production set Y, the boundary $\partial Y_\ell^\perp$ of the normal cone is homeomorphic to $\mathbb{R}^{\ell-2}$ and the map $n_\ell : \partial Y_\ell^\perp \to \partial Y_\ell$ is a homeomorphism.*

This definition is strengthened as follows by the introduction of smoothness:

Definition 11.12. *The firm operates under **smooth** constant returns to scale if, in addition to the properties of Definition 11.11, the boundary $\partial Y_\ell^\perp$ of the normal base $Y_\ell^\perp$ is diffeomorphic to $\mathbb{R}^{\ell-2}$ and the map $n_\ell : \partial Y_\ell^\perp \to \partial Y_\ell$ is a diffeomorphism.*

EXERCISES

11.7. Consider a firm with production set Y where: a) The set Y is a convex cone with vertex $0 \in \mathbb{R}^\ell$; b) The only output of the firm is good ℓ; c) All other $\ell - 1$ goods are inputs necessary to the production process. The production function of that firm is the function $y^\ell = H_\ell(y^1, \ldots, y^{\ell-1})$ such that $y = (y^1, \ldots, y^{\ell-1}, y^\ell)$ is efficient for given $\bar{y} = (y^1, \ldots, y^{\ell-1})$. 1) Show that H_ℓ is a concave function defined on $\mathbb{R}_{++}^{\ell-1}$ that is homogenous of degree one. 2) Show that $Y_\ell = \{y \in \mathbb{R}^\ell \mid H_\ell(y^1, \ldots, y^{\ell-1}) \geq 1\}$ is a convex set. 3) Show that the boundary of Y_ℓ is defined by equation $H_\ell(y^1, \ldots, y^{\ell-1}) = 1$. 4) Assume that H_ℓ is differentiable with first order partial derivatives $\neq 0$. Show that the boundary ∂Y_ℓ is a smooth hypersurface of the hyperplane $\{y \in \mathbb{R}^\ell \mid y^\ell = 1\}$. 5) Give a condition on the second order derivatives of H_ℓ that implies that the set ∂Y_ℓ bounds a strictly convex set. 6) Under that assumption implying strict convexity, show that, given any price system $(p_1, \ldots, p_{\ell-1}) \in \mathbb{R}^{\ell-1}$, there exists a unique price vector p_ℓ (not necessarily equal to 1) such that the firm's profit maximization problem has a solution made of collinear vectors $\lambda n_\ell(p)$, $\lambda \geq 0$, and $n_\ell(p) \in \partial Y_\ell$ uniquely determined by p. 7) Using the map n_ℓ, show that the boundary ∂Y_ℓ is homeomorphic to $\mathbb{R}^{\ell-2}$.

11.8. Show that if the set Y_ℓ is strictly convex, then there is at most one profit maximizing solution $y \in Y_\ell$ for $p \in \partial Y_\ell^\perp$.

11.9. Show that a constant returns to scale firm is smooth if the base Y_ℓ is strictly convex and its boundary is a smooth hypersurface with nonzero Gaussian curvature.

11.10. The production set Y of the linear activity production model is the non-negative linear combination of a finite number of activities a_t with $1 \leq t \leq T$. 1) Show that the production set Y is a convex polyhedron. 2) Show that the set $\Gamma(p)$ of $y \in Y$ that maximize $p \cdot y$ is a facet of the polyhedron Y.

11.6 THE GRAPH OF THE NET SUPPLY CORRESPONDENCE

11.6.1 Definition

The problems in applying the equilibrium manifold approach to the general equilibrium model with constant returns to scale firms will be overcome by substituting to the price set S a larger set, the graph of the net supply correspondence.

Definition 11.13. *The graph of the net supply correspondence Γ is the subset Z of $S \times Y$ that consists of the elements (p, y) such that y maximizes $p \cdot y$ subject to the constraint $y \in Y$.*

The main goal of this section is to get a global structure result for this set. For this, we need to find a convenient coordinate system for the points of the normal base $Y_\ell^\perp$.

11.6.2 Coordinate System for the Normal Base $Y_\ell^\perp$

Let 0_ℓ be the point with coordinates $(0, \ldots, 0, 1) \in \mathbb{R}^\ell$. This point plays the role of the origin of coordinates in the hyperplane $\{p = (p_1, \ldots, p_\ell) \in \mathbb{R}^\ell \mid p_\ell = 1\}$.

Let $p = (\bar{p}, 1) \in Y_\ell^\perp$ and $(\bar{n}_\ell(p), 1) = n_\ell(p)$.

Lemma 11.14. *The segment $[0_\ell, p]$ intersects the boundary $\partial Y_\ell^\perp$ at a unique point $\eta(p)$.*

Proof. For $p \in \partial Y_\ell^\perp$, let $y = n_\ell(p)$. From $p \cdot y = \bar{p} \cdot \bar{y} + 1 = 0$, we have $\bar{p} \cdot \bar{y} = -1$. Let $p' = (\lambda \bar{p}, 1)$ with $0 < \lambda < 1$. It follows that $p' \cdot y = \lambda \bar{p} \cdot \bar{y} + 1 = 1 - \lambda > 0$. This proves that all the interior points of the segment $[0_\ell, p]$ are not in $Y_\ell^\perp$ and, therefore, $\eta(p) = p$.

For $p \in \overset{o}{\widehat{Y^{\perp}_{\ell}}}$, let $y = n_{\ell}(p)$. The same line of reasoning as above shows that the segment $[0_{\ell}, p]$ intersects the boundary $\partial Y^{\perp}_{\ell}$ at the point $\left(\dfrac{1}{\lambda(p)} \bar{p}, 1 \right)$, where $\lambda(p) = -\bar{p} \cdot \bar{n}_{\ell}(p)$. □

Proposition 11.15. *The map* $Y^{\perp}_{\ell} \to \partial Y^{\perp}_{\ell} \times \mathbb{R}_+$ *defined by* $p \to (\eta(p), \lambda(p) - 1)$ *is a homeomorphism.*

Proof. That map is obviously a bijection, is continuous, and its inverse is continuous. □

The pair $(\eta(p), \lambda(p) - 1)$ can be used as a coordinate system for the points $p \in Y^{\perp}_{\ell}$. Note that if p is not in $Y^{\perp}_{\ell}$, we have no guarantee in general that the segment $[0_{\ell}, p]$ is going to intersect the boundary $\partial Y^{\perp}_{\ell}$.

We need to consider explicitly the inverse of the map $p \to (\eta(p), \lambda(p) - 1)$.

Definition 11.16. *The map* $\kappa : \partial Y^{\perp}_{\ell} \times \mathbb{R}_+ \to Y^{\perp}_{\ell}$ *is the inverse map of the map* $p \to (\eta(p), \lambda(p) - 1)$.

Corollary 11.17. *The normal base* $Y^{\perp}_{\ell}$ *is homeomorphic to* $\mathbb{R}^{\ell-2} \times \mathbb{R}_+$.

Proof. This follows from the homeomorphism of the boundary $\partial Y^{\perp}_{\ell}$ with $\mathbb{R}^{\ell-2}$. □

11.6.3 Homeomorphism of the Graph Z with a Euclidean Space

We now extend the global properties of the graph Z of the net supply correspondence of the three examples to the general case of a smooth constant returns to scale firm.

Proposition 11.18. *The graph* Z *of the net supply correspondence of a smooth constant returns to scale firm is homeomorphic to* $\mathbb{R}^{\ell-1}$.

Proof. The graph Z consists of the pairs $(p, y) \in Y^{\perp}_{\ell} \times Y$ where either $p \in \overset{o}{\widehat{Y^{\perp}_{\ell}}}$ and then $y = 0$, or $p \in \partial Y^{\perp}_{\ell}$ and $y = \lambda \, n_{\ell}(p)$ with $\lambda \geq 0$.

The graph Z can therefore be identified with the union of a vertical half-cylinder over the set $\partial Y_\ell^\perp$, the boundary of the normal base $Y_\ell^\perp$, with the normal base itself $Y_\ell^\perp$:

$$Z = \{(p, \lambda) \mid p \in \partial Y_\ell^\perp, \lambda \geq 0\} \cup \{(p, \lambda) \mid p \in Y_\ell^\perp, \lambda = 0\}.$$

Using the coordinate system for the normal base $Y_\ell^\perp$ given in Proposition 11.15, the map from $\partial Y_\ell^\perp \times \mathbb{R}$ into Z defined by

$$(p, \lambda) \rightarrow \begin{cases} (p, \lambda\, n_\ell(p)) & \text{for } \lambda \geq 0, \\ \kappa(p, 1 - \lambda) & \text{for } \lambda < 0, \end{cases}$$

is clearly continuous, bijective, with a continuous inverse. It is a homeomorphism. We conclude by observing that $\partial Y_\ell^\perp$ is homeomorphic to $\mathbb{R}^{\ell-2}$. $\qquad\square$

11.6.4 The Stratified Structure of the Graph Z

The picture of graph Z provided by Proposition 11.18 gets even clearer with the following explicit description of the components or, better, strata of that set. Let us define:

- $Z_0 = \{(p, y) \in Z \mid y = 0\}$;
- $Z_1 = \{(p, y) \in Z \mid p \in \partial Y_\ell^\perp\}$;
- $Z_{10} = Z_0 \cap Z_1$.

We then have:

Proposition 11.19.

- *The set Z_0 can be identified to the closed convex set $Y_\ell^\perp$ and is homeomorphic to $\mathbb{R}^{\ell-2} \times \mathbb{R}_+$;*
- *The set Z_1 can be identified to the half-cylinder $\partial Y_\ell^\perp \times \mathbb{R}_+$ and is homeomorphic to $\mathbb{R}^{\ell-2} \times \mathbb{R}_+$;*
- *The set Z_{10} can be identified to the boundary $\partial Y_\ell^\perp$ and is diffeomorphic to $\mathbb{R}^{\ell-2}$.*
- $Z = Z_0 \cup Z_1$.

Proof. This is obvious. $\qquad\square$

The set Z is known as a stratified set. It is made of two full dimensional strata, the sets Z_0 and Z_1 that are both smooth manifolds with boundary. Their boundary is the set Z_{10}, itself a smooth submanifold of Z_0 and Z_1. The set Z_{10} is also considered to be a stratum of the set Z.

11.7 CONCLUSION

We now have a clear picture of the behavior of a smooth firm under constant returns to scale. This picture will help us to include firms operating under constant returns to scale into the general equilibrium model.

11.8 NOTES AND COMMENTS

The first part of this chapter about production cones is standard.

The focus placed in this chapter on the graph of the net supply correspondence as a way to study the properties of the general equilibrium model with constant returns to scale firms is new.

CHAPTER 12

Equilibrium with Constant Returns

12.1 INTRODUCTION

This chapter is devoted to the study of an equilibrium model where privately owned firms feature either smooth decreasing or constant returns to scale. Profit of the constant returns to scale firms being equal to zero at equilibrium, the equilibrium of the model does not depend on the ownership structure of these firms. In addition, the convex conical production sets of these firms sum up into a convex cone. It is as if the production sector operating under constant returns consists of a unique firm. The general equilibrium model with decreasing and constant returns to scale firms is essentially the same model as the one considered in chapter 10 with the addition of a unique firm operating under constant returns to scale.

Nevertheless, this addition is enough to hamstring the approach of the preceding chapters based on the concept of price system that equates aggregate supply and demand. The solution is to add to that price system the activity of the constant returns to scale firm. That richer concept of equilibrium will enable us to follow essentially the same paths as for the exchange model and the production model with privately owned strictly decreasing returns to scale production. As a consequence, the equilibrium model with constant and decreasing returns to scale firms has essentially the same properties as the exchange model or the equilibrium model with decreasing returns firms.

12.2 DECREASING AND CONSTANT RETURNS: GENERAL CASE

As in chapter 10, the model $\mathcal{M}$ is made in part of m consumers and n smoothly decreasing returns to scale firms. Consumer i is characterized by a demand function $f_i : S \times \mathbb{R} \to \mathbb{R}^\ell$ and an endowment vector $\omega_i \in \mathbb{R}^\ell$. The decreasing returns to scale firm j is defined by its net supply function $g_j : S \to \mathbb{R}^\ell$. The ownership structure $\theta = (\theta_{ij})$ of these firms is exogenously given and fixed. In addition to these consumers and firms, there is a finite number of smooth constant returns to scale firms. As profit maximization for these firms means zero profit, their ownership structure has no effect on the equilibrium of the model and does not need to be specified.

An economy in the model $\mathcal{M}$ is identified to its endowment parameter $\omega = (\omega_i) \in \Omega$, all other characteristics such as demand functions, production sets, or supply functions and ownership structure being fixed. This is summed up in the following:

Definition 12.1. *The general equilibrium model $\mathcal{M}$ with constant and decreasing returns to scale production consists of finite numbers of consumers, of privately owned firms operating under decreasing returns to scale, and of firms operating under constant returns to scale.*

Consumers and firms satisfy the assumptions of the previous chapters. In addition we assume that the aggregate production set, i.e., the sum of all individual production sets satisfy BIBO (bounded inputs, bounded outputs).

12.3 CONSTANT RETURNS: REDUCED FORM

Our goal is to reduce the study of the general version of the model $\mathcal{M}$ to a special and simpler case where there are no smooth decreasing returns to scale firms and just one smooth constant returns to scale firm.

We have seen in chapter 10 how to adjust consumers' demand functions for the activity of the smooth decreasing returns firms that they own. This operation does not depend on the existence or non-existence of constant returns to scale firms. The resulting model contains only consumers and constant returns to scale firms.

The production sets of the constant returns to scale firms are convex cones. The aggregate production set is the sum of these convex cones and is also a convex cone. In addition, this cone carries all the properties that are associated with constant returns to scale firms except possibly smoothness. (The aggregate production set may fail to be smooth even if the individual production sets are smooth because the sum of smooth convex sets is not necessarily smooth.) Nevertheless, convex sets can be approximated or, better, squeezed between two arbitrarily close smooth convex sets. Thanks to this approximation property, there is no significant loss of generality in assuming that the aggregate production set Y is the production set of a smooth constant returns to scale firm as defined in the previous chapter. This unique firm in the model $\mathcal{N}$ carries no subscript.

Definition 12.2. *The production model $\mathcal{N}$ consists of a finite number m of consumers and of a unique constant returns to scale firm.*

Consumer i, with $1 \leq i \leq m$, is characterized by a demand function h_i : $S \times \mathbb{R} \to \mathbb{R}^\ell$. The firm is characterized by its production set Y with which are associated the base Y_ℓ, its boundary ∂Y_ℓ, the normal base $Y_\ell^\perp$, and its boundary $\partial Y_\ell^\perp$. The normalized activity map $n_\ell : \partial Y_\ell^\perp \subset S \to \partial Y_\ell$ associates with the price vector $p \in \partial Y_\ell^\perp$ the normalized profit maximizing activity for that price vector p. The map n_ℓ is a diffeomorphism.

Recall that $\Gamma : S \to \mathbb{R}^\ell$ denotes the net supply correspondence of the constant returns to scale firm and Z its graph, which is identified to a subset of $S \times Y$.

The rest of this chapter is devoted to the definition of a suitable equilibrium concept for the model $\mathcal{N}$ and to the study of this equilibrium concept along the lines of the equilibrium manifold approach.

12.4 EQUILIBRIA OF THE MODEL $\mathcal{N}$

The fact that the net supply correspondence $\Gamma : S \to \mathbb{R}^\ell$ associated with the strict constant returns to scale firm is a correspondence and not a function is a complicating factor for the direct application of the equilibrium manifold approach. We are therefore going to substitute to the price set S the graph Z of the net supply correspondence.

Definition 12.3. *The element* $z = (p, y) \in Z$ *is an* **equilibrium price-activity vector** *of the economy characterized by the endowment vector* $\omega \in \Omega$ *in the model* $\mathcal{N}$ *if equation*

$$\sum_i h_i(p, p \cdot \omega_i) = \sum_i \omega_i + y \tag{1}$$

is satisfied.

This definition expresses the equality of aggregate demand and aggregate supply net of productive activities. It extends Definition 4.5 of the equilibrium price vector for an exchange economy and Definition 10.1 for an economy with decreasing returns to scale production.

12.5 THE EQUILIBRIUM MANIFOLD APPROACH

The program is to study how the equilibrium price-activity vector $z = (p, y) \in Z$ depends on the endowment vector ω when the latter is varied in the parameter space Ω. As we did with exchange economies, we combine into one single element the parameter $\omega \in \Omega$ defining the economy and its equilibrium price-activity vector $z \in Z$.

Definition 12.4. *The element $(z, \omega) \in Z \times \Omega$ is an **equilibrium** of the model $\mathcal{N}$ if $z \in Z$ is an equilibrium price-activity vector associated with the economy ω.*

Definition 12.5. *The equilibrium manifold E of the model $\mathcal{N}$ is the subset of $Z \times \Omega$ consisting of the equilibria $(z, \omega) \in Z \times \Omega$ in the sense of Definition 12.4.*

In other words, the equilibrium manifold E is the subset of $Z \times \Omega$ that is defined by equation

$$\sum_i h_i(p, p \cdot \omega_i) = \sum_i \omega_i + y. \tag{2}$$

The relation between the equilibrium price-activity vector $z \in Z$ and the economy $\omega \in \Omega$ is then captured by the natural projection. Its definition parallels the exchange model.

Definition 12.6. *The natural projection for the model $\mathcal{N}$ is the map $\pi : E \to \Omega$ that is the restriction to the equilibrium manifold E of the projection map $Z \times \Omega \to \Omega$.*

The equilibrium analysis of the model $\mathcal{N}$ can now follow essentially the same path as in the previous chapters: 1) Study of the equilibrium manifold E; 2) Study of the natural projection $\pi : E \to \Omega$.

12.6 THE EQUILIBRIUM MANIFOLD FOR THE MODEL $\mathcal{N}$

Despite its name of equilibrium manifold, the set E **is not a smooth manifold** or a smooth submanifold of $Z \times \Omega$. But its structure is not that bad either. In fact, the equilibrium manifold is a set known as a stratified set, i.e., a set "stratified" into smooth manifolds. We have already seen in the previous chapter that the graph Z of the net supply correspondence of the smooth constant returns to scale firm is a stratified set. It is in fact that stratification that carries over to the equilibrium manifold E. This stratification is also interesting from an economic perspective because it is related to the existence or non-existence of a productive activity of the constant returns to scale production sector of the economy.

12.6.1 A Typology for the Equilibria of $\mathcal{N}$

Definition 12.7. *Let $z = (p, y) \in Z$.*

(i) The equilibrium (z, ω) is of type 0 whenever $y = 0$ (no productive activity);

(ii) The equilibrium (z, ω) is of type 1 whenever $p \in \partial Y_\ell^\perp$ (possibility of non zero productive activity);

(iii) The equilibrium (z, ω) is of type 10 if it is both of type 0 and 1.

We denote by E_0, E_1, and E_{10} the subsets of the equilibrium manifold E consisting of the type 0, type 1, and type 10 equilibria respectively.

Note that an equilibrium of type 10 is simultaneously of type 0 and 1. Such equilibrium is a *transition equilibrium* in the sense that a continuous path in the equilibrium manifold E going from some type 0 equilibrium with no productive activity to a type 1 equilibrium with productive activity will cross a type 10 equilibrium at some point and vice versa.

Let $\mathcal{E}$ denote the exchange model made of the m consumers in the model $\mathcal{N}$. The following proposition offers us an interesting interpretation of the type 0 equilibria:

Proposition 12.8. *Let $((p, y), \omega) \in Z$ be an equilibrium in the model $\mathcal{N}$. It is a type 0 equilibrium if and only if $(p, \omega) \in S \times \Omega$ is an equilibrium of the model $\mathcal{E}$.*

Proof. This is obvious. ∎

The type 0 equilibria are indeed the equilibria of an exchange economy since there is no production at equilibrium.

12.6.2 A Global Coordinate System for the Equilibrium Manifold

Recall that we denote by $\bar{\omega}_i = (\omega_i^1, \ldots, \omega_i^{\ell-1}) \in \mathbb{R}^{\ell-1}$ and $\bar{p} = (p_1, \ldots, p_{\ell-1})$ the components made of the first $\ell - 1$ coordinates of ω_i and p respectively.

Define the map

$$\psi : Z \times \mathbb{R}^m \times \mathbb{R}^{(\ell-1)(m-1)} \to Z \times \mathbb{R}^{\ell m}$$

by

$$\psi(z, (w_1, \ldots, w_{m-1}, w_m), \bar{\omega}_1, \ldots, \bar{\omega}_{m-1}) = (z, (\omega_1, \ldots, \omega_m)),$$

where ω_i^ℓ is determined by

$$\omega_i^\ell = w_i - \bar{p} \cdot \bar{\omega}_i \tag{3}$$

for i varying from 1 up to $m - 1$ and ω_m by the equality

$$\omega_m = \sum_{i=1}^{m} h_i(p, w_i) - \sum_{i=1}^{m-1} \omega_i - y. \tag{4}$$

Proposition 12.9. *The image of the map ψ is the equilibrium manifold E. The map ψ then defines a homeomorphism between E and $Z \times \mathbb{R}^m \times \mathbb{R}^{(\ell-1)(m-1)}$.*

Proof. It suffices to reproduce the proof of Proposition 5.8. □

It is quite remarkable that this proof is almost word for word similar to the exchange model proof. The map ψ is a homeomorphism instead of a diffeomorphism because of the lack of differentiability over $Z_{10} \times \mathbb{R}^m \times \mathbb{R}^{(\ell-1)(m-1)}$.

Corollary 12.10. *A set of global coordinates for the equilibrium manifold E is given by $\left(z, (w_1, \ldots, w_m), \bar{\omega}_1, \ldots, \bar{\omega}_{m-1}\right) \in Z \times \mathbb{R}^m \times (\mathbb{R}^{\ell-1})^{m-1}$.*

Corollary 12.11. *The equilibrium manifold E is homeomorphic to $\mathbb{R}^{\ell m}$.*

Proof. It suffices to observe that $Z \times \mathbb{R}^m \times \mathbb{R}^{(\ell-1)(m-1)}$ is homeomorphic to the equilibrium manifold E by Proposition 12.9 and that Z is homeomorphic to $\mathbb{R}^{\ell-1}$ by Proposition 11.18. □

12.6.3 The Stratified Structure of the Equilibrium Manifold

The stratified structure of the equilibrium manifold E in smooth submanifolds then follows readily from the following:

Proposition 12.12.

(i) *The restriction of the map ψ to $Z_0 \times \mathbb{R}^m \times \mathbb{R}^{(\ell-1)(m-1)}$ is smooth and is a diffeomorphism with E_0;*

(ii) *The restriction of the map ψ to $Z_1 \times \mathbb{R}^m \times \mathbb{R}^{(\ell-1)(m-1)}$ is smooth and is a diffeomorphism with E_1;*

(iii) *The restriction of the map ψ to $Z_{10} \times \mathbb{R}^m \times \mathbb{R}^{(\ell-1)(m-1)}$ is smooth and is a diffeomorphism with E_{10}.*

Proof. This is obvious. □

Corollary 12.13.

(i) E_0 is a smooth manifold with boundary E_{10} diffeomorphic to $\mathbb{R}^{\ell m-1} \times \mathbb{R}_+$;
(ii) E_1 is a smooth manifold with boundary E_{10} diffeomorphic to $\mathbb{R}^{\ell m-1} \times \mathbb{R}_+$;
(iii) E_{10} is a smooth manifold (without boundary) diffeomorphic to $\mathbb{R}^{\ell m-1}$.

The equilibrium manifold E is not a smooth manifold because of lack of differentiability at the points of E_{10}. Nevertheless, the stratified structure defined by the three smooth manifolds E_0, E_1, and E_{10} will suffice for the application of differentiability to the natural projection, the map $\pi : E \to \Omega$.

WHERE ARE THE FIBERS?

One may wonder where the fibers of the equilibrium manifold of the exchange model have gone. They played such a crucial role in unlocking the properties of the equilibrium model in the previous chapters so that, without them or their analog, the study of the equilibrium manifold of the model $\mathcal{N}$ is likely to become much more difficult if not impossible.

The fibers are still there. They are just hidden by the direct formulation of a global coordinate system for the equilibrium manifold E that has been adopted here. This is to be compared to the more pedestrian and intuitive approach to the exchange model where we derived the coordinate system from the picture of the equilibrium manifold as a collection of linear fibers parameterized by the no-trade equilibria. Here, we have followed a more direct route by starting right away with the global coordinate system. With the homeomorphism defined by the map $\psi : Z \times \mathbb{R}^m \times \mathbb{R}^{(\ell-1)(m-1)} \to Z \times \mathbb{R}^{\ell m}$, the fiber of the equilibrium manifold E associated with the price-activity vector $z = (p, y) \in Z$ and the income vector $(w_1, \ldots, w_m)$ is simply the image of the map

$$\psi\big(z, (w_1, \ldots, w_m), \cdot\big) : \mathbb{R}^{(\ell-1)(m-1)} \to E.$$

12.6.4 The No-trade Equilibria for the Model $\mathcal{N}$

We now extend to the production model $\mathcal{N}$ the definition of a no-trade equilibrium. This definition parallels the one for the model with (strictly) decreasing returns to scale production in the sense that individual demands are adjusted for the production activity. In other words, a no-trade equilibrium means that there is no trade at equilibrium but does not mean that there is no production. This observation is particularly important with the constant returns to scale firms because such firms can very well choose inactivity at equilibrium.

Definition 12.14. *The equilibrium* $(z, \omega) \in Z \times \Omega$ *where* $z = (p, y)$ *and* $\omega = (\omega_1, \ldots, \omega_m)$ *is a no-trade equilibrium for the model* $\mathcal{N}$

if $\omega_i = h_i(p, w_i) + y_i$ with $(p, y_i) \in Z$ for $1 \le i \le m$ and $\sum_i y_i = y$. We denote by T the set of no-trade equilibria.

For $y = 0$, there is no production activity by the unique firm. Then, the no-trade equilibrium (z, ω) satisfies the equality $\omega_i = h_i(p, w_i) + y_i$ with $y_i = 0$ for $1 \le i \le m$. We recognize the definition of a no-trade equilibrium for the exchange model.

For a fixed price-activity vector $z = (p, y) \in Z$ and some wealth distribution $w = (w_1, \ldots, w_m) \in \mathbb{R}^m$, the no-trade equilibrium $((p, y), \omega)$ where $\omega_i = h_i(p, w_i) + y_i$ is parameterized by the vector $(y_1, \ldots, y_m)$ such that $y_i \ge 0$ and $\sum_i y_i = y$. These no-trade equilibria all belong to the fiber associated with $(z, (w_1, \ldots, w_m))$ and, at variance with the exchange model, there is therefore more than one no-trade equilibrium in the fibers that are associated with non-zero productive activities. The structure of the no-trade equilibria in such fibers is then given by:

Proposition 12.15. *The set of no-trade equilibria $T(z, (w_1, \ldots, w_m))$ associated with $(z, (w_1, \ldots, w_m))$ is a m-simplex for $y \ne 0$. (Recall that $z = (p, y) \in Z$.)*

Proof. Given $(z, (w_1, \ldots, w_m))$, the associated no-trade equilibrium (z, ω) satisfies $\omega_i = h_i(p, w_i) + y_i$ for $1 \le i \le m$. The activity vector $y_i = \omega_i - h_i(p, w_i)$ is collinear with $y \in Y$. There exists $\lambda = (\lambda_i)$ in the m-dimensional simplex $\{\lambda \in \mathbb{R}^m \mid \sum_i \lambda_i = 1, \lambda_i \ge 0\}$ such that $y_i = \lambda_i y$. We then have $\omega = (\omega_1, \ldots, \omega_m) = (h_1(p, w_1), \ldots, h_m(p, w_m)) + (\lambda_1, \ldots, \lambda_m)y$. The no-trade equilibria are therefore the elements of the m-simplex with vertices $(h_1(p, w_1), \ldots, h_m(p, w_m)) + (0, \ldots, 0, 1, 0, \ldots, 0) y$, with 1 at the i-th coordinate and $1 \le i \le m$. □

This leads us to highlight the center of the simplex $T(z, (w_1, \ldots, w_m))$ for $y \ne 0$.

Definition 12.16. *The no-trade equilibrium $((p, y), \omega) \in Z \times \Omega$ is **symmetric** if $\omega_i = h_i(p, w_i) + y_i$ where $y_1 = \cdots = y_m = y/m$. Let T_s denote the set of symmetric no-trade equilibria.*

Proposition 12.17. *The set of symmetric no-trade equilibria T_s is homeomorphic to $Z \times \mathbb{R}^m$.*

Proof. Consider the map from $\theta : Z \times \mathbb{R}^m \to Z \times \Omega$ defined by

$$\theta((p, y), (w_i)) = \left((p, y), h_i(p, w_i) + \frac{1}{m} y \right)$$

and the map $\phi : T \to Z \times \mathbb{R}^m$ defined by

$$\phi\big((p, y), (\omega_i)\big) = \big((p, y), (p \cdot \omega_i)\big).$$

These maps are obviously continuous. We conclude by observing that $\theta(Z \times \mathbb{R}^m) = T_s$, the set of symmetric no-trade equilibria, and $\phi \circ \theta = \mathrm{id}_{Z \times \mathbb{R}^m}$ and $\theta \circ \phi = \mathrm{id}_{T_s}$. □

Corollary 12.18. *The set of symmetric no-trade equilibria T_s is homeomorphic to $\mathbb{R}^{\ell+m-1}$.*

Proof. This follows from the homeomorphism of Z with $\mathbb{R}^{\ell-1}$ by Proposition 11.18. □

12.6.5 The Volume Element for the Equilibrium Manifold

A first application of the stratified structure of the equilibrium manifold E is the identification of a volume element (or measure) on that set. This part requires some familiarity with the concept of volume element for Riemannian manifolds and details can be skipped in a first reading.

The two strata E_0 and E_1 are submanifolds with boundaries of dimension ℓm of $Z_0 \times \mathbb{R}^{\ell m}$ and $Z_1 \times \mathbb{R}^{\ell m}$ respectively. These two manifolds E_0 and E_1 are subsets of $S \times \mathbb{R}^\ell \times \mathbb{R}^{\ell m}$ and, therefore, are equipped with the Euclidean length (or distance) of that space. That length element defines a measure or volume element on each submanifold E_0 and E_1, a measure that is the analog for these submanifolds of the Lebesgue measure in Euclidean spaces. In addition, these measures coincide on the submanifold that is their intersection, namely $E_{10} = E_0 \cap E_1$. This construction therefore defines a unique measure μ, or volume element, on the equilibrium full manifold $E = E_0 \cup E_1$.

Proposition 12.19. *The set of transition equilibria E_{10} is a closed subset with measure (or volume) zero in the equilibrium manifold E.*

Proof. Closedness is obvious. In addition, the set E_{10} of transition equilibria is a smooth submanifold of codimension one in both E_0 and E_1. It has therefore a measure $\mu(E_{10})$ equal to zero in both smooth manifolds E_0 and E_1 and, therefore, in the equilibrium manifold E. □

12.7 THE NATURAL PROJECTION

12.7.1 Smoothness

The natural projection $\pi : E \to \Omega$ cannot be a smooth map all over its domain because the equilibrium manifold E is not a smooth manifold. But the two subsets E_0 and E_1 that make up the equilibrium manifold E are smooth manifolds. This leads us to:

Proposition 12.20. *The natural projection is smooth on the subset* $E \setminus E_{10}$.

Proof. This follows from the fact that the interior sets $\overset{0}{\widehat{E_0}}$ and $\overset{0}{\widehat{E_1}}$ are both smooth open submanifolds $Z_0 \times \Omega$ and $Z_1 \times \Omega$ respectively. $\qquad\square$

12.7.2 Properness

The most crucial ingredient in the study of the natural projection in the exchange model is its properness, namely that the preimage of every compact set is compact.

Proposition 12.21. *The natural projection* $\pi : E \to \Omega$ *associated with the production model* $\mathcal{N}$ *is proper.*

Proof. The properness property is proved here for the model $\mathcal{M}$ where the decreasing returns to scale firms are explicitly considered even if the constant returns to scale firm is still unique. The reason is due to the fact that, just as in the production model without constant returns to scale firms, properness requires only property (BIBO) (i.e., bounded inputs, bounded outputs in the sense of Definition 10.12) for the aggregate production set.

Let K be a compact subset of Ω. Closedness of $\pi^{-1}(K)$ follows readily from the continuity of the natural projection.

Let $(z^q, \omega^q) \in \pi^{-1}(K)$ where $z^q = (p^q, y^q) \in Z$ is a sequence in $\pi^{-1}(K)$. It suffices that we show that this sequence has a convergent subsequence. Since K is compact, there is no loss in generality in considering a subsequence such that ω^q converges to some $\omega^* \in K$ and the price sequence p^q of $z^q = (p^q, y^q)$ to some $p^* \in \overline{S_\Sigma}$ where $\overline{S_\Sigma} = \{p = (p_j) \in \mathbb{R}_+^\ell \mid \sum_j p_j = 1\}$ is the closed price simplex, itself a compact set. (Note that we switch between the numeraire and the simplex normalization whenever this is convenient; the same notation is used for the price vector in both cases.)

The equilibrium (z^q, ω^q) in the model $\mathcal{M}$ satisfies the equation

$$\sum_i f_i(p^q, p^q \cdot \omega_i^q + p^q \cdot \gamma_i(p^q)) = \sum_i \omega_i^q + \sum_j g_j(p^q) + y^q$$

where $g_j(p^q)$ represents the net supply of the decreasing returns to scale firm j, and $\gamma_i(p^q)$ consumer i's virtual production activity from Definition 10.2.

It follows from the definition of the sequence (z^q, ω^q) that the value of the inner product $p^q \cdot \omega_i^q$ is bounded. In addition, the profit $p^q \cdot \gamma_i(p^q)$ is greater than or equal to 0. This implies that the wealth $p^q \cdot (\omega_i^q + \gamma_i(p^q))$ is bounded from below. It then follows from the property of boundedness from below (property (B) of Definition 3.14) that there exists $B_i \in \mathbb{R}^\ell$ such that the inequality

$$B_i \leq f_i(p^q, p^q \cdot \omega_i^q + p^q \cdot \gamma_i(p^q)) \tag{5}$$

is satisfied for every q and i.

The sequence $\sum_i \omega_i^q$ is also bounded from above by some $A \in \mathbb{R}^\ell$. This implies that the inequality

$$\sum_i B_i \leq \sum_i f_i(p^q, p^q \cdot \omega_i^q + p^q \cdot \gamma_i(p^q)) \leq A + \sum_j g_j(p^q) + y^q \tag{6}$$

is satisfied for all q. This inequality implies that the sequence $\sum_j g_j(p^q) + y^q$ is bounded from below.

Since $\sum_j g_j(p^q) + y^q$ belongs to the aggregate production set $\sum_j Y_j + Y$, a set that satisfies (BIBO), the sequence $\sum_j g_j(p^q) + y^q$ is also bounded from above. It then follows from inequality (6) that the sequence $\sum_i f_i(p^q, p^q \cdot \omega_i^q + p^q \cdot \gamma_i(p^q))$ is also bounded from above. This is incompatible with desirability (A) that is satisfied by at least one demand function since $(f_i) \in \mathcal{E}_c$. □

12.8 REGULAR AND CRITICAL EQUILIBRIA

12.8.1 Definition

The restriction of the natural projection to the open subset $E \backslash E_{10}$ is smooth. We can therefore define a critical point for this map in the usual way: the point (z, ω) is critical if the tangent map $T_{(z,\omega)}\pi$ to the natural projection $\pi : E \backslash E_{10} \to \Omega$ at the point (z, ω) is not onto. This leads us to define a critical equilibrium as:

Definition 12.22. *The equilibrium* $(z, \omega) \in E$ *is critical if it is either a type 10 equilibrium (i.e.,* $(z, \omega) \in E_{10}$*) or if it is a critical point of the restriction of the natural projection to* $E \backslash E_{10}$*.*

We denote by $\mathfrak{S}$ the set of critical equilibria. We also denote by $\mathfrak{S}_0$ (resp. $\mathfrak{S}_1$) the subset that consists of the critical equilibria that belong to $E_0 \backslash E_{10}$ (resp. $E_1 \backslash E_{10}$).

An equilibrium is regular if it is not critical. Therefore, the set of regular equilibria is a subset $\mathfrak{R}$ of $E \backslash E_{10}$. We denote by $\mathfrak{R}_0$ and $\mathfrak{R}_1$ the sets of regular equilibria of type 0 and of type 1 respectively.

12.8.2 Regularity of the No-trade Equilibria

Proposition 12.23. *Every no-trade equilibrium that is not of type 10 is regular.*

Proof. Let $(z, \omega) \in E$ be an equilibrium of type 0 that is not of type 10, i.e., $y = 0$ and $p \in \overset{o}{Y_\ell^\perp}$ where $z = (p, y)$. This equilibrium is regular if and only if it is regular as an equilibrium of the exchange model made of the m consumers. It then suffices to apply the property that the no-trade equilibria of the exchange model are regular to prove that the type 0 no-trade equilibria that are not of type 10 are also regular for the model $\mathcal{N}$.

Let $(z, \omega) \in E$ be an equilibrium of type 1 that is not of type 10, i.e., $y \neq 0$ and $p \in \partial Y_\ell^\perp$. Then, the price vector p is a (locally defined) smooth function $p(\bar{y})$ of $\bar{y} \in \mathbb{R}^{\ell-1}$ where $p(\bar{y}) = -DH_\ell(\bar{y})$ and $y^\ell = H_\ell(\bar{y})$ is the ℓ-th production function of the constant returns to scale firm. The expression $DH_\ell(\bar{y})$ is the gradient or vector of first order derivatives of the production function H_ℓ at the point $\bar{y}$.

Let $\bar{y} \to F(\bar{y}) = \sum_i h_i(p(\bar{y}), p(\bar{y}) \cdot \omega_i) - y - \sum_i \omega_i \in \mathbb{R}^\ell$ denote the aggregate excess demand function. Let $\bar{F}(\bar{y})$ denote the first $\ell - 1$ coordinates of $F(\bar{y})$. The equilibrium (z, ω) is regular if and only if the Jacobian matrix $\dfrac{D\bar{F}}{D\bar{y}}(z, \omega)$ is invertible. We have

$$\frac{D\bar{F}}{D\bar{y}}(z, \omega) = \sum_i \frac{D\bar{h}_i}{D\bar{y}} - I$$

where I is the identity matrix. The application of the chain rule gives us

$$\sum_i \frac{D\bar{h}_i}{D\bar{y}} = \left(\sum_i \frac{D\bar{h}_i}{Dp} \right) \left(\frac{Dp}{D\bar{y}}(\bar{y}) \right).$$

At a no-trade equilibrium, the matrices $\dfrac{D\bar{h}_i}{Dp}$ are negative definite as being individual Slutsky matrices; their sum is negative definite. Matrix $\dfrac{Dp}{D\bar{y}}(\bar{y})$ is equal to $-\dfrac{D^2 H_\ell}{D\bar{y}^2}(\bar{y})$ and is negative definite by the smooth strict convexity of the base Y_ℓ of the production set Y. This implies that matrix $\sum_i \dfrac{D\bar{h}_i}{D\bar{y}}$ is invertible. $\qquad\square$

Remark 5. The fact that a type 10 no-trade equilibrium is critical is essentially an artifact of our definition of criticality that includes the type 10 equilibria. In the current setup, this is not too important because the set E_{10} of type 10 equilibria is closed with measure zero in the equilibrium manifold E.

Remark 6. The regularity of the no-trade equilibria needs the negative definiteness of the individual Slutsky matrices, not their symmetry. In other words, individual preferences do not have to be transitive.

12.8.3 Genericity of Regular Equilibria

Proposition 12.24. *The set of regular equilibria $\mathfrak{R}$ is an open subset with full measure of the equilibrium manifold E .*

Proof. We give only a quick sketch of the proof because it parallels the proof of Proposition 8.10.

Step 1. Using the expression of the natural projection in terms of the global coordinate system for the equilibrium manifold E, we observe that the set of critical equilibria $\mathfrak{S}(z, (w_1, \ldots, w_m))$ in the fiber associated with $(z, (w_1, \ldots, w_m)) \in (Z \setminus Z_{10}) \times \mathbb{R}^m$ given is defined by a polynomial equation. This set is therefore a semi-algebraic set.

Step 2. The semi-algebraic set $\mathfrak{S}(z, (w_1, \ldots, w_m))$ is the union of a finite family of smooth manifolds in the fiber. The main point is to show that the dimension of these submanifolds is strictly less than the dimension $(\ell - 1)(m - 1)$ of the fiber. Assume that there are strata of dimension $(\ell - 1)(m - 1)$: each full-dimensional stratum has a non-empty interior. This implies that the polynomial function whose zeros are the critical equilibria is equal to zero on some non empty open set and is therefore identically equal to zero over the full fiber. This implies that the no-trade equilibria of the fiber are also critical, a contradiction with Proposition 12.23.

Step 3. The set of critical equilibria $\mathfrak{S}(z, (w_1, \ldots, w_m))$ has therefore measure zero in the fiber associated with $(z, (w_1, \ldots, w_m)) \in (Z \setminus Z_{10}) \times \mathbb{R}^m$.

Step 4. It follows from Fubini's theorem on integration by parts that the measure of the set of critical equilibria $\mathfrak{S} = E_{10} \cup \mathfrak{S}_0 \cup \mathfrak{S}_1$ is equal to the integral

$$\int_{(z,(w_1,\ldots,w_m))\in(Z\setminus Z_{10})\times\mathbb{R}^m} \mu(\mathfrak{S}(z, (w_1, \ldots, w_m))) d\mu,$$

hence to zero. □

Corollary 12.25. *The set of critical equilibria $\mathfrak{S}$ is a closed subset of measure zero of the equilibrium manifold E.*

Proof. The set of critical equilibria S is the complement in E of the set of regular equilibria $\mathcal{R}$ that is open with full measure. □

12.9 Degrees of the Natural Projection

The proof of the following proposition exploits properties of the degree of a proper map that are usually handled by techniques of algebraic topology. However, Milnor's approach through differential topology can also be used in this set up with minor adaptations. The proof can be skipped in a first reading.

Proposition 12.26. *The modulo 2 degree and the Brouwer degree are defined for the natural projection $\pi : E \to \Omega$.*

Proof. The argument goes as follows. The natural projection is a map from E into Ω. The domain E is homeomorphic to, and the range Ω, equal to $\mathbb{R}^{\ell m}$. In addition, the map $\pi : E \to \Omega$ is proper. The Alexandroff's compactification of $\mathbb{R}^{\ell m}$ (this amounts to adjoining a point at infinity to $\mathbb{R}^{\ell m}$, namely the point $\{\infty\}$) is the sphere $S^{\ell m}$. The proper map $\pi : E \to \Omega$ has then a continuous extension $\tilde{\pi} : E \cup \{\infty\} \to \Omega \cup \{\infty\}$ to the Alexandroff's compactifications of E and Ω. That extension is also such that $\tilde{\pi}(\{\infty\}) = \{\infty\}$. We are therefore reduced to a continuous map from a sphere into itself. Degrees, the modulo 2 degree and the topological degree, are then defined for such maps by looking at the cohomology groups of the sphere. □

The fact that $\tilde{\pi}^{-1}(\infty) = \{\infty\}$ plays no role in the definition of the degree of the extended map $\tilde{\pi}$. This property will become crucial when interpreting the degree of $\tilde{\pi}$ in terms of the number of elements, signed or non-signed, in the preimage $\pi^{-1}(\omega)$ of suitably chosen elements $\omega \in \Omega$. The value of the modulo 2 and Brouwer degrees of the natural projection will be computed in section 12.13.

12.10 REGULAR AND SINGULAR ECONOMIES

12.10.1 A Property of the Volume Element of the Equilibrium Manifold

The following proposition tells us that the volume element of the equilibrium manifold cannot increase by taking its image by the natural projection. The proof of that property can be skipped in a first reading. Indeed, we do not need such a strong version of this property in order to show that the set of singular economies has measure zero.

Proposition 12.27. *Let λ be the Lebesgue measure on Ω and μ the volume element on the equilibrium manifold E. For any compact subset K of the equilibrium manifold E, the inequality $\lambda(\pi(K)) \leq \mu(K)$ is satisfied.*

Proof. The natural projection $\pi : E \to \Omega$ can be identified to the restriction to E of the orthogonal projection from $(S \times \mathbb{R}^\ell) \times \Omega$ to Ω. Orthogonal projections do not increase length. Therefore, the volume element does not increase through orthogonal projection, which implies the inequality $\lambda(\pi(K)) \leq \mu(K)$. □

12.10.2 The Set of Singular Economies S

Proposition 12.28. *The image $\pi(E_{10})$ of the set of transition equilibria by the natural projection is a closed subset of measure zero in Ω.*

Proof. It follows from the properness of the natural projection that the image of a closed set is closed. Therefore $\pi(E_{10})$ is closed in Ω. In addition, the set E_{10} has its volume equal to zero in the equilibrium manifold E. It then follows from Proposition 12.19 that its image has measure zero in Ω. □

Definition 12.29. *The set of singular economies S is the image by the natural projection of the set of critical equilibria of type 0 and 1 and of the set E_{10} of transition equilibria.*

In other words, $S = \pi(\mathfrak{S}_0) \cup \pi(\mathfrak{S}_1) \cup \pi(E_{10})$.

Proposition 12.30. *The set of singular economies S is contained in a closed subset of with measure zero in Ω.*

Proof. The closure in E of the sets of critical equilibria $\mathfrak{S}_0$ and $\mathfrak{S}_1$ have measure zero in the equilibrium manifold E. The closed set E_{10} has also measure zero. The images of these three sets by the natural projection are closed since π is proper. In addition, they have measure zero by Proposition 12.27. This implies that the set S is contained in a closed set with measure zero. $\qquad\square$

Remark 7. Proposition 12.30 could also be proved by the direct application of Sard's theorem to the natural projection restricted to E_0 and E_1 respectively.

12.10.3 The Set of Regular Economies $\mathcal{R}$

Definition 12.31. *The economy ω is regular if it is not singular. Let $\mathcal{R}$ denote the set of regular economies.*

Proposition 12.32. *The set of regular economies $\mathcal{R}$ contains an open subset of Ω with full measure in Ω.*

Proof. The set of regular economies $\mathcal{R}$ is the complement in Ω of the set of singular economies S, a closed set with measure zero. $\qquad\square$

12.11 UNIQUENESS OF EQUILIBRIUM OVER $\pi(T)$

Proposition 12.33. *Equilibrium is unique for every $\omega \in \pi(T)$.*

Proof. By definition, we have $\omega_i = h_i(p, p \cdot \omega_i) + y_i$ for $1 \leq i \leq m$. We argue by contradiction. Let $z' = (p', y') \neq z = (p, y) \in Z$ such that

$$\sum_i h_i(p', p' \cdot \omega_i) = \sum_i \omega_i + y'.$$

First, let us assume $p' = p$. Then, the above equality implies

$$\sum_i h_i(p, p \cdot \omega_i) = \sum_i \omega_i + y',$$

which is to be compared to

$$\sum_i \omega_i = \sum_i (h_i(p, p \cdot \omega_i) + y_i) = \sum_i h_i(p, p \cdot \omega_i) + \sum_i y_i.$$

It then follows that $y' = \sum_i y_i = y$ so that $z' = z$, a contradiction.

Let $p' \neq p$. The price vector p' belonging to $Y_\ell^\perp$ and y_i to the cone Y, then $p' \cdot y_i \leq 0$. Taking the inner product of the equality

$$h_i(p, p \cdot \omega_i) = \omega_i + y_i$$

by the price vector p' yields the inequality

$$p' \cdot h_i(p, p \cdot \omega_i) \leq p' \cdot \omega_i.$$

The strict inequality

$$p \cdot h_i(p', p' \cdot \omega_i) > p \cdot \omega_i$$

then follows from (WARP). Adding up all these strict inequalities yields

$$p \cdot \sum_i h_i(p', p' \cdot \omega_i) > p \cdot \sum_i \omega_i;$$

hence

$$p \cdot \left(\sum_i \omega_i + y' \right) > p \cdot \sum_i \omega_i,$$

which implies in turn the strict inequality

$$p \cdot y' > 0,$$

a contradiction with the assumption that p belongs to the normal cone $Y^\perp$ to the production set Y. □

Remark 8. This proof is just the extension to the equilibria of the model $\mathcal{N}$ (with a smooth constant returns firm) of the uniqueness of equilibrium for ω being an equilibrium allocation of the exchange model $\mathcal{E}_c$. It includes as a special case the uniqueness of equilibrium when ω is the projection of a no-trade equilibrium of the exchange model $\mathcal{E}_c$.

12.12 THE NATURAL PROJECTION AS A FINITE COVERING OF THE SET OF REGULAR ECONOMIES

Proposition 12.34. *The natural projection $\pi : E \to \Omega$ defines a covering of the set of regular economies.*

Proof. This is obvious given the developments of the previous chapters. □

It is difficult to illustrate Proposition 12.34 by accurate pictures because the dimension of the parameter space Ω is equal to $m \times \ell$, a number that is greater than or equal to $2 \times 2 = 4$ when total resources are variable. Fixing total resources (which we haven't done in this book) as in the Edgeworth box reduces this minimal dimension to 2. Then, with two goods and, therefore, a price set S with numeraire normalized price vectors having dimension one, it is possible to come up with a three-dimensional representation of the equilibrium manifold E and of the natural projection $\pi : E \to \Omega$. Here, the price-activity set Z is still homeomorphic to $\mathbb{R}$ but its representation as $z = (p, y)$ involves both the price vector p and the activity vector y, which puts us into a two-dimensional space and $2 + 2 = 4$, not very easy to represent by a picture.

An accurate picture of the equilibrium manifold E and the parameter space Ω requires us to restrict the parameter space Ω to one dimension. This can be done by having endowments in some line in the plane of the Edgeworth box. The following picture is a three-dimensional representation of such a situation. It illustrates the stratified structure of the equilibrium manifold E and also the possibility of multiple equilibria, several type-zero equilibria coexisting with a type-one equilibrium.

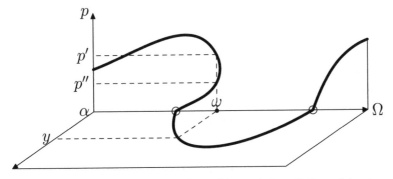

Figure 12.1 Equilibrium manifold with equilibria $(p', 0)$, $(p'', 0)$, and (α, y) associated with $\omega \in \Omega$

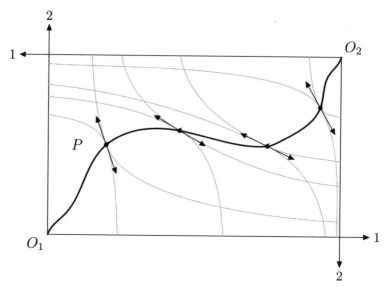

Figure 12.2 The standard Edgeworth box and its set of Pareto optima

The following pictures show us how the standard Edgeworth box representation of a two-good two-consumer economy with fixed total resources is modified by the introduction of a constant returns to scale firm.

In the first picture, consumers' preferences are represented by the usual indifference curves found in all textbooks (and consumption restricted to be positive). The set of Pareto optima is the set of points where the indifference curves are tangent to one another. The budget lines are defined by these common tangent lines at the Pareto optima.

The firm with production set Y operates under constant returns to scale in the case of one input (good 1) and one output (good 2) if $Y = \{(y^1, y^2) \in \mathbb{R}^2 \mid \alpha y^2 \leq -y^1, y^1 \leq 0, \alpha > 0\}$. The efficient boundary of Y is the line $y^2 = -\alpha y^1$. The set $Y_2^{\perp}$ is the set $\{(p_1, 1) \in \mathbb{R}^2 \mid p_1 \geq \alpha\}$. This eliminates from the picture of the Edgeworth box in the exchange case the budget lines associated with price vectors $(p_1, 1)$ where $p_1 < \alpha$. Instead, we have budget lines that are perpendicular to the price vector $(\alpha, 1)$. Consumers' indifference curves are generally tangent to these lines in different points, a difference that represents the activity y of the constant returns to scale firm.

The Pareto optima, i.e., the points of the contract curve that are still equilibrium allocations after the introduction of the constant returns to scale firm are those with supporting price vector $p = (p_1, 1)$ with $p_1 \geq \alpha$. Those that satisfy $p_1 < \alpha$ are in regions where the Engel curve of the

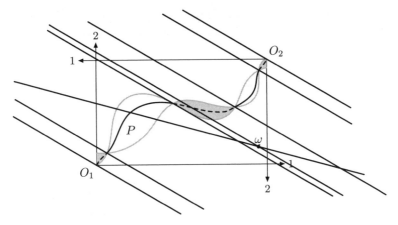

Figure 12.3 The Edgeworth box with production and its budget lines

first consumer is below the Engel curve of the second consumer. These regions are colored in gray in figure 12.3. Endowments ω in those gray areas have a unique equilibrium, actually a no-trade equilibrium.

Note that in the case of two goods, $\ell = 2$, an economy can have at most one type-one equilibrium (i.e., with productive activity). It can easily be seen that this peculiarity of the two-good case does not extend to a larger number of goods where multiple type-one equilibria can be associated with the same economy.

12.13 VALUES OF THE NATURAL PROJECTION DEGREES

Proposition 12.35. *The degree modulo 2 degree of the natural projection is equal to one.*

Proof. We have seen that degrees can be defined for the natural projection. We now have a way of computing them. It suffices to pick a regular economy ω that is the projection of a no-trade equilibrium (z, ω) of type zero. Since this no-trade equilibrium is regular for the natural projection restricted to E_0, ω is a regular economy and the preimage $\pi^{-1}(\omega)$ contains only one element. $\square$

Proposition 12.36. *Let $\omega \in \mathcal{R}$. The number of equilibria $\#\pi^{-1}(\omega)$ is odd. This number is locally constant and constant over every pathconnected component of $\mathcal{R}$.*

Proof. This follows from the modulo two degree of the natural projection being equal to one combined with the covering defined by the natural projection. □

Remark 9. We could compute by the same technique the topological or Brouwer degree of the natural projection $\pi : E \to \Omega$.

12.14 CONCLUSION

The general picture of an equilibrium model with firms operating under smooth decreasing and constant returns to scale remains essentially the same as for the exchange model with the central role played by the intensity of exchange as a factor explaining the properties of equilibria.

Therefore the properties of this model go a long way beyond the generic finiteness and continuity of equilibria or the homeomorphism of the equilibrium manifold with a Euclidean space. The role played by the intensity of trade at equilibrium as a cause for discontinuities of productive activity is a new and important result. By the same token and contrary to some old beliefs, the existence of production with constant returns to scale does not prevent by itself the possibility of multiple equilibria if there are more than two goods.

12.15 NOTES AND COMMENTS

The definition of an index for the special case of the linear activity model appears in [40]. The first statement and proof of Proposition 12.34 for economies with firms operating under smooth constant returns to scale is from Mas-Colell [46].

All the other properties developed in this chapter are new.

Postscript

THE TOPICALITY OF THE STANDARD MODEL

The general equilibrium model studied in this book, a model that we can call the standard model, offers us a description of modern economies with their competitive markets and firms that is sufficiently general to be economically relevant without being too complex to make its study intractable. Many simpler models exist, but their relevance is doubtful at best because those models are too simplistic. There also exist models that are more complex than the standard model, but these models are so difficult to study that not many of their properties have been identified.

The standard model has been around for quite some time. It was first formulated by Walras almost 150 years ago [67]. It is the unique subject of Debreu's quintessential book published 50 years ago [23]. All graduate textbooks in microeconomics devote their first chapters to the standard model. One could expect the standard model to have become history. Nevertheless, the standard model is still the workhorse of many applications of economic theory. Welfare economics in general, and cost-benefit analysis in particular, rely on considerations formulated within the set-up of the standard model. Models dealing with taxation are minor variations on the standard model. The computable general equilibrium models developed during the last 20 years directly apply the standard model to planning and development issues in real-world economies. The topicality of the standard model has never been higher and justifies the thorough study of its properties.

BEYOND THE EQUILIBRIUM MANIFOLD APPROACH

The study of the standard model in this book has followed the equilibrium manifold approach. This approach has given us a remarkable picture of the relations between market (equilibrium) prices and the fundamentals of the economy. Such a picture was not available a generation ago. Despite the success of the equilibrium manifold approach, we should not forget that there are often multiple ways to extract information from an equation system. For example, there are at least three approaches to classical mechanics: Newton's laws of motion, Lagrangian mechanics, and Hamiltonian mechanics. Some properties are captured more easily through one approach than through another. The situation is similar with the standard model. There is an alternative approach to the equilibrium manifold approach. It starts by interpreting the solution set of the equilibrium equation as the intersection of two smooth manifolds. One of these manifolds is linear and depends only on the endowment parameter that characterizes an economy in the model. The other manifold is fixed because it is independent of the endowment parameter and it captures the most treacherous part of the equilibrium equation, its non-linearities. This explains the fruitfulness of this alternative approach in questions dealing with the number of equilibria for example. For original sources, see [15] and [16]. For applications to the theory of economic fluctuations, see [18].

Putting the Standard Model in Perspective

The study of the mathematical properties of the standard model would be incomplete if that model were not put in perspective. Of particular interest is the place of the model in the history of economic models and ideas. Walras' original treatise [67, 68] and his correspondence [37] make excellent background readings. Schumpeter's panorama of the ideas that led to the development of the standard model remains to this day unsurpassed [60] (see especially chapter 7, *Equilibrium Analysis,* pp. 951–1073). The evolution of the standard model towards the more complex second-generation models is already perceivable in the two major books by Hicks and Samuelson [33, 55].

Applying the Standard Model to Second-generation General Equilibrium Models

The second-generation models that have appeared during the last 50 or 60 years retain the main aspects of the standard model such as preference maximization under budget constraints and production subject to technological feasibility. But they generally offer a more detailed and specific treatment of time and uncertainty. For example, in the overlapping-generations model, consumers have finite lifespans in an infinitely lived economy. In the temporary equilibrium model markets are open for only some of the goods, and economic agents have to substitute forecasts to actual market prices for the goods for which no markets are open. In models with asset markets, economic agents face multiple budget constraints reflecting the complex nature of the risk they are facing.

A very active field of economic theory deals with the study of these complex second-generation models. Their equation systems have many similarities with the equilibrium equation of the standard model, which is hardly surprising, a proximity that explains that the properties of the second-generation models can sometimes be inferred from those of the standard model. Skills acquired in the study of the standard general equilibrium model are then invaluable. In addition and quite remarkably, properties that have no analog in the standard model are often derived from purely mathematical properties of the standard general equilibrium model. Study of these second-generation models would be almost impossible without a thorough understanding of the standard model.

Notation

A.1 POINTS, VECTORS, INNER PRODUCT

The point $x = (x^1, x^2, \ldots, x^\ell) \in \mathbb{R}^\ell$ is identified with the vector with the same coordinates. In matrix notation, the point (or vector) x is represented by default by a column matrix.

A.1.1 Inner Product of Two Vectors

The inner product of the vectors x and y is written indifferently as $x \cdot y$ (vector notation) or as $x^T y = y^T x$ (matrix notation).

A.2 GRADIENT

The gradient vector of the smooth function $u_i : \mathbb{R}^\ell \to \mathbb{R}$ at x_i is denoted by $Du_i(x_i)$. In matrix form, it is the column matrix

$$Du_i(x_i) = \begin{bmatrix} \dfrac{\partial u_i}{\partial x^1}(x_i) \\ \vdots \\ \dfrac{\partial u_i}{\partial x^\ell}(x_i) \end{bmatrix}. \tag{1}$$

A.2.1 Normalized Gradient

The definition of the normalized gradient reflects the choice of the numeraire normalization by $p_\ell = 1$.

The normalized gradient vector of the smooth function u_i at x_i is denoted by $D_n u_i(x_i)$ and is equal to

$$D_n u_i(x_i) = \frac{1}{\dfrac{\partial u_i}{\partial x^\ell}(x_i)} \, Du_i(x_i). \tag{2}$$

The ℓ-th coordinate of the normalized gradient vector $D_n u_i(x_i)$ is equal to 1.

The gradient and normalized gradient vectors $Du_i(x_i)$ and $D_n u_i(x_i)$ are collinear.

A.3 SECOND-ORDER DERIVATIVES AND THE HESSIAN MATRIX OF A SMOOTH FUNCTION

A.3.1 Definition of the Hessian Matrix

The Hessian matrix of the smooth function $u_i : \mathbb{R}^\ell \to \mathbb{R}$ at $x_i \in \mathbb{R}^\ell$ is the square $\ell \times \ell$ matrix denoted by $D^2 u_i(x_i)$ whose coefficients are the second order derivatives of the function u_i at x_i:

$$D^2 u_i(x_i) = \begin{bmatrix} \dfrac{\partial^2 u_i}{(\partial x^1)^2} & \cdots & \dfrac{\partial^2 u_i}{\partial x^1 \partial x^k} & \cdots & \dfrac{\partial^2 u_i}{\partial x^1 \partial x^\ell} \\ \vdots & \cdots & \vdots & \cdots & \vdots \\ \dfrac{\partial^2 u_i}{\partial x^h \partial x^1} & \cdots & \dfrac{\partial^2 u_i}{\partial x^h \partial x^k} & \cdots & \dfrac{\partial^2 u_i}{\partial x^h \partial x^\ell} \\ \vdots & \cdots & \vdots & \cdots & \vdots \\ \dfrac{\partial^2 u_i}{\partial x^\ell \partial x^1} & \cdots & \dfrac{\partial^2 u_i}{\partial x^\ell \partial x^k} & \cdots & \dfrac{\partial^2 u_i}{(\partial x^\ell)^2} \end{bmatrix}.$$

The Hessian matrix $D^2 u_i(x_i)$ is symmetric.

If the function u_i is concave (quasi-concave is not sufficient for that!) or strictly concave, then the Hessian matrix is everywhere negative semi-definite. Conversely, the Hessian matrix has to be negative definite in order for the function u_i to be strictly concave.

Point-set Topology

The following properties of point-set topology are used in various places of the main text.

B.1 PROPER MAPS

Definition B.1. *Let X and Y be two metric spaces. The continuous map $f : X \to Y$ is proper if the preimage $f^{-1}(K)$ of every compact set K is compact.*

Proposition B.2. *Let $f : X \to Y$ be a proper map. Then the direct image of every closed subset of X is closed in Y.*

Proof. Let F be a closed subset of X. Let $y^0 = \lim_{q \to \infty} y^q$ where y^q belongs to $f(F)$. There exists therefore some $x^q \in F$ such that $y^q = f(x^q)$, with $q \geq 1$. It also follows from the definition of a convergent sequence that the set $K = \{y^0\} \cup (\bigcup_q \{y^q\})$ is compact. Therefore, the preimage $f^{-1}(K)$ is compact. The sequence (x^q) belongs to the compact set $f^{-1}(K)$. There exists a subsequence that converges to some $x^0 \in f^{-1}(K)$. From now on, we consider only this subsequence. The limit x^0 of the sequence (x^q) belongs to F since F is closed. The continuity of f implies

$$f(x^0) = \lim_{q \to \infty} f(x^q) = \lim_{q \to \infty} y^q = y^0,$$

which proves that y^0 belongs to F. $\qquad\square$

Smooth Manifolds

C.1 THE IMPLICIT FUNCTION THEOREM

Theorem C.1. *Let* (f_i) *be a collection of* n *real-valued functions defined in a neighborhood* $U \times V$ *of the point* $(x^*, y^*) = (x_1^*, \ldots, x_k^*, y_1^*, \ldots, y_n^*)$ *in* $\mathbb{R}^k \times \mathbb{R}^n$. *The functions* f_i *are smooth,* $f_i(x^*, y^*) = 0$ *for* $1 \leq i \leq n$ *and the Jacobian matrix* $\left[\dfrac{\partial f_i}{\partial y_j} \right]_{1 \leq i, j \leq n}$ *is invertible at* (x^*, y^*). *Then, there exists an open neighborhood* $W_0 \subset U$ *of* x^* *such that, for every open, connected neighborhood* $W \subset W_0$ *of* x^*, *there exists a unique system of* n *smooth real-valued functions* $g_i(x) = y_i$ *defined on* W, *continuous, and such that* $g_i(x^*) = y_i^*$ *for* $1 \leq i \leq n$ *and*

$$f_i(x, g_1(x), \ldots, g_n(x)) = 0.$$

The implicit function theorem holds true if the assumption of smoothness for the functions f_i is replaced by r-times continuous differentiability, with $r \geq 1$, or by analyticity.

For a proof, see [28], (10.2.1).

C.2 SMOOTH MANIFOLDS AND SUBMANIFOLDS

The subset $X \subset \mathbb{R}^N$ is a *smooth manifold* of dimension n if every $x \in X$ possesses a neighborhood $W \cap X$ that is diffeomorphic to the Euclidean space $\mathbb{R}^n$. Any diffeomorphism $g : \mathbb{R}^n \to W \cap X$ is called a *parameterization* of the domain $W \cap X$. The open set $W \cap X$ is known as a chart of X at the point x and the coordinates of $\mathbb{R}^n$ as defining a local coordinate system.

If X and Z are two manifolds embedded in $\mathbb{R}^N$ and satisfying $Z \subset X$, then Z is a *submanifold* of X. As a special case, the manifold X is itself a submanifold of X. Every open subset of X is a submanifold of X. If Z is a submanifold of X, the codimension of Z in X is, by definition, equal to $\dim X - \dim Z$.

C.3 SMOOTH MAPPINGS, IMMERSIONS, AND SUBMERSIONS

Let $f: X \to Y$. Let $y = f(x)$, with $x \in U$ and $y \in V$ where U and V are charts of X and Y. Using the local coordinates defined by these charts, the open sets U and V can be identified to $\mathbb{R}^p$ and $\mathbb{R}^q$ respectively and the map f to a smooth map $f: \mathbb{R}^p \to \mathbb{R}^q$. The Jacobian matrix Df_x of that map at the point x defines a linear map (also denoted by Df_x) from $\mathbb{R}^p$ to $\mathbb{R}^q$.

C.3.1 Immersions

Definition C.2. *The map $f: X \to Y$ is an immersion at $x \in X$ if Df_x is an injection, i.e., is one-to-one. If f is an immersion at every point $x \in X$, f is an immersion.*

C.3.2 Embeddings

Definition C.3. *An embedding $f: X \to Y$ is an immersion that is both injective and proper.*

The following property is an obvious consequence of the definition:

Proposition C.4. *An embedding is an immersion that is also a homeomorphism between its domain and its image.*

Proposition C.5. *Let $f: X \to Y$ be an embedding. The image $f(X)$ is a submanifold of Y that is diffeomorphic to X by the map f.*

Proof. See [29], Proposition (16.8.4). □

Lemma C.6. *Let $\varphi: X \to Y$ and $\psi: Y \to X$ be two smooth maps between smooth manifolds such that the composition $\phi \circ \psi: Y \to Y$ is the identity map id_Y. Then, the set $Z = \psi(Y)$, the image of the map ψ, is a smooth submanifold of X that is diffeomorphic to Y.*

Proof. The strategy is to show that the map $\psi: Y \to X$ is an embedding. This will then imply that its image Z is a submanifold of X diffeomorphic to Y. We have therefore to show that ψ is an immersion and a homeomorphism between its domain and its image.

To prove the homeomorphism property, we first observe that ψ viewed as a map from Y to $Z = \psi(Y)$ is onto. From $\varphi \circ \psi = \mathrm{id}_Y$ follows that ψ is also an injection, hence a bijection. Let $\varphi \mid Z$ denote the restriction of φ to Z. The relation $\varphi \circ \psi = \mathrm{id}_Y$ implies $(\varphi \mid Z) \circ \psi = \mathrm{id}_Y$; with ψ

being a bijection between Y and Z, its inverse map is therefore equal to $\varphi \mid Z$. The definition of the induced topology of Z implies that the maps $\varphi \mid Z : Z \to Y$ and $\psi : Y \to Z$ are continuous as a consequence of the continuity of the maps $\varphi : X \to Y$ and $\psi : Y \to X$.

To prove the immersion, pick $y \in Y$. The relation $\varphi \circ \psi = \mathrm{id}_Y$ yields, by taking the derivative maps, the relation

$$D_{\psi(y)}\varphi \circ D_y\psi = \mathrm{id}_{T_y(Y)},$$

where $T_y(Y)$ denotes the tangent space to the manifold Y at y. Therefore, the linear map between the tangent spaces $D_y\psi : T_y(Y) \to T_{\psi(y)}(X)$ is an injection. □

C.3.3 Submersions

Definition C.7. *The map $f : X \to Y$ is a submersion at $x \in X$ if Df_x is a surjection, i.e., is onto. The map f is a submersion if it is a submersion at every point $x \in X$.*

Singularities of Smooth Maps

D.1 CRITICAL AND REGULAR POINTS

Let $f: X \to Y$ be a smooth map between two smooth manifolds X and Y, with $\dim X = p$ and $\dim Y = q$. Let $x \in X$ be given and let $y = f(x)$. There exist open subsets U and V of X and Y such that $x \in U$, $y \in V$ and $f(U) \subset V$. In addition, these subsets are diffeomorphic to $\mathbb{R}^p$ and $\mathbb{R}^q$ respectively.

The diffeomorphisms of U with $\mathbb{R}^p$ and V with $\mathbb{R}^q$ define so-called local coordinate systems for X and Y at x and y respectively. Using these local coordinates, the map f restricted to the open set U becomes represented by q real-valued functions of p real variables. The derivative of that map is then the Jacobian matrix of these q real-valued functions with respect to their p real variables. This is a $q \times p$ matrix with q rows and p columns. We denote this matrix by Df_x.

Definition D.1. *The point $x \in X$ is regular if the Jacobian matrix of $f: X \to Y$ at x is onto. The point $x \in X$ is critical if it is not regular.*

If $x \in X$ is regular, the rank of the Jacobian matrix Df_x is equal to q, the dimension of Y. A critical point is characterized by the rank of Df_x that is strictly less than q.

Proposition D.2. *The set of critical points of $f: X \to Y$ is closed.*

Proof. This is obvious. ☐

Corollary D.3. *The set of regular points of $f: X \to Y$ is open.*

D.2 SINGULAR AND REGULAR VALUES

Definition D.4. *The point $y \in Y$ is a singular value of the smooth map $f: X \to Y$ if it is the image of a critical point.*

Therefore, if y is singular, there exists some $x \in X$ such that $f(x) = y$ and x is a critical point of the map f.

Definition D.5. *The point $y \in Y$ is a regular value of the smooth map $f : X \to Y$ if it is NOT a singular value.*

It follows from this definition that a "regular value" $y \in Y$ of the map $f : X \to Y$ is not necessarily a "value" of that map in the sense that the preimage $f^{-1}(y)$ may very well be empty at a regular value.

D.3 SARD'S THEOREM

There are no general theorems about the structure of the set of critical points of a smooth map except that of being a closed set. This set can be the empty set or the full set. The situation is very different with the set of singular values.

Proposition D.6. (Sard) *The set of singular values Σ of a smooth map $f : X \to Y$ has measure zero.*

Proof. See, e.g., [48], pp. 16–19, or [32], pp. 202–207 or [29], section 16.23. □

D.4 THE REGULAR VALUE THEOREM

Proposition D.7. *Let $f : X \to Y$ be a smooth map between smooth manifolds. Let $y \in Y$ be a regular value of f. Then, the preimage $f^{-1}(y)$ is a smooth submanifold of X, with $\dim f^{-1}(y) = \dim X - \dim Y$.*

Proof. See for example, [48], Lemma 1 of chapter 2, p. 11 or [32], chapter 1, p. 21. □

D.5 THE CASE WHERE $\dim X = \dim Y$

D.5.1 Inverse Mapping Theorem
We now assume $\dim X = \dim Y$.

Proposition D.8. (Inverse function theorem) *Let $f : X \to Y$ and $x \in X$ be a regular point of X. Then, there exists an open neighborhood U of x such that $V = f(U)$ is an open subset of Y (with $y = f(x) \in V$) and the restriction $f \mid U$ defines a diffeomorphism between U and V.*

Proof. See [28], Proposition (10.3.1). □

Often, the inverse mapping theorem is used in the following form. Let $x \in X$ be such that the linear map defined by the Jacobian matrix Df_x for some local coordinate system is invertible. Then, the map f is actually a local diffeomorphism. In other words, the "invertibility" of the linearized form of the map f implies the local "invertibility" of the map f itself.

D.6 COVERINGS

D.6.1 Fibrations

Definition D.9. *A fibration is a triple* (X, B, p) *where X and B are smooth manifolds, p is a* surjective *smooth map from X onto B that satisfies the following "local triviality" condition:*
For every $b \in B$, there exists an open neighborhood U of $b \in B$, a smooth manifold F, and a diffeomorphism $\phi : U \times F \to p^{-1}(U)$ that satisfies the relation

$$p\big(\phi(y, t)\big) = y$$

for every $y \in U$ and $t \in F$.

The fiber space is X, the base B and the map p the projection. For every $b \in B$, the set $p^{-1}(b)$ is a closed submanifold of X known as the fiber of b. It follows from the local triviality property that there exists a neighborhood U of b such that $p^{-1}(b)$ and $p^{-1}(b')$ are diffeomorphic for $b' \in U$.

D.6.2 Coverings

Definition D.10. *A covering of B is a fiber bundle $p : X \to B$ such that the fibers $p^{-1}(b)$ are discrete.*

The projection map $p : X \to B$ in a covering is then a local diffeomorphism that is a surjection.

Proposition D.11. *Let $f : X \to Y$ be a smooth map between smooth manifolds where X is connected and Y simply connected. If f is surjective and a local diffeomorphism, then f is a diffeomorphism.*

Proof. See for example [29], (16.28.4). $\qquad\qquad\square$

D.7 SURJECTIVITY OF MAPS WITH NON-ZERO MODULO 2 DEGREE

Proposition D.12. *The smooth proper map* $f : X \to Y$ *where* $\dim X = \dim Y$ *with a modulo 2 degree equal to 1 is onto.*

Proof. The proof proceeds by contradiction. Assume that the map f: $X \to Y$ is not onto. There exists some $y \in Y$ that does not belong to the image $f(X)$. The preimage $f^{-1}(y)$ is therefore empty. This element y cannot be the image of a critical point of the map $f : X \to Y$ because this element $y \in Y$ is not the image of any point at all. Therefore, y is not a value of the map f. By definition, this implies that $y \in Y$ is a regular value of that map f. This implies that the number of elements of the set $f^{-1}(y)$ is odd by the definition of the degree. This is a contradiction with the fact that this set is also empty, and hence has a number of elements equal to zero. □

EXERCISE

D.1. Let $f : \mathbb{R} \to \mathbb{R}$ be a smooth proper map. Let y^0 and y^1 be two regular values of f and assume $y^0 < y^1$. Let $G = \{(x, y) \in \mathbb{R}^2 \mid y = f(x)\}$ be the graph of f. let $D^0 = \{(x, y) \in \mathbb{R}^2 \mid y = y^0\}$ and $D^1 = \{(x, y) \in \mathbb{R}^2 \mid y = y^1\}$ be the two horizontal lines associated with y^0 and y^1. Draw the graph G of f.

1. Show that the graph G is transverse to the lines D^0 and D^1.
2. Prove that the sets $G \cap D^0$ and $G \cap D^1$ are finite.
3. Let Γ be the intersection of G with the horizontal band $\{(x, y) \in \mathbb{R}^2 \mid y^0 \leq y \leq y^1\}$ in between the two lines D^0 and D^1. Prove that Γ consists of arcs joining either a point of D^0 to a point of D^1 or a point of D^0 to a point of D^0 or a point of D^1 to a point of D^1.
4. Show that the difference $\#f^{-1}(y^0) - \#f^{-1}(y^1)$ is divisible by 2.

Convexity

E.1 CONVEX AND STRICTLY CONVEX SETS

A subset X of $\mathbb{R}^n$ is *convex* if for every pair of points a and b in X, the segment $[a, b] = \{(1 - t)a + tb \mid t \in [0, 1]\}$ is contained in X. The linear manifold $L(X)$ generated by the convex set X is the smallest linear submanifold of $\mathbb{R}^n$ that contains X. The dimension of the convex set X is the dimension of the linear manifold $L(X)$. The *relative interior* of the convex set X is the interior of X for the topology of $L(X)$. The convex set X is *strictly convex* if for every pair of points a and b in X, the interior of the segment $[a, b]$ is contained in the relative interior of the convex set X.

E.2 QUASI-CONCAVE FUNCTIONS

The function $u : \mathbb{R}^n \to \mathbb{R}$ is *convex* if the inequality $u((1 - t)x + ty) \le (1 - t)u(x) + tu(y)$ is satisfied for every x and y in $\mathbb{R}^n$ and $t \in [0, 1]$. The function u is *convex* if and only if the set

$$X_u = \{(x, \alpha) \mid u(x) \le \alpha \text{ and } x \in \mathbb{R}^n\}$$

is a convex subset of $\mathbb{R}^n \times \mathbb{R}$.

The function $u : \mathbb{R}^n \to \mathbb{R}$ is *strictly convex* if the inequality

$$u((1 - t)x + ty) < (1 - t)u(x) + tu(y)$$

is satisfied for $x \ne y$ in $\mathbb{R}^n$ and t belonging to the open interval $(0, 1)$. The function $u : \mathbb{R}^n \to \mathbb{R}$ is *strictly convex* if and only if the set X_u is a strictly convex subset of $\mathbb{R}^n \times \mathbb{R}$.

The function $u : \mathbb{R}^n \to \mathbb{R}$ is *quasi-convex* (resp. *strictly quasi-convex*) if the set $X_u(\alpha) = \{x \in \mathbb{R}^n \mid u(x) \le \alpha\}$ is convex (resp. strictly convex) for every $\alpha \in \mathbb{R}$. The function u is *concave* (resp. *strictly concave, quasi-concave, strictly quasi-concave*) if the function $-u$ is convex (resp. strictly convex, quasiconvex, strictly quasi-convex).

Proposition E.1. *The function $u : \mathbb{R}^n \to \mathbb{R}$ is strictly quasi-concave if and only if the inequality*

$$u(x_1) < u((1 - t)x_1 + tx_2)$$

is satisfied for any $x_1 \ne x_2 \in \mathbb{R}^n$, with $u(x_1) \le u(x_2)$ and $t \in (0, 1)$.

The condition is necessary. Assume that u is strictly quasi-concave. Take $x_1 \neq x_2 \in \mathbb{R}^n$ with $u(x_1) \leq u(x_2)$ and let $t \in (0, 1)$. Let $\alpha = u(x_1)$. The set $Y_u(\alpha) = \{x \in \mathbb{R}^n \mid \alpha \leq u(x)\}$ contains x_1 and x_2. Its strict convexity implies that $(1 - t)x_1 + tx_2$ belongs to the interior of $Y_u(\alpha)$, which implies the strict inequality

$$\alpha = u(x_1) < u\big((1 - t)x_1 + tx_2\big).$$

The condition is sufficient. It suffices that we show that the set $Y_u(\alpha)$ is strictly convex for every $\alpha \in \mathbb{R}$. Take $x_1 \neq x_2 \in Y_u(\alpha)$. There is no loss of generality in assuming $\alpha \leq u(x_1) \leq u(x_2)$. This inequality implies for $t \in (0, 1)$ the inequality

$$\alpha \leq u(x_1) < u((1 - t)x_1 + tx_2),$$

from which follows that $(1 - t)x_1 + tx_2$ belongs to the interior of $Y_u(\alpha)$, which proves that this set is strictly convex. $\qquad \square$

Proposition E.2. *The smooth function $u : \mathbb{R}^n \to \mathbb{R}$ is strictly quasi-concave if and only if for any $x_1 \neq x_2 \in \mathbb{R}^n$ with $u(x_1) \leq u(x_2)$, the following strict inequality is satisfied:*

$$Du(x_1)^T(x_2 - x_1) > 0. \qquad (1)$$

The condition is necessary. Define $Z = x_2 - x_1$. By the strict quasi-concavity of u, we have

$$u(x_1) < u(x_1 + tZ) \qquad (2)$$

for $t \in (0, 1)$.

The derivative of $t \to u(x_1 + tZ)$ at $t = 0$ is equal to $Du(x_1)^T Z$. It is also the limit, when t tends to zero, of

$$\frac{u(x_1 + tZ) - u(x_1)}{t},$$

which is greater than or equal to zero from inequality (2). This implies $Du(x_1)^T Z \geq 0$.

The strict quasi-concavity of u therefore implies the following property:

$$\left. \begin{array}{c} u(x_1) \leq u(x_1 + Z) \\ Z \neq 0 \end{array} \right\} \implies Du(x_1)^T Z \geq 0. \qquad (3)$$

We now prove that $Du(x_1)^T Z = 0$ is impossible. Assume the contrary. There exists a sequence (Z^q) that satisfies the two conditions

$$\begin{cases} \lim_{q \to \infty} Z^q = Z, \\ Du(x_1)^T Z^q < 0. \end{cases} \tag{4}$$

The second inequality in (4) can be rewritten as $Du(x_1)^T(tZ^q) < 0$. It then follows from (3) that this inequality is compatible only with the strict inequality $u(x_1 + tZ^q) < u(x_1)$, with $t \in (0, 1)$. By going to the limit, this yields the inequality

$$u(x_1 + tZ) \leq u(x_1),$$

which contradicts Proposition E.1.

The condition is sufficient. We establish the strict quasi-concavity of u by showing that for $x_1 \neq x_2 \in \mathbb{R}^n$, $u(x_1) \leq u(x_2)$, the strict inequality

$$u(x_1) < u((1 - t)x_1 + tx_2)$$

is satisfied for $t \in (0, 1)$.

We consider the function of $t \in [0, 1] \to u((1 - t)x_1 + tx_2)$. This function is continuous. Its minimum is reached at some $t_0 \in [0, 1]$. Let us show that t_0 is equal to 0 or 1.

Assume the contrary, i.e., $0 < t_0 < 1$. Let $x_0 = (1 - t_0)x_1 + t_0x_2$. By the definition of t_0, we have

$$u(x_0) \leq u(x_1),$$

$$u(x_0) \leq u(x_2).$$

The application of inequality (1) yields

$$\begin{cases} Du(x_0)^T(x_1 - x_0) > 0, \\ Du(x_0)^T(x_2 - x_0) > 0. \end{cases} \tag{5}$$

But we also have $x_1 - x_0 = -t_0(x_2 - x_1)$ and $(x_2 - x_0) = (1 - t_0)(x_2 - x_1)$. From $-t_0 < 0$ and $1 - t_0 > 0$, we get a contradiction between the two strict inequalities (5).

This implies that the minimum of $u((1 - t)x_1 + tx_2)$ can be reached only for $t = 0$ or $t = 1$. From $u(x_1) \leq u(x_2)$ it follows that the minimum value of $u(x_1 + t(x_2 - x_1))$ is $u(x_1)$. The combination with the above argument yields the strict inequality $u(x_1) < u((1 - t)x_1 + tx_2)$ for $0 < t < 1$. $\quad\square$

Corollary E.3. *Let $u : \mathbb{R}^n \to \mathbb{R}$ be a strictly quasi-concave function. The inequality $Du(x_1)^T(x_2 - x_1) \le 0$ for $x_1 \ne x_2 \in \mathbb{R}^n$ implies the strict inequality $u(x_2) < u(x_1)$.*

Proof. This is obvious. $\quad\square$

E.3 Smooth Quasi-concavity and Second-Order Derivatives

In this section, we consider the second order derivatives of the strictly quasi-concave function $u : \mathbb{R}^\ell \to \mathbb{R}$. This will lead us to strengthen marginally the concept of strict quasi-concavity into what we call smooth quasi-concavity in the case of utility functions.

We recall that $D^2u(x)$ denotes the $n \times n$ Hessian matrix defined by the second-order derivatives of u. The vector $Z \in \mathbb{R}^n$ is identified to a column matrix.

Proposition E.4. *The restriction of the quadratic form $Z \to Z^T D^2u(x)Z$ to the hyperplane $\{Z \in \mathbb{R}^n \mid Du(x)^TZ = 0\}$ is negative semidefinite for every $x \in \mathbb{R}^n$ if the smooth function $u : \mathbb{R}^n \to \mathbb{R}$ is strictly quasi-concave.*

Proof. The inequality $Du(x)^T tZ = 0$ combined with Corollary E.3 implies the strict inequality $u(x + tZ) < u(x)$ for $t \ne 0$. The function $t \in [0, 1] \to u(x + tZ)$ has an absolute maximum at $t = 0$. This implies that its second derivative at $t = 0$ is negative or equal to zero. This takes the form $Z^T D^2u(x)Z \le 0$. $\quad\square$

Proposition E.5. *The smooth function $u : \mathbb{R}^n \to \mathbb{R}$ is strictly quasi-concave if the restriction of the quadratic form $Z \to Z^T D^2u(x)Z$ for $Z \in \mathbb{R}^n$ to the hyperplane $\{Z \in \mathbb{R}^n \mid Du(x)^TZ = 0\}$ is negative definite for every $x \in \mathbb{R}^n$.*

Proof. The strategy is to show that the condition stated in Proposition E.5 implies the sufficient condition for strict quasi-concavity of Proposition E.2.

Let $x_1 \neq x_2 \in \mathbb{R}^n$ with $u(x_1) \leq u(x_2)$ and let us show that the inequality $Du(x_1)^T(x_2 - x_1) > 0$ is satisfied.

We argue by contradiction. Assume $Du(x_1)^T(x_2 - x_1) \leq 0$. Let $Z = x_2 - x_1$ and consider the function $t \in [0, 1] \to u((1 - t)x_1 + tx_2) = u(x_1 + tZ)$. From $Du(x_1)^TZ \leq 0$, we have either $Du(x_1)^TZ < 0$ or $Du(x_1)^TZ = 0$. Let us prove that, in both cases, there exists $t_1 > 0$ such that $u(x_l + t_1 Z) < u(x_1)$. The derivative of $u(x_1 + tZ)$ at $t = 0$ is equal to $Du(x_1)^TZ$. If $Du(x_1)^TZ = 0$, then the second derivative, equal to $Z^T D^2 u(x_1)Z$, is < 0 by assumption. Therefore, $t = 0$ is a local maximum, and there exists $t_1 > 0$ such that $u(x_l + t_1 Z) < u(x_1)$. If $Du(x_1)^TZ < 0$, then $u(x_1 + tZ)$ is a strictly decreasing function of t in a neighborhood of 0. Once again, there exists $t_1 > 0$ such that $u(x_1 + t_1 Z) < u(x_1)$.

The continuous function $t \in [0, 1] \to u(x_1 + tZ)$ reaches its absolute minimum for some $t_0 \in [0, 1]$. From $u(x_1 + t_0 Z) < u(x_1) \leq u(x_2)$, this minimum cannot be reached at $t_0 = 0$ or $t_0 = 1$ so that we have $0 < t_0 < 1$. The derivative of $u(x_1 + tZ)$ at t_0 is equal to $Du(x_0)^TZ$ (with $x_0 = x_1 + t_0 Z$), and must be equal to 0. The second derivative, equal to $Z^T D^2 u(x_0)Z$, is strictly negative by assumption, a condition sufficient for t_0 to be a local maximum, hence a contradiction. $\qquad\square$

Definition E.6. *The function $u : \mathbb{R}^n \to \mathbb{R}$ is smoothly quasi-concave if it satisfies the condition of Proposition E.5.*

Proposition E.7. *A smoothly quasi-concave function is strictly quasi-concave.*

Proof. This follows readily from Proposition E.5. $\qquad\square$

Proposition E.8. *The function $u : \mathbb{R}^n \to \mathbb{R}$ is smoothly quasi-concave if and only if, for any $x \in \mathbb{R}^n$, the only solution to*

$$\begin{cases} Z^T D^2 u(x)Z \geq 0 \\ Du(x)^TZ = 0 \end{cases}$$

is $Z = 0 \in \mathbb{R}^n$.

Proof. This is obviously equivalent to Proposition E.5. $\qquad\square$

E.4 BORDERED HESSIAN OF A SMOOTHLY QUASI-CONCAVE FUNCTION

Definition E.9. *The bordered Hessian matrix associated with the function $u : \mathbb{R}^n \to \mathbb{R}$ at $x \in \mathbb{R}^n$ is the $(n+1) \times (n+1)$ matrix*

$$H(x) = \begin{bmatrix} D^2 u(x) & Du(x) \\ Du(x)^T & 0 \end{bmatrix}.$$

The bordered Hessian matrix is symmetric like the Hessian matrix $D^2 u(x)$. The determinant of that matrix, however, has an interesting and useful property if u is smoothly quasi-concave.

Proposition E.10. *Let $u : \mathbb{R}^n \to \mathbb{R}$ be a monotone and smoothly quasi-concave function. Its bordered Hessian matrix $H(x)$ is invertible for every $x \in \mathbb{R}^n$.*

Proof. We argue by contradiction. Assume $\det H(x) = 0$. There exists a column matrix $X \in \mathbb{R}^{n+1}$ with

$$X^T = (X^1, X^2, \ldots, X^n, X^{n+1}) \neq 0$$

such that $H(x)X = 0$. Let $\bar{X}^T = (X^1, X^2, \ldots, X^n)$. Block matrix multiplication gives us

$$D^2 u(x)\bar{X} + X^{n+1} Du(x) = 0, \tag{6}$$

$$Du(x)^T \bar{X} = 0. \tag{7}$$

The left matrix multiplication of equality (6) by the matrix $\bar{X}^T$ yields the equality

$$\bar{X}^T D^2 u(x)\bar{X} + X^{n+1}\bar{X}^T Du(x) = 0. \tag{8}$$

Given the equality (7), equality (8) becomes

$$\bar{X}^T D^2 u(x)\bar{X} = 0.$$

The combination with

$$Du(x)^T \bar{X} = 0,$$

implies that $\bar{X}$ is equal to 0. Equality (6) then implies

$$X^{n+1} Du(x) = -D^2 u(x)\bar{X} = 0,$$

from which follows $X^{n+1} = 0$. This proves that the column matrix X is equal to 0, a contradiction with the assumption $X \neq 0$. $\qquad\square$

Remark 10. The condition for the quadratic form defined by the Hessian matrix $D^2u(x)$ restricted to the tangent plane $Du(x)^T Z = 0$ to the surface $\{y \in \mathbb{R}^n \mid u(y) = u(x)\}$ at the point x to be negative definite can be interpreted as the non-vanishing of the Gaussian curvature of the hypersurface $\{y \in \mathbb{R}^n \mid u(y) = u(x)\}$ at the point x. For a proof in the context of utility functions and indifference (hyper)surfaces, see [25].

E.5 RECESSION CONE OF A CONVEX SET

Let C be a convex subset of $\mathbb{R}^\ell$. The recession cone of C is the set $0^+C = \{t \in C \mid t + C \subset C\}$. For references, see [53].

Proposition E.11. *The recession cone of a closed convex set is closed and convex.*

Proposition E.12. *The closed convex set C is bounded if and only its recession cone is equal to 0.*

EXERCISE

E.1 Let C be a convex subset of $\mathbb{R}^\ell$. Let $x \in C$. Define $N(x) = \{t \in \mathbb{R}^\ell \mid x + \lambda t \in C \text{ for any } \lambda > 0\}$. Show that $N(x)$ coincides with the recession cone 0^+C.

Miscellany

F.1 DIMENSION OF SEMI-ALGEBRAIC SETS

Definition F.1. *A semi-algebraic subset of $\mathbb{R}^n$ is defined by a finite number of polynomial equalities and inequalities. An algebraic set is a special case in the sense that it is defined by polynomial equalities.*

A remarkable property of semi-algebraic sets is that they are stratified sets. More specifically, a semi-algebraic set is the union of a finite number of smooth connected manifolds [19], Proposition (2.5.1). It is then possible to define the dimension of each manifold and the dimension of the semi-algebraic set is the dimension of the manifolds of highest dimension in that decomposition. See also [20], section 2.8, pp. 44–48.

References

[1] N. Al-Najjar. Non-transitive smooth preferences. *Journal of Economic Theory*, 60:14–41, 1993.

[2] V. Arnold. *Catastrophe Theory*. Springer, Heidelberg, 3rd edition, 1992.

[3] K.J. Arrow. Le role des valeurs boursières pour la répartition la meilleure des risques. In *Econométrie. Fondements et applications de la théorie du risque en économétrie*, Paris, 1953. CNRS.

[4] K.J. Arrow. The role of securities in the optimal allocation of risk-bearing. *Review of Economic Studies*, 31:91–96, 1964.

[5] K.J. Arrow and G. Debreu. Existence of an equilibrium for a competitive economy. *Econometrica*, 22:265–290, 1954.

[6] K.J. Arrow and F.H. Hahn. *General Competitive Analysis*. Holden-Day, San Francisco, 1971.

[7] A.B. Atkinson and J.E. Stiglitz. *Public Economics*. McGraw-Hill, London, 1980.

[8] R. Auspitz and R. Lieben. *Untersuchung über die Theorie des Preises*. Duncker und Humblot, Leipzig, 1889.

[9] R. Auspitz and R. Lieben. Die mehrfachen Schnittpunkte zwischen der Angebots- und der Nachfragekurve. *Zeitschrift für Volkswirtschaft, Sozialpolitik und Verwaltung*, 17:607–616, 1908.

[10] Y. Balasko. Connexité de l'espace des équilibres d'une famille d'économies. *Revue Francaise d'Automatique, Informatique, Recherche Opérationnelle*, 5:121–123, 1973.

[11] Y. Balasko. The graph of the Walras correspondence. *Econometrica*, 43:907–912, 1975.

[12] Y. Balasko. Some results on uniqueness and on stability of equilibrium in general equilibrium theory. *Journal of Mathematical Economics*, 2:95–118, 1975.

[13] Y. Balasko. Connectedness of the set of stable equilibria. *SIAM Journal of Applied Mathematics*, 35:722–728, 1978.

[14] Y. Balasko. Economies with a finite but large number of equilibria. *Journal of Mathematical Economics*, 6:145–147, 1979.

[15] Y. Balasko. A geometric approach to equilibrium analysis. *Journal of Mathematical Economics*, 6:217–228, 1979.

[16] Y. Balasko. *Foundations of the Theory of General Equilibrium*. Academic Press, Boston, 1988.

[17] Y. Balasko. The set of regular equilibria. *Journal of Economic Theory*, 58:1–9, 1992.

[18] Y. Balasko. *The Equilibrium Manifold. Postmodern Developments of the Theory of General Economic Equilibrium*. MIT Press, Cambridge, MA., 2009.

[19] R. Benedetti and J-J. Risler. *Real Algebraic and Semi-Algebraic Sets.* Hermann, Paris, 1990.

[20] J. Bochnak, M. Coste, and M-F. Roy. *Géométrie Algébrique Réelle.* Springer, Berlin, 1987.

[21] D. Cass and K. Shell. Do sunspots matter? *Journal of Political Economy,* 91:193–227, 1983.

[22] A.A. Cournot. *Recherches sur les Principes Mathématiques de la Théorie des Richesses.* Hachette, Paris, 1838. English translation by N.T. Bacon, Macmillan, New York, 1897.

[23] G. Debreu. *Theory of Value.* Wiley, New York, 1959.

[24] G. Debreu. Economies with a finite set of equilibria. *Econometrica,* 38:387–392, 1970.

[25] G. Debreu. Smooth preferences. *Econometrica,* 40:603–615, 1972.

[26] G. Debreu. Economic theory in the mathematical mode. *American Economic Review,* 74:267–278, 1984.

[27] F. Delbaen. *Lower and upper hemi-continuity of the Walras correspondence.* PhD thesis, Free University of Brussels, 1971.

[28] J. Dieudonné. *Foundations of Modern Analysis.* Academic Press, New York, 1960.

[29] J. Dieudonné. *Treatise on Analysis,* volume 3. Academic Press, New York, 1973.

[30] H. Eggleston. *Convexity.* Cambridge University Press, Cambridge, 1966.

[31] G. Fuchs. Private ownership economies with a finite number of equilibria. *Journal of Mathematical Economics,* 1:141–158, 1974.

[32] V. Guillemin and A. Pollack. *Differential Topology.* Prentice-Hall, Englewood Cliffs, NJ., 1974.

[33] J.R. Hicks. *Value and Capital.* Clarendon Press, Oxford, 1st edition, 1939.

[34] J.R. Hicks. *Value and Capital.* Clarendon Press, Oxford, 2nd edition, 1946.

[35] W. Hildenbrand and M. Jerison. The demand theory of the weak axioms of revealed preference. *Economics Letters,* 29:209–213, 1989.

[36] H.S. Houthakker. Revealed preference and the utility function. *Economica,* 17:159–174, 1950.

[37] W. Jaffe, editor. *Correspondence of Léon Walras and Related Papers, Vol. III.* North-Holland, Amsterdam, 1965.

[38] W.S. Jevons. *The Theory of Political Economy.* Macmillan, London, 1871.

[39] E. Jouini. The graph of the Walras correspondence. The production economies case. *Journal of Mathematical Economics,* 22:139–147, 1993.

[40] T.J. Kehoe. An index theorem for general equilibrium models with production. *Econometrica,* 48:1211–1232, 1980.

[41] T.J. Kehoe. Regularity and index theory for economies with smooth production technologies. *Econometrica,* 51:895–918, 1983.

[42] T. Kihlstrom, A. Mas-Colell, and H. Sonnenschein. The demand theory of the weak axiom of revealed preferences. *Econometrica,* 44:971–978, 1976.

[43] T. Koopmans. *Three Essays on the State of Economic Science.* McGraw Hill, New York, 1957.

[44] T.C. Koopmans. Analysis of production as an efficient combination of activities. In T.C. Koopmans, editor, *Activity Analysis of Production and Allocation*, pages 33–97, New York, 1951. Wiley.

[45] M. Magill and M. Quinzii. *Theory of Incomplete Markets*. MIT Press, Cambridge, MA., 1995.

[46] A. Mas-Colell. On the continuity of equilibrium prices in constant returns production economies. *Journal of Mathematical Economics*, 2:21–33, 1975.

[47] L.W. McKenzie. On equilibrium in Graham's model of world trade and other competitive systems. *Econometrica*, 22:147–161, 1954.

[48] J. Milnor. *Topology from the Differentiable Viewpoint*. Princeton University Press, Princeton, 2nd edition, 1997.

[49] H. Nikaido. *Convex Structures and Economic Theory*. Academic Press, New York, 1968.

[50] V. Pareto. *Cours d'Economie Politique*. Rouge, Lausanne, 1896.

[51] V. Pareto. *Manuel d'Economie Politique*. Rouge, Lausanne, 1909.

[52] J. Quah. Weak axiomatic demand theory. *Economic Theory*, 29:677–699, 2006.

[53] T.R. Rockafellar. *Convex Analysis*. Princeton University Press, Princeton, 1970.

[54] P.A. Samuelson. A note on the pure theory of consumer's behaviour. *Economica*, 5:61–71, 1938.

[55] P.A. Samuelson. *Foundations of Economic Analysis*. Harvard University Press, Cambridge, MA., 1947.

[56] P.A. Samuelson. Consumption theory in terms of revealed preference. *Economica*, 15:243–253, 1948.

[57] P.A. Samuelson. The pure theory of public expenditure. *Review of Economics and Statistics*, 36:387–389, 1954.

[58] P.A. Samuelson. An exact consumption loan model of interest with or without the social contrivance of money. *Journal of Political Economy*, 66:467–482, 1959.

[59] S. Schecter. On the structure of the equilibrium manifold. *Journal of Mathematical Economics*, 6:1–7, 1979.

[60] J.A. Schumpeter. *History of Economic Analysis*. Allen and Unwin, London, 1954.

[61] S. Smale. Global analysis and economics IV: Finiteness and stability with general consumption sets and production. *Journal of Mathematical Economics*, 1:119–128, 1974.

[62] R. Thom. *Stabilité Structurelle et Morphogénèse*. Benjamin, Reading, MA., 1972.

[63] R. Thom. *Structural Stability and Morphogenesis*. Benjamin, Reading, MA., 1975.

[64] M. Tvede. *Overlapping Generations Economies*. Macmillan, Houndmills, UK., 2010.

[65] H. Uzawa. Preference and rational choice in the theory of consumption. In K.J. Arrow, S. Karlin, and P. Suppes, editors, *Mathematical Methods in*

the Social Sciences, chapter 9, pages 129–148. Stanford University Press, Stanford, 1960.

[66] A. Wald. Über einige Gleichungssysteme der Mathematischen Ökonomie. *Zeitschrift für Nationalökonomie*, 7:637–670, 1936.

[67] L. Walras. *Eléments d'Economie Politique Pure*. Corbaz, Lausanne, 1st edition, 1874.

[68] L. Walras. *Elements of Pure Economics*. (English translation by W. Jaffe of the definitive 1924 French edition). Allen and Unwin, London, 1954.

Index

activity (vector), 71, 83–88; efficient, 84, 89; inactivity or zero, 86, 109
aggregate demand, 39, 40, 97
aggregate excess demand, 39, 60
aggregate supply, 39, 40, 97
allocation: equilibrium, 11, 75, 78, 79, 140; set of preferred, 8, 12
asset markets, 146

BIBO: and the existence of a profit maximizing solution, 110; for the net supply function, 104; for production sets, 104–107, 110, 125, 133, 134. *See also* production
binary relation, 6; antisymmetric, 6; complete, 6; reflexive, 6; symmetric, 6; transitive, 6

commodity: bundle, 2, 19; space, 5; vector, 2
comparative statics, 37, 38
connected component, 39, 47, 48, 54, 66, 67, 74–76, 78, 80, 81, 143. *See also* connectedness
connectedness, 35, 47, 55, 75, 76, 157, 166. *See also* pathconnected component; point-set topology
consumer theory: demand-based, 31
consumer's demand, 39; existence of, 20; first-order conditions satisfied by, 21; as a smooth function, 24, 25; uniqueness of, 20
consumption set, 5, 6, 8
continuous path, 47, 48, 69, 128. *See also* pathconnected component
contractible space, 47, 48, 55. *See also* point-set topology
convex polyhedron, 85

convex production technology, 85. *See also* production set
convex sets: approximation by smooth convex sets of, 85, 111, 125
convexity: of the normal cone, 113; of preferences, 5, 10, 16, 26, 27, 36, 39; of the profit function, 91; of a set, 85, 159
correspondence, 109, 112; equilibrium correspondence, 81; net supply, 109, 112, 115, 119–123, 126, 127
covering map, 35, 65, 141, 144, 157. *See also* point-set topology; smooth map
critical equilibrium, 45, 58, 59, 72, 79, 134, 135, 137. *See also* critical point; natural projection
critical point, 43, 45, 60, 72, 134, 135, 155, 156, 158. *See also* critical equilibrium; smooth map

degree: modulo, 2, 69–72, 79, 137, 138, 143, 144, 157, 158; topological or Brouwer, 70–72, 79, 137, 138, 143, 144, 157, 158. *See also* proper map
demand function, 19, 23, 39, 124; aggregate, 39, 40, 97; as a diffeomorphism, 35; first-order derivatives of, 27; production adjusted, 96, 98, 99, 100; properness of, 62; property (A) or desirability for, 19, 28, 62; property (B) or boundedness from below of, 17, 19, 27, 32, 62; property (ND) or negative definiteness of the Slutsky matrix of, 19, 29, 31, 36, 39, 74, 77, 100; property (NSD) or negative semidefiniteness of the